ARCO

SPECIAL AGENT
DEPUTY U.S. MARSHAL

TREASURY ENFORCEMENT AGENT

10TH EDITION

ARCO

SPECIAL AGENT
DEPUTY U.S. MARSHAL

TREASURY ENFORCEMENT AGENT

10TH EDITION

Eve Steinberg

THOMSON

ARCO

Australia • Canada • Mexico • Singapore • Spain • United Kingdom • United States

An ARCO Book

ARCO is a registered trademark of Thomson Learning, Inc., and is used herein under license by Peterson's.

About The Thomson Corporation and Peterson's

With revenues of US$7.2 billion, The Thomson Corporation (www.thomson.com) is a leading global provider of integrated information solutions for business, education, and professional customers. Its Learning businesses and brands (www.thomsonlearning.com) serve the needs of individuals, learning institutions, and corporations with products and services for both traditional and distributed learning.

Peterson's, part of The Thomson Corporation, is one of the nation's most respected providers of lifelong learning online resources, software, reference guides, and books. The Education Supersite[SM] at www.petersons.com—the internet's most heavily traveled education resources—has searchable databases and interactive tools for contacting U.S.-accredited institutions and programs. In addition, Peterson's serves more that 105 million education consumers annually.

For more information, contact Peterson's, 2000 Lenox Drive, Lawrenceville, NJ 08648; 800-338-3282; or find us on the World Wide Web at: www.petersons.com/about

Tenth Edition

ISBN 0-7645-6104-9

Printed in the United States of America

10 9 8 7 6 5 4 3   02

CONTENTS

Foreword   ix

PART ONE

Law Enforcement Careers with the Department of the Treasury and the U.S. Marshals Service

Bureau of Alcohol, Tobacco, and Firearms   3

Mission 3
Functions and Activities 3
Arson and Explosives Enforcement.. 4
Technology 5
Training 6
Qualifications 6

Internal Revenue Service   9

Mission of Criminal Investigation 9
Mission of Inspection.. 11

U.S. Customs Service   15

Mission 15
Functions and Activities 15
Training 19
Qualifications 20

U.S. Secret Service   21

Mission 21
Historical Review 21
Functions and Activities 23
Information Technology in the Service Today 24
Training 25
Qualifications 26

U.S. Marshals Service   27

Mission 27
Functions and Activities 27
Training 30

PART TWO
Federal Law Enforcement Training

The Federal Law Enforcement Training Center 35

Operations 35

Marana Facility 35

Programs 35

Staff 37

Facilities 37

The Criminal Investigator Training Program 39

Length of Program 39

Standard Daily Schedule 39

Student Evaluation 39

Written Examinations 40

Practical Exercises 40

Firearms Training 40

Distinguished Graduate Designation 41

Course Information 41

Behavioral Science Division 46

Enforcement Operations Division 47

Enforcement Techniques Division 48

Legal Division 50

Computer and Economic Crime Division 51

Driver and Marine Division 52

Firearms Division 53

Physical Techniques Division 54

PART THREE
The Treasury Enforcement Agent Exam

Sample Questions: The TEA Exam 59

Part A—Verbal Reasoning Questions 59

Part B—Arithmetic Reasoning Questions 61

Part C—Problems for Investigation 62

First Model Examination 67

Part A—Verbal Reasoning Questions 67

Part B—Arithmetic Reasoning Questions 76

Part C—Problems for Investigation 81

After Taking the First Model Exam 90

Second Model Examination   105

Part A—Verbal Reasoning Questions 105

Part B—Arithmetic Reasoning Questions 116

Part C—Problems for Investigation 121

After Taking the Second Model Exam 131

PART FOUR
Skills and Strategies for the TEA Exam

Verbal Reasoning   147

Exercise 1 147

Exercise 2 151

Exercise 3 154

Arithmetic Reasoning   165

Ratio and Proportion 165

Work Problems 173

Distance 180

Interest 188

Taxation 197

Profit and Loss 203

Payroll 211

Formula Questions 218

Problems for Investigation   225

Exercise 1 225

Exercise 2 228

Exercise 3 230

Exercise 4 233

Test-Taking Techniques   241

Tips for Examination Day 241

Self-Descriptive Inventories   243

The Interview   251

Tips for a Successful Interview 252

FOREWORD

Some years ago, I decided on a career in federal law enforcement, and I have never regretted that decision. After qualifying for a position as a Treasury Enforcement Agent, I received an appointment as a Special Agent with the U.S. Secret Service. My career was rewarding beyond my earliest expectations. Since retirement, I continue to be involved with Treasury law enforcement as a consultant. So when I talk about exciting and challenging law enforcement career opportunities within the Department of the Treasury, I do so from personal knowledge and with a deep sense of pride.

The law enforcement bureaus of the Treasury Department—Alcohol, Tobacco, and Firearms; U.S. Customs Service; Internal Revenue Service; and the U.S. Secret Service—are in the forefront of the fight against crime on a national level. Every day the news media report on the activities of these bureaus as their Special Agents arrest persons with illegal weapons and explosives, seize shipments of illicit drugs, arrest "white-collar" criminals for tax evasion, or thwart an attempt against the life of the President of the United States.

These are just a few of the many activities of the Treasury bureaus that offer careers for men and women interested in law enforcement on the federal level. Let me elaborate further on the specific responsibilities of these bureaus.

Special Agents with the Bureau of Alcohol, Tobacco, and Firearms (ATF) investigate violations of federal firearms and explosives laws, the illicit production of liquor, and the sale of untaxed tobacco products. Their investigative caseload includes activities such as: bombings; arson-for-profit schemes affecting interstate commerce; and the illicit sale, illegal possession, and criminal use of firearms. Often their firearms investigations result in arrests of persons using illegal weapons to protect illicit drug activity, while their expertise with explosive devices requires them to investigate cases of suspected arson in the destruction of large facilities like hotels and warehouses.

The U.S. Customs Service is the lead federal law enforcement agency in efforts to prevent illegal drugs from entering the United States—one of the greatest challenges facing law enforcement today. In addition to this priority responsibility, Customs Special Agents investigate smuggling of arms and sophisticated technology, money laundering, counterfeit merchandise, child pornography, and myriad other violations of federal laws.

The primary focus of Special Agents with the Internal Revenue Service is tax fraud. They investigate attempts to cheat the federal government by defeating or evading the tax laws of the United States. Persons found guilty of tax fraud represent the full spectrum of our society, ranging from the common criminal making illegal income to legitimate business persons, often referred to as "white-collar criminals." Tax fraud cases involve a complex and painstaking investigative process requiring accounting and auditing skills, as well as criminal investigative training.

Secret Service agents have diverse responsibilities—both protective and investigative. They protect the President and others, as well as investigate persons who threaten those they protect. In addition, they investigate the counterfeiting of U.S. currency and the forgery of government checks and bonds. Recent legislation added new investigative responsibilities relevant to the U.S. monetary system that include electronic fund transfer fraud, credit and debit card fraud, and computer fraud.

To effectively meet the challenges of the major law enforcement responsibilities, Treasury bureaus often share information and expertise and join forces against organized crime, drug trafficking, and white-collar crime. They also combine personnel resources for the purpose of protecting candidates in the race for the White House.

From my own experience of more than three decades with Treasury law enforcement, I understand why young men and women choose to join the ranks of Special Agent. I, too, experienced that special feeling of having been selected from among countless applicants. And because the Treasury's enforcement efforts have a major impact on the public safety of our nation, there is immense sense of pride associated with public service as a Special Agent of the Department of the Treasury.

To become a Special Agent with one of these challenging federal agencies, it is important that you not only pass the Treasury Enforcement Examination, but that you also score well on the exam. By so doing, you can become one of the best qualified among the large number of applicants competing for these positions.

This comprehensive study guide is designed to assist you in attaining your goal of becoming a member of the Treasury Agent team—a proud and rewarding career.

John W. Warner, Jr.

Assistant to the Director (Retired)

U.S. Secret Service

ONE

Law Enforcement Careers with the Department of the Treasury and the U.S. Marshals Service

CONTENTS

Bureau of Alcohol, Tobacco, and Firearms   3

Internal Revenue Service   9

U.S. Customs Service   15

U.S. Secret Service   21

U.S. Marshals Service   27

BUREAU OF ALCOHOL, TOBACCO, AND FIREARMS

Mission

The Bureau of Alcohol, Tobacco, and Firearms (ATF) is an agency of the Department of the Treasury with approximately 4,000 employees—special agents, inspectors, auditors, laboratory personnel, and support persons located throughout the United States. It has both law enforcement and regulatory responsibilities.

The mission of ATF is to do the following:

- Curb the illegal traffic in and criminal use of firearms by effectively enforcing federal firearms laws.
- Investigate violations of federal explosives laws, bombings, and arson-for-profit schemes, and remove safety hazards caused by improper and unsafe storage of explosive materials.
- Regulate the alcohol, tobacco, firearms, and explosives industries.
- Trace the origin and movement of firearms recovered by law enforcement agencies worldwide.
- Assure the collection of all alcohol and tobacco tax revenues and obtain voluntary compliance with alcohol and tobacco tax laws.
- Suppress commercial bribery, consumer deception, and other prohibited trade practices in the alcoholic beverage industry.
- Suppress the illicit manufacture and sale of alcoholic beverages.
- Assist the states in their effort to eliminate interstate trafficking in, sale of, and distribution of cigarettes in avoidance of state taxes.

Functions and Activities

LAW ENFORCEMENT

ATF Special Agents investigate violations of federal explosives laws, including most bombings and many arson-for-profit schemes affecting interstate commerce. ATF also investigates violations of federal firearms laws in an effort to prevent illicit trafficking, illegal possession, and criminal use of firearms. Other ATF responsibilities include investigating violations of the Federal Alcohol Administration Act and interstate smugglers of non-tax-paid cigarettes.

With the enforcement of firearms, arson, and explosives laws, ATF is able to target career criminals, organized crime figures, members of violent extremist groups, and major narcotics dealers. ATF is also charged with tracking and control of outlaw motorcycle gangs and illegal movement of firearms in international traffic.

COMPLIANCE

ATF's compliance responsibilities include the licensing of nearly 248,000 firearms and explosives dealers, manufacturers, and importers. Inspection of firearms licensees' records assists ATF's investigative responsibilities. For example, during a task force on drugs in Miami, ATF inspection of licensee records identified 300 illegal sales, 450 potential traffickers, and 1,500 questionable purchases for further investigation.

It is also ATF's responsibility to determine if criminals have infiltrated legal liquor businesses through hidden ownership, since organized crime often becomes involved in legitimate businesses in order to launder money from its criminal activities.

ATF protects the consumer in a number of ways, such as assuring that alcoholic beverage labels accurately reflect the contents and include warning statements; monitoring liquor advertising for improprieties; conducting market area surveys to identify illegal trade practices; ensuring safe and secure storage of explosives by high-risk users; informing the nation about fetal alcohol syndrome; working to eliminate foreign regulatory obstacles to U.S. wine exports; and conducting a nationwide sampling program to detect and remove potentially hazardous or adulterated liquor products from the marketplace.

SUPPORT

With responsibilities that are both law enforcement and regulatory, ATF is supported by a laboratory system that operates to ensure health, safety, and the integrity of the alcoholic beverage industry, and conducts forensic services in behalf of criminal investigations involving explosives and arson crimes.

Arson and Explosives Enforcement

NATIONAL RESPONSE TEAMS

ATF has developed, equipped, and trained four National Response Teams (NRTs) capable of responding within 24 hours to assist in major bombing and arson investigations anywhere in the United States.

Each team includes 10 ATF Special Agents trained in investigative techniques particular to arson and bombings, a forensic chemist, a cause-and-origin specialist, and an expert in explosives technology. In addition, trucks outfitted with state-of-the-art equipment can be driven to the scene or loaded aboard U.S. Coast Guard planes and flown to the site.

When an NRT arrives on the scene, a command center is established and immediate coordination with local authorities begins. ATF Agents and fire officials start the tedious process of reconstructing the scene, identifying the seat of the blast, sifting debris, searching for evidence, canvassing the area for witnesses, tracking the purchase of the components, determining the cause of the fire, conducting on-scene interviews, and, often, making the arrests.

Evidence is sent to the ATF laboratory where specialists help to reconstruct the crime scene. The lab technicians also look for evidence linking the crime to a suspect. Laser equipment searches glass or plastic containers, doorknobs, or parts of the incendiary device for latent fingerprints. Materials handled or owned by a suspect are compared to materials found at the crime scene. Many of the techniques used in forensic labs to detect accelerants were pioneered by ATF chemists.

Audit Specialists with expertise in arson fraud complete the complex suspect chase.

THE ARSON TASK FORCE

The Arson Task Force concept consists of pooling the resources of state and local police, fire service personnel, and ATF Special Agents to provide a unified and concentrated attack on arson. Specialized training for task force participants addresses the latest techniques and skills associated with arson investigations.

Motives for arson vary, as does the degree of sophistication of arson-for-profit schemes, but the vast majority involve insurance fraud, revenge, and extortion. ATF's enforcement efforts are directed toward arson-for-profit schemes that tend to target industrial and commercial activities. Perpetrators of arson-for-profit may be members of organized crime, white-collar criminals, or members of organized "arson rings."

ATF works jointly with state and local authorities who are experiencing a significant arson problem, particularly when the magnitude of the problem extends beyond their jurisdictional authority or resource capability.

FEDERAL FIREARMS LAWS

The Armed Career Criminal Act, the Comprehensive Crime Control Act of 1984, and amendments to the federal firearms laws give ATF valuable tools to get armed career criminals off the streets. These statutes subject the repeat offender and armed drug trafficker to mandatory prison sentences.

In 1987, ATF created a national project entitled "Project Achilles," so named because, from a law enforcement perspective, current laws make possession of a firearm the criminal's most vulnerable point. Hence, the career criminals who carry firearms are the targets of these Project Achilles task forces that are set up around the country.

The success of the task forces has a major impact on reducing crime because those responsible for committing the crimes will be behind bars for long periods of time with no chance for parole or probation.

DRUG ENFORCEMENT EFFORTS

Because of its firearms jurisdiction, ATF participates in the Organized Crime Drug Enforcement Task Force (OCDETF) program. This national multiagency task force was organized in 1982 to coordinate the federal government's efforts in the war against drugs. In addition to ATF, member agencies include DEA, FBI, Immigration and Naturalization Service (INS), Customs, IRS, U.S. Marshals Service, U.S. Coast Guard, and the U.S. Attorney's Office.

Technology
FIREARMS TRACING CENTER

ATF's Tracing Center, located in the suburbs of Washington, D.C., traces approximately 40,000 firearms a year for local, state, and federal law enforcement agencies. The tracing of firearms is an integral part of ATF's activities and has aided law enforcement in the identification of suspects involved in illegal use or trafficking of firearms, narcotics-related violations, and homicide investigations.

NATIONAL LABORATORY CENTER

Located in Rockville, Maryland, ATF's National Laboratory Center supports both law enforcement and compliance activities.

Forensic chemists provide a full range of analyses using the latest scientific equipment and techniques. They examine intact and functional explosive devices and debris to identify theft components. Their findings are often relayed to agents still working the scene of a suspected arson or explosion.

New laser devices retrieve fingerprints that might have gone undetected using conventional methods. Portable hydrocarbon detectors called "sniffers" allow the investigator to examine the scene for the presence of accelerants. Computer aid in the testing of fire-scene samples results in more accurate readings. The ATF National Laboratory also provides arson training for state and local chemists in arson accelerant detection.

The ATF Laboratory is also responsible for handling the chemical analysis of alcoholic beverages in order to protect the consumer and maintain the integrity of the alcoholic beverage industry.

NATIONAL EXPLOSIVES TRACING CENTER

To fulfill its responsibility for tracing explosives, ATF maintains a liaison with the explosives industry. A trace involves checking with the manufacturer concerning explosive materials recovered at a crime scene.

Training

Special Agent training involves formal classroom instruction supplemented by on-the-job training.

Appointees undergo approximately eight weeks of intensive training in general law enforcement and investigative techniques in Criminal Investigator School at the Federal Law Enforcement Training Center in Glynco, Georgia. Subjects of study include rules of evidence, surveillance techniques, undercover assignments, arrest and raid techniques, and the use of firearms.

Agents later attend New Agent Training, where they receive highly specialized training in their duties as ATF Agents. Subjects relate to the laws enforced by ATF, case-report writing, firearms and explosives nomenclature, bomb scene search, arson training, and link analysis.

Successful completion of both training courses is mandatory for all newly-hired ATF Special Agents.

ATF provides training in the investigation of complex, profit-motivated arson schemes for state and local law enforcement officers. The Advanced Arson-for-Profit Investigative Training program is also conducted at the Federal Law Enforcement Training Center at Glynco. The course concentrates on investigative techniques beyond the point of cause and origin determination, and involves workshops and classes dealing with topics such as financial investigative techniques, motives of the arsonist, and the role of the insurance industry.

ATF also provides an undercover investigative techniques training program for state and local law enforcement officers at the training center at Glynco.

Qualifications

Special Agent candidates must:

- be United States citizens;
- be at least 21, but under 37 years of age;

- be able to successfully pass a thorough background investigation;
- pass the Treasury Enforcement Agent examination;
- have:

  a) four years of study successfully completed at a college or university, or completion of all requirements for a bachelor's degree, or

  b) one year of general experience and two years of specialized experience (responsible criminal investigative experience);
- be in excellent physical condition and pass a comprehensive medical examination by a licensed physician;
- have distant vision without correction at least 20/100 in each eye; and
- pass a pre-employment drug screening examination.

INTERNAL REVENUE SERVICE

The primary role of the Internal Revenue Service (IRS) is the collection of taxes in a fair and impartial manner. The IRS's goal is to achieve the highest possible degree of voluntary compliance with the internal revenue laws of the United States.

Two divisions work to ensure the integrity of the nation's tax collection system. They are 1) Criminal Investigation and 2) Inspection.

Mission of Criminal Investigation

The mission of IRS's Criminal Investigation Division is to ensure voluntary compliance with the internal revenue laws by conducting investigations of suspected tax offenders. The taxes collected in the U.S. support the federal budget, and the United States' domestic fiscal programs are closely allied to this budget. Thus, the amount of revenue collected is a barometer of the overall economic strength of the nation.

Because of its importance to the effective functioning of the U.S. government, the prompt, fair, and vigorous enforcement of its tax laws is imperative. The investigation and apprehension of tax evaders not only serves to protect the public revenues, but also warns potential tax evaders against attempts to defeat the United State's system of voluntary tax compliance.

The criminal aspects of federal tax violations are the particular concern of the Criminal Investigation function. Criminal Investigation activities cover a wide range of tax-law enforcement, including individual and corporate income taxes, withholding and excise taxes, and other miscellaneous taxes. Violations of certain provisions of the Bank Secrecy Act also fall into this realm.

FUNCTIONS AND ACTIVITIES

The investigation of people with illegal income is only one aspect of Criminal Investigation enforcement activity that attempts to ensure compliance among all groups of taxpayers. Investigations have resulted in individuals being convicted for tax evasion in almost every occupation, profession, and segment of the economy and have also resulted in convictions of many corporations.

Prosecution of racketeers for tax evasion cuts at the profit from illegal activities, the "lifeblood" of organized crime. It is this profit that has enabled organized crime to finance illicit activities, as well as to invest in legitimate businesses.

Strike Force

Criminal Investigation contributes to the federal government's fight against organized crime by participating in the Federal Organized Crime Strike Force Program, a coordinated multi-agency effort directed at traditional organized crime. Strike forces are located in fifteen major cities and are headed by a Strike Force attorney-in-charge from the U.S. Attorney's Office. Criminal Investigation has been a part of all of the strike forces since their inception in 1966.

Drug Task Forces

Organized Crime Drug Enforcement Task Forces, instituted in 1982 by then-President Ronald Reagan, combine the financial investigative expertise of IRS Criminal Investigation with the expertise of the FBI, DEA, ATF, and Customs in joint investigations reaching the highest levels of narcotics trafficking organizations. The ability of Criminal Investigation Special Agents to determine an individual's net worth and to penetrate the methods sophisticated drug traffickers use to disguise the ownership of their assets has enabled these task forces to identify and target the previously undetected "respectable" drug traffickers in society—those professionals who use front companies and middlemen to insulate themselves from physical involvement in drug trafficking enterprises.

Other Investigative Activities

In addition, Special Agents are assigned on a full time basis to the Office of National Drug Control Policy, the El Paso Intelligence Center (EPIC), INTERPOL and the INTERPOL-U.S. National Central Bureau, the Customs Financial Analysis Division, and the Treasury Department headquarters.

TRAINING

The training program consists of five phases, two of which take place at the agent's post of duty. These are Introductory Special Agent Training, a self-instructional course, and On-the-Job Training. The other three phases (which include Tax Law for Criminal Investigators, Criminal Investigator Training, and Special Agent Investigative Techniques), are taught at the Federal Law Enforcement Training Center (FLETC) in Glynco, Georgia, and require a total of 21 weeks.

Continuing Professional Education training is offered to update Special Agents with regard to new or revised laws, policies, and procedures and includes topics such as data processing, electronic surveillance, and money laundering as it relates to tax havens.

QUALIFICATIONS

The basic qualification for the Special Agent position is three years of accounting and related business experience. Four years of college-level study or a bachelor's degree may be substituted for the experience if the study included fifteen semester hours in accounting and nine semester hours in related business subjects.

In addition to meeting the basic requirements, it is necessary to establish eligibility on the Treasury Enforcement Agent Examination, a written test used to measure investigative aptitudes.

Individuals who, in addition to the above qualifications, also possess a law degree or a master's degree in police science, criminology, law enforcement, or business administration may enter at a somewhat higher salary.

Any physical condition or disease that interferes with the full performance of the duties of a Special Agent is disqualifying.

Vision must be at least 20/200 in each eye, correctable to at least 20/20 in one eye and 20/30 in the other.

Before entrance on duty, an applicant must undergo a pre-employment medical examination and be medically suitable to efficiently perform the full duties of this position without hazard to himself or herself and others.

Applicants must not have reached their 37th birthday in order to be considered for this position.

Mission of Inspection

Inspection is a "fact-finding" organization with no direct responsibility for, or authority over, employees in the operating activities of the Internal Revenue Service. Management officials are charged with the responsibility for taking appropriate actions on Inspection reports.

The two Inspection functions consist of:

1. Internal Audit—A professional auditing staff that conducts independent review and appraisal of IRS operations.
2. Internal Security—An investigative service that assures the maintenance of the highest standards of honesty, integrity, loyalty, security, and conduct among Internal Revenue Service employees.

The functions of each of these two Inspection divisions are primarily separate, and each is manned by a separate staff. However, the detection and deterrence of fraud and corruption within IRS programs is a joint effort of both divisions.

INTERNAL AUDIT FUNCTIONS AND ACTIVITIES

The Internal Audit function is the combined result of a legal requirement, a Treasury Department Directive that prescribes the basic requirement for internal audit of financial, accounting, and other operations as a service to management and Internal Revenue Service policy. The significant value of the IRS's operations to the nation requires the maintenance of an effective system of internal control, including an independent internal audit organization that has broad but well-defined examining and reporting responsibilities.

To provide maximum benefit to IRS management, audit emphasis is placed on the examination of those operations most closely connected with the collection of tax revenues and the administration and enforcement of tax laws. Internal Auditors use computer analysis applications and sampling techniques in auditing these activities.

The Internal Audit program extends beyond the verification of an activity's compliance with the Manual and other written instructions. This broad program covers all organizations and activities of the IRS and includes a determination as to whether the policies, practices, procedures, and controls at all levels of management adequately protect the revenue and are being efficiently and effectively carried out. In addition, these audit tests determine whether taxpayers are treated fairly and equitably.

Internal Audit's responsibilities in the Integrity Program of the IRS include reviewing work and actions of employees suspected of or alleged to have committed breaches of integrity and assisting in joint investigations with Internal Security of taxpayers and tax practitioners suspected of collusion with IRS employees.

Internal Audit provides the Commissioner and his staff with a factual and candid appraisal of the manner in which the various organizations are carrying out their assigned functions and a picture entirely independent of that afforded by direct organizational reporting.

TRAINING

Internal Auditors participate in a continuing program of professional development, receiving on-the-job training in a wide variety of auditing assignments. Classroom instruction includes auditing standards and techniques, internal controls of key IRS activities, management policies, and the organization and function of IRS, including the extensive system of automatic data processing.

After gaining experience, Internal Auditors receive advanced training in audit techniques including computer audit training. Internal Audit's rotation policy is designed to ensure that assignments provide Auditors with experience in a variety of IRS program areas. Also, Internal Audit has a Continuing Professional Development program to ensure that Auditors maintain their skills and their knowledge of the latest techniques and issues throughout their careers.

QUALIFICATIONS

To qualify at the GS-5 level, four years of college-level study, which includes twenty-four semester hours of accounting or eighteen semester hours of accounting and six semester hours of business law, are required. In lieu of four years of college-level study, completion of the requisite accounting courses and four years of professional accounting experience, or completion of the requisite accounting courses and a combination of professional accounting experience and college-level education equivalent to four years, may be substituted.

To qualify at the GS-7 level, the following requirements must be met:

- Standing in the upper third of the class;
- 2.90 or better average in all courses completed at the time of application or completed during the last two years of study;
- B+ (3.5) or better average in accounting and auditing courses completed at the time of application or completed during the last two years of study;
- Election to membership in a national scholastic society which meets the minimum requirements of the Association of College Honor Societies; and
- One year of professional accounting, auditing, or appropriate student trainee experience; or
- Completion of one year of graduate study in accounting or related fields.

To qualify at the GS-9 level, completion of all requirements for a Master's degree in accounting or related fields at an accredited college or university is required.

INTERNAL SECURITY

The Internal Security Division is essentially a fact-finding organization. The purpose of any Internal Security investigation is to resolve the allegations involved and present the facts of the investigation to the appropriate official for criminal prosecution or administrative adjudication. All information contained in an Internal Security report of investigation has to be obtained from records or documents, interviews of third-party witnesses or the subject of the investigation, or the personal observations of the Inspector. These reports of investigation contain no personal opinions of Inspectors and make no recommendations whatsoever regarding possible disciplinary actions against employees.

Internal Security reports of investigations concerning administrative matters are submitted by Inspection to the appropriate Service official who is authorized to adjudicate the issues. Investigations involving criminal matters are referred to the U.S. Attorney for consideration as to prosecution.

FUNCTIONS AND ACTIVITIES

To accomplish its mission of maintaining the highest levels of integrity within the Service, Internal Security has been delegated numerous responsibilities and functions. These include the following:

- Investigations of complaints or information indicating criminal acts on the part of Service employees, such as bribery, embezzlement, disclosure or unauthorized use of tax information, and conflicts of interest.
- Investigations of persons outside the Service who try to bribe or otherwise improperly influence Service employees or whose actions otherwise affect the integrity of the Service.
- Investigations of threats, assaults, or forcible interference against Service personnel.
- Probes and tests of high-risk integrity areas to detect corruption involving Service personnel and activities. Information developed in these probes and tests is used to alert managers and employees to potential integrity hazards.
- Investigations of serious administrative misconduct by IRS personnel.
- Background investigations of applicants or appointees to all types of technical positions in the Service, all nontechnical positions in higher grades, and positions involving the handling of funds or the ability to adjust tax accounts.
- Investigations of personnel of certain other Treasury agencies.
- Background investigations of applicants who apply for special enrollment to represent taxpayers before the Service.
- Investigations of complaints of unethical or other improper conduct on the part of attorneys, CPAs, and other persons enrolled to practice before the Service.
- Certain tort investigations of accidents involving Service employees or property.
- Special investigations and studies when requested by the Office of the Secretary of the Treasury, the Inspector General, Treasury Department, the Commissioner, or other officials.
- Special assignments, such as assisting the U.S. Secret Service in the protection of dignitaries.

Bribery

One of the greatest threats to the integrity of the IRS is attempted bribary of IRS employees by taxpayers and practitioners. When a bribe attempt is reported by an employee, Internal Security immediately initiates an investigation into the matter. In almost all bribery cases, the employee plays an active role in the investigation. Investigations are designed to identify and develop prosecutable cases against those who try to corrupt employees.

To a lesser but equally serious extent, there have been cases where practitioners, and persons purporting to be practitioners, have solicited money from clients under the guise of having to pay off employees of the IRS, when in fact, no IRS employee has solicited or received any such payment.

Embezzlement

Internal Security investigates cases involving embezzlement, disclosure or unauthorized use of tax information, and conflicts of interest. Embezzlement by employees is one of Internal Security's most challenging functions. Through sophisticated use of IRS computers, discovery of loopholes in audit systems, or manipulation of accounting procedures, some employees have found ways to circumvent IRS's various controls and have embezzled funds from the Service or taxpayers. These cases present unusual challenges because, unlike bribery, there is often no one to report the crime, and there is no obvious evidence that an embezzlement has occurred. Realizing this, Internal Security, often in conjunction with Internal Audit, conducts probes and tests of high-risk integrity areas to detect corruption involving Service personnel and activities. In this way, criminal activity can be identified for investigation *during* its commission instead of *after* the fact. These probes also give Inspection an opportunity to uncover undetected frauds.

QUALIFICATIONS

The qualification requirements for entry at GS levels 5, 7, and 9 are identical to those for Internal Auditors.

U.S. CUSTOMS SERVICE

Mission

The U.S. Customs Service is one of the U.S. government's major revenue producers and the lead federal agency in drug interdiction. Customs also monitors and protects the nation's perimeters to thwart attempts to bring all types of illicit merchandise into the country, while enforcing over 400 laws for more than 40 federal agencies.

An agency of the Department of the Treasury, the U.S. Customs Service is divided into 45 districts and areas with responsibilities at more than 300 ports of entry and headquarters in Washington, D.C. Customs also maintains offices in various U.S. embassies and consulates overseas.

The Customs mission today is to do the following:

- Assess and collect Customs duties, excise taxes, fees, and penalties due on imported goods.
- Prevent fraud and smuggling.
- Control carriers, persons, and cargo entering and departing the United States.
- Intercept illegal high-technology exports to proscribed destinations.
- Cooperate with other federal agencies in suppressing the traffic in illicit narcotics and pornography.
- Enforce international transportation reporting requirements of the Bank Secrecy Act.
- Protect the American public by enforcing auto safety and emission control standards, flammable fabric restrictions, and animal and plant quarantine requirements on imports.
- Protect U.S. business and labor by enforcing laws and regulations dealing with copyrights, trademarks, and quotas.

Functions and Activities

Within the U.S. Customs Service, three principal offices have an impact on the enforcement and regulatory operations of the agency. They are Commercial Operations, Inspection and Control, and Enforcement.

OFFICE OF COMMERCIAL OPERATIONS

In carrying out its border protection mission, Customs must balance the responsibility of enforcement with the requirement to facilitate the legitimate movement of passengers and cargo into the United States.

Working with the world trade community and the international transportation industry, Customs has implemented numerous automated systems and techniques to expedite the flow of commerce. For example, Customs' Automated Commercial System (ACS) is a joint public/private sector computerized data processing and telecommunications system linking customhouses and members of the import trade community with the Customs computer.

Customs uses the data captured by the system in many ways, including the control and release of cargo; commodity classification and valuation decisions; collection of duty, taxes, fees, and other revenue; and enforcement of trade laws and regulations.

Commercial Operations personnel collect fines and penalties and process seizures and forfeitures under the import laws and export control laws. Import Specialists work with Inspectors to enforce tariff and trade laws and to prevent commercial fraud.

The Office of Laboratories and Scientific Services within the Office of Commercial Operations develops testing programs to enforce intellectual property rights, including rights that apply to copyrighted computers, software programs, and video game motherboards. Their work is often done in cooperation with private industry.

Field laboratories provide technical support for a number of specialized enforcement operations, such as counterfeit products, concentrating on textiles, steel, petroleum, or fasteners.

Customs' mobile laboratories expedite the movement of cargo through ports of entry without compromising enforcement.

COMMERCIAL FRAUD

The Customs Fraud Investigation Center (CFIC), part of the Office of Enforcement, was established in 1983 to expand Customs efforts in the areas of textiles, steel, electronics, and quota fraud. It is a multidisciplined element whose primary function is to support the total Customs effort in combatting commercial fraud.

A Fraud Detection Section was established within the Headquarters Office of Commercial Operations in 1986 to interact with the commercial community and field offices in such commercial fraud-related areas as country-of-origin, marking, trademark, and copyright violations.

In 1987, Customs initiated a new industry liaison program to improve the flow of investigative information to Customs concerning all types of commercial fraud violations. One example is the counterfeit fasteners program. This program is directed toward stopping the importation of counterfeit and mismarked bolts and fasteners that are causing a safety hazard to the public and to military personnel. Investigative efforts have also been directed toward other types of counterfeit merchandise and trademark violations.

A new Office of Commercial Fraud Enforcement was formed in the spring of 1988 by the Office of Enforcement, and the CFIC was renamed the Commercial Fraud Enforcement Center (CFEC). Import Specialists and Intelligence Analysts joined the fraud effort along with Special Agents and Inspectors.

OFFICE OF INSPECTION AND CONTROL

Protecting 96,000 miles of U.S. land, air, and sea borders, and more than 300 ports of entry, the U.S. Customs Service performs many functions aimed at controlling carriers, persons, and articles entering and leaving the United States.

This phase of the Customs operation is the most visible and has the dual purposes of (1) facilitating travelers and commerce, and (2) enforcing federal laws concerning international travel and commercial activity.

Customs Inspectors process persons, baggage, cargo, and mail, and assess and collect Customs duties, excise taxes, fees, and penalties levied on imported merchandise. Their efforts often uncover violations of federal law such as drug smuggling and counterfeiting trademark items. Consequently, they work closely with the Customs Office of Enforcement and other federal law enforcement agencies.

CARGO PROCESSING

The Customs Service processes approximately 8.5 million commercial entries into the United States each year, of which 6 million are processed through the Automated Commercial System (ACS) Cargo

Selectivity Module. The primary goal of this module is to move low-risk shipments quickly and easily and target high-risk and trace-sensitive imports for close scrutiny. This selectivity system has also been effective in seizures of cocaine smuggled in shipping containers.

AIRPORT PASSENGERS

The Office of Inspection and Control also utilizes a strategy of selectivity in order to achieve both effective enforcement and passenger facilitation. The essential elements of Inspection and Control selectivity are inspectional skills and automation.

Passenger Analysis Teams (PAT) consist of Inspectors who are trained in analyzing and using advance flight and passenger information. Included in PAT are "rover" Inspectors who are skilled in behavioral analysis techniques. They select and interview arriving passengers to determine whether a more thorough examination is needed.

The PAT teams evaluate intelligence information contained in automated systems such as the Treasury Enforcement Communications System (TECS), the National Crime Information Center (NCIC), and the National Automated Immigration Lookout System (NAILS). In addition, they analyze international sources of information through INTERPOL to determine the risk potential of flights and passengers.

Analytical data is also available to PAT teams through the APIS/EDIFACT (Advanced Passenger Information System/Electronic Data Interchange for Administration, Commerce and Transport) and the IBIS (Interagency Border Inspection System). These systems provide data on arriving flights and passengers.

Under APIS/EDIFACT, the air carrier transmits flight and passenger information via computer interface to Customs. With advance information, the "rover" can identify the selected passenger and perform a thorough examination.

IBIS is a system that combines the databases of other law enforcement agencies with Customs' TECS database and is used in conjunction with APIS/EDIFACT to retrieve information on arriving flights and passengers.

CANINE ENFORCEMENT PROGRAM

With the growth of drug smuggling, Customs has turned to detector dogs to enhance its inspection effectiveness. Today, the Customs Canine Enforcement Program, which consists of nearly 300 teams of dogs and handlers, is the most cost-effective narcotics interdiction program in the Customs Service, accounting for more than 73,000 narcotic seizures with a street value in excess of $10 billion.

OFFICE OF ENFORCEMENT

The Office of Enforcement is responsible for enforcing the nation's import and export laws. Customs Special Agents delve into smuggling attempts, fraudulent entry of merchandise, undervaluation, cargo theft and pilferage, neutrality violations, the illegal export of sophisticated technology to restricted nations, and money laundering activities.

Customs Special Agents are cross-designated with DEA drug investigative authority to combat drug smuggling. In April 1990, an agreement was reached with DEA to "cross-designate" an additional 1,000 Customs Special Agents with the authority to investigate narcotics violations as they relate to border interdiction.

Enforcement personnel utilize sources of information (informants), computers, electronic surveillance equipment, and polygraph examinations in support of their investigative activities. All enforcement offices are linked with one another, including inspectors, ports of entry, etc., through an enforcement computer network known as the Treasury Enforcement Communications System (TECS). This allows immediate access to critical information, quick referral of investigative leads, and rapid exchange of investigative information.

BLUE LIGHTNING OPERATIONS

Acting as a catalyst, the Customs Service, in 1985, combined the resources of more than 200 federal and nonfederal law enforcement agencies to form the Blue Lightning Strike Force to disrupt marine drug smuggling operations. The control center for this operation was opened in Miami, Florida, in 1986.

In 1987, two additional Blue Lightning Operation Center (BLOC) sites were established—one in Houston, Texas, and the other in Gulfport, Mississippi. Houston coordinates the marine enforcement activities along the coastal area from Mexico to Louisiana, while Gulfport is responsible for the coastal area in Mississippi, Louisiana, and Alabama.

Using radar mounted on towers, condominiums, and tethered aerostats, the three BLOC sites provide 24-hour radar coverage from the Mexico border along the Gulf coast, the west coast of Florida, the Florida Keys, and the east coast of Florida to Cape Kennedy.

Upon identifying a suspect vessel, BLOC personnel, utilizing a common and standardized radio network, contact one of the many marine or land-based law enforcement resources under the BLOC umbrella. These resources might include Customs' high-speed interceptors or aircraft from one of the member agencies. After the agencies are contacted, BLOC continues to communicate with the units, providing vectoring and intelligence updates.

Through loan/use agreements, and asset sharing, Customs provides assorted vessels and voice privacy radios to state and local agencies. In addition, more than 1,600 agents and officers from other agencies have received training in Customs laws and regulations. Once trained, these agents act as cross-designated Customs officers when performing under the direct control of a BLOC facility.

CURRENCY/MONEY LAUNDERING PROGRAM

The Customs Financial Enforcement Program is comprised of Special Enforcement Programs (BUCKSTOP), Customs Joint Financial Task Forces, the Organized Crime Drug Enforcement Task Forces (OCDETF), Undercover Operations, the International Money Laundering Investigative Network, and the Commissioner's International Money Laundering Initiative (CIMLI).

BUCKSTOP is a national inbound/outbound currency enforcement program of the Office of Enforcement and the Office of Inspection and Control, which is responsible for the interception of currency and negotiable monetary instruments in the process of being transported into or out of the United States without being properly reported.

PORNOGRAPHY ENFORCEMENT

In 1983, the President identified obscene and pornographic materials imported into the United States as a national enforcement priority, with special attention on the problem of child pornography. The Child Pornography and Protection Unit (CPPU) was created in October, 1985, and now functions as the national clearinghouse for the international enforcement of child pornography laws by the U.S. Customs Service. The CPPU has established a network of child pornography investigators who regularly work in task force groups in all Customs domestic and foreign field offices.

EXPORT ENFORCEMENT

Although Customs has been enforcing export laws since its inception, the Export Administration Act of 1979 has given Customs statutory authority to enforce export laws and exclusive jurisdiction over foreign investigations of export violations. This enforcement effort is a permanent part of Customs' mission, with both inspectional and investigative personnel dedicated to export enforcement activity.

Customs' most effective enforcement initiative to control the illegal export of valuable strategic technology to restricted nations is a proactive investigative stance involving carefully designed covert operations to disrupt smuggling conspiracies before they can harm national security. Covert operations have resulted in a number of high profile arrests and seizures involving major violations of the Arms Export Control Act (AECA) and the Export Administration Amendments Act (EAAA).

AVIATION PROGRAM

In the late 1960s, Congress authorized the establishment of the Customs air interdiction program in response to smugglers using aircraft to bring narcotics into the United States along the southern border. By 1971, Customs had acquired its first sensor-equipped aircraft, stationing them at tactical interdiction units in Miami, Florida; Corpus Christi, Texas; Tucson, Arizona; and San Diego, California. Today, the Customs National Aviation Center in Oklahoma City, Oklahoma, manages the 17 operational field offices that make up the Customs Aviation Program.

The five phases of air interdiction identified by Customs are detection, sorting, interception, tracking, and apprehension. The resources needed to accomplish these activities include the Lockheed P-3AEW, Lockheed P-3, Cessna Citation II, and the Customs High Endurance Tracker (CHET) fixed-wing aircraft. Other resources include the Command, Control, Communications, and Intelligence (C3I) Centers, radar aerostats, and the Black Hawk helicopter.

CUSTOMS NATIONAL AVIATION CENTER

The Customs National Aviation Center (CNAC) is the operational field headquarters of the Office of Aviation Operations. It provides operational, administrative, and logistical control and accountability over all nationally deployed Customs aviation resources.

Training

Basic enforcement training is held at the U.S. Customs Service Academy at the Federal Law Enforcement Training Centers in Glynco, Georgia, and Marana, Arizona. Basic Special Agent school includes courses in such areas as fraud, smuggling, export investigations, and child pornography, as well as surveillance practices, physical fitness, and firearms.

Specialized training for Customs enforcement personnel includes training in undercover work, intelligence, physical surveillance, and marine and air law enforcement.

Training programs in basic supervisory skills for mid-level and senior managers, as well as professional staff development, are also offered by the Academy. In addition, a program on "Officer Professionalism," which provides guidance on how to perform inspectional duties in a businesslike and professional manner, is offered to all inspectional personnel.

For Commercial Operations, the Import Specialists receive basic, intermediate, and specialized training. Programs for Regulatory Auditors; Entry Unit personnel; Fines, Penalties, and Forfeiture Officers; and Paralegals are also provided by the Academy.

The Academy's computer training facilities provide hands-on Automated Commercial System (ACS) instruction in all Customs major operational training programs. Legal training in such topics as border search, arrest authority, and major statutes enforced by Customs is routinely provided to Customs Officers.

Qualifications

Customs offers a number of career opportunities in the enforcement area. These include Special Agent, Inspector, Pilot, Canine Enforcement Officer, and other specialized positions that support enforcement.

To qualify, an applicant must be a U.S. citizen, under 37 years of age (for Special Agent position); pass an appropriate physical examination; pass a personal background investigation and drug test; and have at least one year of progressively responsible experience that demonstrates skill in effectively dealing with people, collecting pertinent facts, and writing reports. No less than four years (for Special Agents) or two years (for Investigators) of specialized criminal investigative experience is also needed, plus the ability to analyze and evaluate evidence and to make oral/written presentations of personally conducted investigations. Comparable experience in situations that call for tact, judgement, and resourcefulness will be considered. One scholastic year of education above high school equals nine months of work experience. Educational achievement in accounting or criminal justice/law enforcement is desirable.

Candidates must successfully complete 14 weeks of enforcement training at the Federal Law Enforcement Training Center in Glynco, Georgia. This consists of written and physical tests, as well as graded practical exercises, including one on firearms proficiency.

Candidates must be willing to travel, to work overtime, and to work under stressful conditions, and must be available for temporary and permanent assignments to a variety of geographic areas. They will also be required to carry weapons and to qualify regularly with firearms.

U.S. SECRET SERVICE

Mission

The mission of the Secret Service, an agency within the U.S. Department of the Treasury, encompasses both investigative and protective responsibilities. The protection of the President of the United States and other dignitaries is the Service's primary responsibility. Additionally, the U.S. Secret Service investigates counterfeiting of U.S. currency, forgery of government bonds and other obligations, credit and debit card fraud, and computer crimes.

Historical Review

THE INVESTIGATIVE MISSION

The U.S. Secret Service is the oldest general law enforcement agency of the federal government. In 1861, the United States was faced with both a Civil War and a growing monetary crisis. At that time there was no national currency; state governments issued their paper money through banks within their own states. The notes were printed in numerous designs, and it was difficult for the public to become familiar with the wide array of paper money then in circulation. Estimates from that period indicate that as much as one-third to one-half of all paper currency in circulation was counterfeit.

In 1863, the U.S. government introduced a new national currency that was uniform in design and printed with the very latest equipment. Treasury Department officials thought the new currency would be difficult for counterfeiters to duplicate and pass on to the public. They were wrong, however, and the new "greenbacks," as they were commonly called, were counterfeited and circulated extensively.

Counterfeiting continued to flourish despite the efforts of state and local law enforcement authorities and private investigators. Although the U.S. Constitution empowered Congress to provide for the *punishment* of counterfeiters of the securities and current coin of the United States, there was no concentrated national effort to deal with the problem.

Consequently, on July 5, 1865, the Secret Service was created for the purpose of suppressing counterfeiting of U.S. currency. William P. Wood was sworn in by Treasury Secretary McCulloch as the first Chief of the Secret Service Division, and Secret Service headquarters was established in Washington, D.C.

The scope of responsibilities assigned to the Secret Service broadened in 1867, when Congress provided funds for the purpose of "detecting persons perpetrating frauds against the government." The frauds in question initially involved "back pay and county claims" but within a few years included investigations of the Ku Klux Klan, nonconforming distillers, smugglers, mail robbers, land frauds, and a number of other infractions against federal laws.

At the request of President Theodore Roosevelt in 1905, the Secret Service assisted the Department of Justice with an investigation that exposed widespread fraudulent homestead claims by western cattle barons and coal and lumber companies. Findings also disclosed that prominent and powerful politicians were involved in these fraudulent practices. As a result of the investigation, two members of Congress were indicted and millions of acres of land were recovered for the government.

Many politicians charged that the Secret Service had no right to investigate matters outside the realm of the Treasury Department and urged that action be taken to prevent other departments of the government from borrowing Secret Service agents for investigative purposes. Congress limited the Secret Service's activities by restricting their appropriations, and all investigations of the western land frauds were discontinued.

Seeking other ways to utilize the experienced Secret Service investigators for matters not related to Treasury business, President Roosevelt transferred eight of them to the Department of Justice on July 1, 1908, creating what is now known as the Federal Bureau of Investigation.

THE PROTECTIVE MISSION

The assassination of President William McKinley in 1901 was the third such tragedy in U.S. history. The first occurred on April 14, 1865, when President Abraham Lincoln was shot by John Wilkes Booth. The second assassination ended the life of President James A. Garfield in 1881.

Following the death of President McKinley, the Secretary of Treasury and the Secretary to the President directed the Secret Service to assume the responsibility of protecting the life of the President. Thus began the second mission of the Secret Service, a mission which today is the agency's primary responsibility. Permanent authority for this function did not come until years later, however.

During a period in 1950, when the White House was undergoing renovation, President and Mrs. Truman took up official residence at the Blair House, a historic home on Pennsylvania Avenue close to the White House. On the afternoon of November 1, two Puerto Rican nationalists attempted to assassinate the President. Although their attempt failed, a member of the White House Police was killed. Congress later passed legislation providing the Secret Service with permanent authority to continue its protective and investigative missions.

The assassination of President John F. Kennedy in Dallas, Texas, on November 22, 1963, greatly affected the way the Secret Service would operate on future protective missions. Almost a year after the assassination, the President's Commission on the Assassination, more commonly known as the Warren Commission, submitted its report to President Lyndon B. Johnson. Those findings gave specific recommendations for the protection of presidents. These included an increase in the number of Special Agents assigned to presidential protection; expansion of Special Agent training; further development of the protective intelligence function; and increased liaison with other federal agencies, as well as with state and local law enforcement entities. The Service also added new technical security equipment, automatic data processing, and improved communications equipment.

Candidate Protection: Following the assassination of Robert F. Kennedy on June 5, 1968, President Lyndon B. Johnson saw that appropriate legislation was immediately passed for Secret Service protection of presidential candidates.

THE UNIFORMED DIVISION

On May 14, 1930, Congress gave the supervision of the White House Police to the Chief of the Secret Service. This action was prompted by the entrance of an unexpected and unknown visitor to the White House dining room.

On November 15, 1977, the name of the uniformed force officially became the U.S. Secret Service Uniformed Division, conforming to the law enforcement status and authority of the organization.

Functions and Activities

THE PROTECTIVE FUNCTION

Today, the Secret Service is authorized to protect:

- the President, the Vice President (or other officer next in line of succession to the Office of President), the President-elect, and Vice President-elect;
- the immediate families of the above individuals;
- former presidents and their spouses for their lifetimes, except that protection of a spouse will terminate in the event of remarriage;
- children of former presidents until age 16;
- visiting heads of foreign states or governments and their spouses traveling with them, other distinguished foreign visitors to the United States, and official representatives of the United States performing special missions abroad; and
- major presidential and vice presidential candidates, and within 120 days of the general presidential election, the spouses of such candidates.

PROTECTIVE RESEARCH

Protective research is inherent in all security operations. Protective Research Technicians and Engineers develop, test, and maintain technical devices and equipment needed to secure a safe environment for the Service's protectees.

Agents and Specialists assigned to protective research also evaluate information received from other law enforcement and intelligence agencies regarding individuals or groups who may pose a threat to protectees. Such information is critical to the Service's protective planning.

CANDIDATE AND FOREIGN DIGNITARY PROTECTION

In 1968, Congress authorized the Secret Service to protect major candidates and nominees for President and Vice President of the United States. Under the law, eligibility for Secret Service protection is determined by a committee of House and Senate leaders who make recommendations to the Secretary of the Treasury. Protection is also authorized for the spouses of presidential and vice presidential nominees for up to 120 days preceding the national election.

In 1976, Congress also authorized Secret Service protection for visiting heads of state of foreign governments.

THE INVESTIGATIVE FUNCTION

The Secret Service is the agency responsible for monitoring the integrity of U.S. currency, not only in the United States, but also abroad. It accomplishes this aspect of its mission through the services of its foreign liaison offices which are now located in Paris, Rome, London, Bonn, and Bangkok.

As new methods and mechanisms evolve for handling financial transactions involving U.S. currency, the Service's investigative jurisdictions must expand. Computer crimes spawned by 20th century technological advances are emerging as a major concern for law enforcement. Consequently, in addition to investigating the counterfeiting of certain government identification documents and devices and theft and forgery of U.S. government checks and bonds, Special Agents today investigate major cases involving credit and debit card fraud, computer fraud, automated teller machine fraud, telephone fraud involving long-distance calls, and electronic fund transfer fraud.

Two laws stemming from the 1984 Comprehensive Crime Control Act, commonly referred to as the Credit Card Fraud Act and the Computer Fraud Act, make it a federal violation to use "access devices" fraudulently. The term "access device" includes credit and debit cards, automated teller machine (ATM) cards, computer passwords, personal identification numbers (PINs) used to activate ATM machines, credit or debit card account numbers, long-distance access codes, and, among other things, the computer chips in cellular car phones that assign billing.

To protect users of these transaction devices, in 1986, Congress empowered the Secret Service, along with other federal law enforcement agencies, to investigate fraud and related activities in connection with "federal-interest" computers.

Another area of high technology targeted by criminals is the telecommunications industry. Industry trade organizations estimate that fraud costs long-distance telephone companies about $500 million per year—or about one percent of the industry's total revenue.

Information Technology in the Service Today

In the 1970s, the Service developed the Master Central Index (MCI) to share information among its more than 100 locations around the country and elsewhere in the world. MCI allows the cross-referencing of all investigative data and provides access to other related databases within the Service and in other law enforcement agencies.

The Secret Service currently operates the DES-secured (Digital Encryption Signal), all-satellite, VSAT (Very Small Aperture Terminal) information network. Through this network, the Service staffs in field offices and resident agencies access large, centralized databases of shared Secret Service information, as well as the National Crime Information Center (NCIC) and the National Law Enforcement Telecommunications Systems (NLETS). The network also provides facsimile transmission and electronic mail capabilities.

TECHNICAL SECURITY DIVISION (TSD)

The Technical Security Division is comprised of Special Agents, Security Specialists, Electronic Technicians, and Engineers. This operation supports headquarters, field offices, and the protective details through new concepts in lock, alarm, and video systems, access control, bollards, and hydraulic gates. In its protection of the President and others, TSD handles chemical, biological, radiological, and nuclear concerns. It is involved in water security, fire protection, hazardous materials, and munitions counter-measures and is responsible for the Service's air space monitoring programs.

While providing the traditional physical security measures, TSD develops new investigative equipment for the field offices. Also through its field support, it maintains, stores, and distributes equipment to the field as needed for the protective and investigative missions.

FORENSIC SERVICES DIVISION (FSD)

The Forensic Services Division consists of four branches and includes specialists in fingerprinting, visual information, graphic arts, and audio visual. In the Division are Document Analysts, Scientific/Technical

Photographers, Evidence Control Technicians, Identification Clerks, and Special Agent/Polygraph Examiners.

Today's FSD is monitoring technological developments that will allow computerized recognition of handwriting and is involved in the development of computerized voice recognition.

THE UNIFORMED DIVISION TODAY

Today, the Uniformed Division is divided into three branches: the White House Branch, the Foreign Missions Branch, and the Administration and Program Support Branch.

Uniformed Division Officers in the White House Branch are responsible for security at the Executive Mansion, the Treasury Building, the Treasury Annex and grounds, and the Old and New Executive Office Buildings. Uniformed Division Officers clear all visitors, provide fixed posts, and patrol the White House grounds.

The Foreign Missions Branch of the Uniformed Division safeguards foreign diplomatic missions in the Washington, D.C., area. Officers maintain foot and vehicular patrols in areas where embassies are located. They are assigned to fixed posts at locations where a threat has been received or at installations of countries involved in tense international situations. This branch also provides security at the Vice President's residence and at the Blair House when foreign dignitaries are in residence.

Uniformed Division Officers have additional duties closely involving them in almost every phase of the Service's protective mission.

The Administration and Program Support Branch Officers support the entire Service and operate magnetometers at the White House and at other sites to prevent persons from bringing weapons into secure areas.

Uniformed Division canine teams respond to bomb threats, suspicious packages, and other situations where explosive detection is necessary. The Uniformed Division countersniper team performs still other important security functions.

Training

New agents begin their training as soon as they enter their first field office. There they become acclimated to the agent's way of life. Each field office designates experienced agents who are responsible for assisting the new agents.

The agents begin their structured training, as do all Treasury agents, at the Federal Law Enforcement Training Center in Brunswick (Glynco), Georgia, as part of an eight-week general investigative training course.

They then attend a nine-week Special Agent Training Course at Special Agent Training and Employee Development Division Headquarters, Washington, D.C. There they learn about protection, investigations, and intelligence, and participate in extensive simulation training and testing.

Once the new agents have successfully completed the Special Agent Training Course, they again return to the field office to complete their formal On-the-Job Training (OJT) program. At the end of the agent's first year, the Special Agent in Charge of the field office makes a determination whether or not to retain the new agent.

Officers attend the courses at Glynco and specialized training at the Secret Service training facilities at the James J. Rowley Training Center, Laurel, Maryland. Other training includes instruction in computer systems, management courses, and specialized instruction. Support Personnel also receive training in these areas.

Qualifications

SPECIAL AGENT

Prior to being considered for a Special Agent position, candidates must pass the Treasury Enforcement Agent Examination. Candidates may apply at the nearest Secret Service field office. A limited number of qualified applicants will be called for a series of in-depth interviews. They must complete a polygraph examination as a condition of employment and may be asked to participate in a drug screening program.

Applicants must also undergo a thorough background investigation. Selected applicants should be prepared to wait an extended period of time for vacancies to occur. All appointees must be less than 37 years of age at the time of entrance to duty.

Because Special Agents must be in excellent physical condition, applicants must pass a comprehensive medical examination, provided by the Secret Service, prior to appointment. Weight must be in proportion to height. Distant vision must be at least 20/40 in each eye uncorrected and 20/20 in each eye corrected. Near vision must be at least 20/40 corrected.

A bachelor's degree from an accredited college or university in any field of study meets the minimum requirements for appointment at the GS-5 grade level. One additional year of specialized experience, superior academic achievement (defined as a grade point average of 2.9 or higher on a 4.0 scale), or one year of graduate study in a directly related field meets the requirements for appointment at the GS-7 grade level. In some cases an applicant may be accepted with a minimum of three years of experience, two of which are in criminal investigation, or with a comparable combination of experience and education.

UNIFORMED DIVISION

Uniformed Division applicants must be United States citizens and have a high school diploma or equivalent. They must possess a valid automobile driver's license and qualify for Top Secret clearance. Applicants must be less than 37 years of age when appointed to a Uniformed Division Officer position. Prior to being considered, they must pass a written exam. Qualified applicants then receive a personal interview and must complete a polygraph examination as a condition of employment.

Applicants must pass a comprehensive medical examination, which is provided at no cost to the applicant. Vision must be at least 20/40 in each eye, correctable to 20/20. Weight must be in proportion to height.

Selected applicants should be prepared to wait an extended period of time while a thorough background investigation is conducted.

U.S. MARSHALS SERVICE

Mission

The U.S. Marshals Service is the oldest federal law enforcement agency in the United States, having been instituted in 1789 to enforce federal laws that were administered in behalf of federal interests at the local level.

Marshals and Deputies of the Marshals Service operate both as officers of the federal courts and as law enforcement agents of the Executive Branch within the 94 federal judicial districts and the Superior Court of the District of Columbia.

The Marshals Service provides direct support to the federal courts by protecting members of the judiciary, providing security for court facilities, executing court orders, disbursing funds, and collecting fees relating to court activities. In addition, the Marshals Service has custody of federal prisoners and provides for their appearance in court, as well as their transportation to and between federal prison facilities.

The Marshals Service is also responsible for arresting federal fugitives, protecting endangered government witnesses and their families, and administering the National Asset Seizure and Forfeiture program that maintains custody and control of seized money and property acquired with the proceeds of certain illegal activities.

Functions and Activities

COURT SECURITY

In the 94 judicial districts, the principal mission of the Marshals Service is to ensure security and maintain decorum within the courtroom as well as to provide personal protection for judicial officers, witnesses, and jurors away from the court facilities when warranted.

An increase in the number of threats against members of the judiciary, U.S. attorneys, and other court officers has prompted the Marshals Service to provide round-the-clock personal protection for many court officials.

Marshals Service court security personnel provide technical assistance in the use of the latest security techniques in all phases of sensitive judicial proceedings, threat situations, judicial conferences, and courtroom and general courthouse security.

The Marshals Service administers contracts for Court Security Officers (CSOs) who provide perimeter security at court facilities throughout the nation. In one year, they prevented more than 137,800 weapons from being carried into federal courthouses.

FEDERAL FUGITIVES

The U.S. Marshals Service has primary jurisdiction nationwide in matters involving escaped federal prisoners; probation, parole, and bond default violators; and certain other related felony cases.

More than 16,000 fugitive felons and three-quarters of the federal fugitives returned to custody each year are apprehended by the Marshals Service.

In 1983, the Marshals Service began its "15 Most Wanted" list of the most dangerous career criminals sought by the Service.

The Marshals Service has also become the primary agency responsible for the return of American fugitives apprehended in foreign countries as well as foreign fugitives believed to be in the United States. In addition, the Marshals Service has representatives at the INTERPOL-U.S. National Central Bureau, at INTERPOL headquarters in France, and at the El Paso Intelligence Center (EPIC), which is operated by the Drug Enforcement Administration.

PRISONER CUSTODY

The U.S. Marshals Service assumes custody of individuals arrested by all federal agencies. On an average day, more than 13,000 unsentenced prisoners are in the custody of the Marshals Service in an estimated 825 federal, state, and local jails throughout the nation.

Upon receipt from the court, each prisoner is processed by the Marshals office, a function that includes assigning a prisoner control number; taking fingerprints and photographs; and establishing criminal and personal data records, property records, medical records, and other data. Checks are made through the National Crime Information Center (NCIC) to determine if there are other outstanding charges. Requests for name and fingerprint checks are forwarded to the FBI. More than 90,000 prisoners were processed by the Marshals Service in a recent year.

To house all these prisoners, the Marshals Service contracts with state and local governments to rent space for federal prisoners. As a result, more than two-thirds of the prisoners in Marshals Service custody are detained in state and local facilities. In return for this guaranteed space for federal prisoners, the Service provides Cooperative Agreement Program (CAP) funds to improve local jail facilities and expand jail capacity. Since 1982, the Service has awarded more than $87.7 million to counties and municipalities under CAP agreements.

PRISONER TRANSPORTATION

The U.S. Marshals Service is responsible for the transportation of federal prisoners from the time of their arrest until incarceration. With the help of the Bureau of Prisons, the Marshals Service also transfers sentenced prisoners between correctional institutions.

The Marshals Service National Prisoner Transportation System (NPTS) transports more than 107,000 prisoners a year between two or more judicial districts via coordinated air and ground systems. Most of these prisoners are transported aboard Service-owned and -operated aircraft and vehicles.

PRISONER AIRLINE

The Marshals Service fleet of aircraft, which includes two Boeing 727 airplanes, is used to move prisoners nationwide not only for the Marshals Service but also for the Bureau of Prisons and the Immigration and Naturalization Service. In addition, the Marshals Service has entered into an agreement with the U.S. Army to transport Army prisoners, both nationally and internationally.

Operating from its "hub" in Oklahoma City, Oklahoma, this aircraft transport system serves 33 cities and is the only government-operated, scheduled passenger airline in the nation. To ensure security, Deputy Marshals are stationed throughout the aircraft, and prisoners wear handcuffs and leg irons in the confines of the aircraft. Ground security is provided by Deputy Marshals and Bureau of Prison Guards at each airport transfer point. If prisoners cannot be moved in one day, they are housed overnight at various Bureau of Prison facilities around the country.

On a "space-available" basis, the Marshals Service also assists state and local law enforcement agencies in transporting non-federal prisoners between different jurisdictions.

WITNESS PROTECTION

Government witnesses and their immediate dependents whose lives are in danger as a result of their testimony against organized crime and major criminals receive protection under the Marshals Witness Security Program (WITSEC).

The procedure for admitting a witness to the WITSEC program typically involves obtaining a court-ordered name change and providing new identities with authentic documentation for the witness and family. Among the types of assistance provided to the witness are housing, medical care, job training, and employment. Subsistence funding to cover basic living expenses is also provided while the program participants become self-sufficient in the relocation area.

The Marshals Service provides 24-hour protection to all witnesses while they are in a "threat" environment and upon their return to a danger area for pretrial conferences, testimony at trials, or other court appearances.

NATIONAL ASSET SEIZURE AND FORFEITURE

Under the National Asset Seizure and Forfeiture (NASAF) program, the U.S. Marshals Service is responsible for the management and disposal of seized and forfeited assets that had been purchased with the proceeds of drug trafficking and organized crime.

The Marshals Service is currently managing more than $1.35 billion worth of property seized from criminals. Seized assets include cars, boats, and aircraft; residential and commercial real properties as diverse as horse farms, recording studios, golf courses, banks, historic mansions, restaurants, and retail stores; cash, jewelry, precious metals, and a host of other items.

Seized assets must be secured, inventoried, appraised, stored, and otherwise maintained. Forfeited assets must be prepared for sale or other disposition in accordance with law. Much of the work in maintaining and disposing of seized assets is accomplished through professional managers and commercial vendors under contract with the Marshals Service or through court-appointed trustees. These property management sources range from independent professional appraisers to large property management firms.

Forfeited property is disposed of in various ways, such as public sale or other commercially feasible means; transfer to federal, state, or local law enforcement agencies for official use; and salvage, scrap, or destruction, as appropriate.

In the case of forfeited property to be sold, a variety of marketing and sales options are used, ranging from the traditional Marshals' sale to using brokers, sales agents, and other commercial liquidation services. Classified advertising sections of local newspapers provide public notice of forfeited property to be sold by the Marshals Service.

All forfeited currency and all money received from the sale of forfeited property is deposited in the Justice Assets Forfeiture Fund. The primary purpose of the Fund is to ensure that enough money is available for the expenses related to the seizure and forfeiture of additional property.

In addition, under the Equitable Sharing Program, money from the Fund is shared with state and local law enforcement agencies that participated in the investigations that led to the forfeiture.

A portion of the surplus receipts from the Fund are transferred to the Bureau of Prisons for prison construction. Federal prison space, therefore, is being expanded with the help of money seized from drug traffickers and organized crime figures.

EXECUTION OF COURT ORDERS

The U.S. Marshal, through the deputies, is responsible for serving the process from the U.S. Courts, including summonses and complaints in civil actions, subpoenas in both civil and criminal actions, writs of habeas corpus, and writs of attachment.

SPECIAL OPERATIONS

The Special Operations Group (SOG), the Air Operations Branch, and the Missile Escort Program constitute the Service's Special Operations function.

A force of Deputy U.S. Marshals, known as SOGs, respond to emergency situations, such as civil disturbances, terrorist incidents, or hostage situations where there is a violation of federal law or when federal property is endangered.

The Deputy Marshals in SOG have their "alert equipment" with them at all times and can arrive fully equipped and self-supporting at any target location within six hours after receiving the order to assemble.

SOG members are volunteers for this duty. They undergo extensive training in tactics and weaponry at Camp Beauregard, the SOG training center near Pineville, Louisiana. These full-time Deputy Marshals are assigned to district offices throughout the nation and are part of the regular Deputy staffing complement. However, they are on call 24 hours a day in the event SOG forces are deployed.

THE AIR OPERATIONS BRANCH

The Air Operations Branch, centered in Oklahoma City, Oklahoma, operates aircraft used for transporting prisoners. The Branch also transports SOG teams and other Marshals Service personnel in response to emergency situations and conducts flights to foreign countries for prisoner exchanges.

THE MISSILE ESCORT PROGRAM

The Missile Escort Program provides security and law enforcement assistance to the Department of Defense and U.S. Air Force during the movement of Minuteman and Cruise missiles between military facilities.

Training

Training in the U.S. Marshals Service occurs at three levels: Basic, Advanced, and Special Operations. The Service operates the U.S. Marshals Service Training Academy at the Federal Law Enforcement Training Center (FLETC), Glynco, Georgia, and a second facility for its Special Operations Group and for other federal and non-federal agencies at Camp Beauregard, Louisiana.

BASIC DEPUTY MARSHAL TRAINING

U.S. Marshal candidates must successfully complete 14 weeks of intensive basic training at the Service's Academy. For the first 8 weeks, candidates attend the Criminal Investigator training program conducted for 56 different law enforcement organizations, including the U.S. Secret Service, the Naval Investigative Service, the Bureau of Alcohol, Tobacco, and Firearms, the Internal Revenue Service, and the U.S. Customs Service.

Candidates who successfully complete the first training phase enter the Basic Deputy U.S. Marshal training, which is focused specifically on those skills required by the Service. This six-week portion of the program covers judicial protection, prisoner transportation, witness security, fugitive investigations and apprehensions, and execution and enforcement of court orders.

SPECIALIZED AND ADVANCED TRAINING

Within three years of entry on duty, Deputy U.S. Marshals receive additional training in key operational areas such as asset seizure and forfeiture, enforcement operations, court security, and witness security. Moreover, the Advanced Deputy U.S. Marshals training program is a four-week course designed to enhance the deputy's knowledge, skills, and proficiency in all operational areas.

The specialized Protective Services School is a two-week program dedicated to "dignitary" protection. This school was established to train personnel responsible for the Witness Security Program.

The Fugitive Course is a two-week training session focusing primarily on narcotic fugitive investigations, clandestine labs, and narcotics trafficking.

SPECIAL OPERATIONS—CAMP BEAUREGARD

Training for the Service's Special Operations Group (SOG) members is conducted by Marshals Service personnel at the Service's facility in Camp Beauregard, Louisiana. SOG deputies are trained in varied disciplines such as building entry and search techniques, helicopter operations (repelling and employment), confrontation management (both urban and rural), operational planning, small unit tactics, bomb recognition, emergency care, etc.

Under the sponsorship of the Anti-Terrorism Assistance Program of the U.S. Department of State, nearly 300 police personnel from Mexico, Ecuador, Honduras, Costa Rica, Bolivia, the Philippines, and Colombia have received training in counterterrorism, advanced specialized police tactics, and personal protection from SOG personnel.

A CAREER AS A DEPUTY U.S. MARSHAL

To qualify as a Deputy U.S. Marshal, applicants must:

- be U.S. citizens;
- be between the ages of 21 and 37;
- have a bachelor's degree, or three years of responsible experience, or an equivalent combination of education and experience;
- pass the TEA examination;
- complete an oral interview;

- be in excellent physical condition;
- permit a background investigation; and
- complete a rigorous 14-week basic training program at the U.S. Marshals Service Training Academy.

For further information, contact:

U.S. Marshals Service
Personnel Management Division Law Enforcement Recruiting Branch
600 Army Navy Drive
Arlington, VA 22202-4210
Telephone: (202) 307-9437

TWO

Federal Law Enforcement Training

CONTENTS

The Federal Law Enforcement Training Center   35

The Criminal Investigator Training Program   39

THE FEDERAL LAW ENFORCEMENT TRAINING CENTER

The Federal Law Enforcement Training Center (FLETC) is an interagency training facility that was established in 1970 to serve the training needs of the federal enforcement community. This bureau within the Department of the Treasury provides training for police officers and criminal investigators from almost 60 federal organizations.

Operations

The Department of the Treasury was selected as the center's lead agency because at that time it had the largest number of personnel to be trained and had been conducting training in its own enforcement school. Thus, the nucleus of the new training center was formed, and training operations began in temporary facilities in the Washington, D.C., area in 1970. The former Glynco Naval Air Station near Brunswick, Georgia, was selected as the site for the permanent facility, and the center relocated to Glynco during the summer of 1975.

Although it was primarily designed for residential training operations, the center conducts limited export training at other locations. This option is exercised when the programs being conducted do not require any specialized facilities and when regional-geographical concentrations of personnel can be identified.

Marana Facility

In 1984, the Bureau of Indian Affairs (BIA) requested FLETC to assume responsibility for operating an FLETC Indian Police Academy at the Pinal Air Park, about 30 miles northwest of Tucson, Arizona. Basic training for BIA and tribal police personnel is conducted there as a satellite operation of FLETC's Glynco headquarters. The Marana facility is also used by FLETC and participating agencies as a site for short-term, advanced training of personnel located in the western United States. Customs service advanced training is conducted at Marana.

Programs
BASIC TRAINING

The majority of the students' weeks of training at the center is devoted to basic programs for criminal investigators and police officers who have the authority to make arrests and carry firearms. These programs provide students with a combination of classroom instruction and "hands-on" practical exercises. These exercises often involve hired role-players who act as victims, witnesses, and suspects. The students apply their classroom knowledge in exercises that include a scenario and simulate typical situations encountered on the job.

The criminal investigator students are from such agencies as the Bureau of Alcohol, Tobacco, and Firearms; Customs Service; Internal Revenue Service; Marshals Service; Secret Service; and the various staffs of the Federal Government's Inspectors General. The course length is eight weeks.

ADVANCED TRAINING

The center provides the facilities, equipment, and support services to conduct advanced and specialized training for both uniformed police officers and criminal investigators. This training may be conducted entirely by center personnel, participating agency personnel, or a combination of center and agency personnel. The courses vary in length depending on the subjects being taught. Examples of advanced training programs conducted by the center are: advanced law enforcement photography; firearms instructor training; white collar crime; marine law enforcement; archeological resources theft protection; and computer fraud and data processing investigations.

Examples of agency-conducted advanced programs are the Immigration and Naturalization Service offerings in anti-smuggling for its criminal investigators and anti-smuggling officers, and the Internal Revenue Service offerings for its investigators in tax fraud investigative training.

TOPICS OF STUDY

Following is a description of the eight major instructional areas for officers and investigators participating in center programs.

Legal: Learning the rules and principles of law, especially as they relate to investigation, detention, arrest, and search and seizure, provides working guidelines for police officers and criminal investigators. Frequent changes in the law make it particularly important for officers to be well informed in order to arrest suspects properly, gather admissible evidence, and give proper respect to the rights of individuals.

Enforcement Techniques: Students learn and apply such techniques as fingerprinting, description and identification, law enforcement photography, and collection and preservation of evidence. In the laboratory sessions, such skills as lifting and rolling fingerprints and identifying narcotics are practiced.

Behavioral Science: Officers and investigators are taught awareness of individual, group, social, and cultural motivators and their effect on human behavior. They become conscious of the sources of potential human relations problems and examine alternative means of preventing and resolving conflicts. They also learn to recognize the various sources of stress and how to employ appropriate coping mechanisms in dealing with stress. The students must be able to defuse crisis and non-crisis situations in a safe and humane manner.

Hired role-players are used in these exercises, as well as in those for developing interviewing techniques. Videotape equipment is used extensively in practical exercises on interviewing a witness so that students can play back the tapes made of their interviews prior to the instructor's critique.

Enforcement Operations: Students acquire a basic working knowledge of the various operational procedures specific to their job functions as either criminal investigators or uniformed police officers. The former receive instruction in using techniques such as working with informants, conducting a surveillance, executing search warrants, and working undercover operations. The latter receive instruction in radio communications, notetaking, report writing, and various operational skills and patrol procedures.

Specialty training is provided in the areas of computers, firearms, physical techniques, and driver specialties for officers and investigators in the basic and advanced programs.

Computer/Economic Crime: Just as the development of advanced computer technology has proven to be beneficial and cost effective for large and small businesses throughout the United States, it has been adopted by the criminal element in this country for the same reasons. To help investigators detect and combat computer crimes and crimes where the computer has been used by the criminals to maintain illegal business records, FLETC has programs to teach computer skills to investigators of the various law enforcement organizations. The Computer/Economic Crime Division provides instruction in the investigation of white collar crime and the understanding and employment of computers as investigative tools. The division personnel teach courses in the following basic and advanced programs: white collar crime; computer fraud and data processing investigation; procurement and contract fraud; and a series of microcomputer programs for investigators and auditors.

Firearms: The students are introduced to the safe and accurate operation of a weapon. Fundamental training is done on silhouette-shaped targets designed to teach area of aim. After students learn how to shoot, the remainder of the courses provides realistic training in judgment shooting. The majority of the training is with .38 caliber revolvers, but familiarization with shoulder weapons is also provided.

Physical Techniques: This program provides training in the physical activities often involved with law enforcement. Motivation to proper physical conditioning, arrest techniques, and self-defense are taught in addition to emergency medical procedures and water survival.

Driver and Marine: The center's basic driver training program consists of three phases designed to teach vehicle limitations, sharpen skills in recognition of traffic hazards, and improve reflexes and decision-making ability. One phase, defensive driving, consists of negotiating a series of obstacles at slow speeds. The second phase is skid control taught on a water slick skid pan. The third phase of the course is highway response driving. Training in the operation of four-wheel-drive vehicles is also provided for officers of such agencies as the National Park Service, Border Patrol, and Customs Service, because they are required to use these vehicles in the performance of their duties.

Another part of this division is the marine aspect that provides advanced-level instruction in the center's Marine Law Enforcement Training Program. A variety of subjects is included in the program, all geared toward teaching the handling of small boats in the law enforcement environment; among the topics are navigation, the rules of the road, mechanical troubleshooting, pursuit, board and search, and firing from aboard a boat.

Staff

The training staff of the center is made up of experienced instructors who have a minimum of five years of law enforcement experience. A portion of the instructors are federal officers and investigators on detailed assignment to the center from their parent agencies. This mix of permanent and detailed instructors creates a balance of experience and fresh insight from the field.

Facilities

Many facilities that were used by the Navy have been adapted by the center. These include classrooms, dormitories, recreation facilities, dining hall, and administrative and logistical support facilities. To supplement these, a construction program, which was formally begun in November, 1977, has been completed. It includes: a new classroom building; a new ninety-six-point indoor firing range; a new driver training course; additional physical specialties facilities; an addition to the existing dining hall.

The new classroom building also houses various special-purpose areas—the library, language laboratory, an interviewing techniques complex, and various criminalistics teaching laboratories for rolling and lifting fingerprints and testing narcotics. The indoor firing range provides eight separate ranges of twelve firing points each. Classrooms and weapons cleaning areas are also conveniently located in the range building. The new driver-training complex provides the ability to create more realistic situations for training in defensive driving, skid control, and highway driving. The physical specialties complex is a combination of existing and new buildings, which provide space for the many activities conducted there. The existing dining hall has been remodeled and greatly expanded to double the seating capacity.

During 1985, Glynco reaffirmed its commitment to exploit the latest technologies by applying automated data processing and computer technology to law enforcement training and increasing administrative applications. A long-range plan that has established a method and timetable for designing, staffing, and implementing several new computer systems was developed and approved. The new facilities and systems have greatly enhanced the center's goal of providing high quality, cost-effective training for the men and women who enforce our federal laws.

THE CRIMINAL INVESTIGATOR TRAINING PROGRAM

The techniques of criminal investigation are essential to the work of the police officer, the uniformed guard, the patrol officer, and the Special Agent. For this reason, all Special Agent trainees pass through the Criminal Investigator Training Program before they receive the more specialized training that is specific to their particular duties in their own bureaus.

The Federal Law Enforcement Training Center's Criminal Investigator Training Program provides, on an interagency basis, a program of instruction that fulfills all the basic criminal investigative training requirements necessary for responsible and competent job accomplishment. Rather than being agency specific, the program aims to help individuals attain the common denominator of the duties, skills, and tasks that are expected of all investigators, regardless of agency affiliation.

In today's changing world, criminal investigators are faced with a variety of situations that, in addition to demanding traditional law enforcement skills, require an awareness of or expertise in human behavior, modern technology, cultural sensitivity, law, and other interdisciplinary approaches to effective law enforcement. The Criminal Investigator Training Program is designed to meet these training needs and others, as identified through constant program monitoring and ongoing research, as well as through information on new procedures and techniques received from participating organizations.

Length of Program

The Criminal Investigator Training Program consists of forty training days, excluding weekends and federal holidays. There are a total of 333 course hours in the program, covered in 8 weeks of training. The duration of the total program is 357 hours.

Standard Daily Schedule

Morning Session*	7:30 A.M. to 11:30 A.M.
Lunch	11:30 A.M. to 12:30 P.M.
Afternoon Session*	12:30 P.M. to 4:30 P.M.

Student Evaluation

The Criminal Investigator Training Program cognitive testing system consists of five examinations: three legal examinations and two comprehensive examinations. In addition, the student is expected to

*Classes are fifty minutes in length with breaks scheduled according to subject matter being presented and the status of practical exercise activity.

satisfactorily complete a series of practical exercises and homework assignments. Satisfactory completion of all examinations, practical exercises, and assignments is required for graduation from the Criminal Investigator Training Program.

Written Examinations

The student is required to achieve a score of at least 70 percent on each of the 5 written examinations. The student is allocated a total of one hour and forty-five minutes to complete each examination. Immediately following each examination, a fifteen-minute examination review is conducted, allowing the students to assess their performance on the examination. Official results of examinations are posted as soon as possible after the completion of the examination. Each individual student's grade is maintained in confidentiality as far as fellow classmates are concerned. Student examination scores are available to the student's agency through official channels.

In the event a student fails to achieve a score of at least 70 percent on any written examination, the student will be placed on academic probation. During this period, additional assistance will be made available to the student, upon request, in the form of counseling, out-of-class study assignments, and personal instructional sessions. The student must take a remedial examination covering the same subjects as the original failed examination within three working days of the failure date. The student must successfully pass this remedial examination to remain eligible for graduation.

A student may be placed on academic probation once after failing a regularly scheduled examination. In the event a student fails a second regularly scheduled examination (or fails to achieve a passing score on *any* remedial examination), the student will not be eligible for graduation from the Criminal Investigator Training Program.

Practical Exercises

The second component of the CITP evaluation system is the measurement of skills acquired during training. A student must satisfactorily complete all phases of the practical exercises to successfully complete the training program.

The practical exercises are designed to provide the student with as much individual attention and instruction as possible. This area involves the development of psychomotor skills and the basic knowledge needed to perform at least minimally in the occupational role.

Evaluation of student performance is made during various practical exercises. Performance will be judged by the student's actual ability to satisfactorily complete the required tasks.

The center employs the practice of providing two remedial examinations for all practical exercises. If a student fails to achieve mastery in any practical exercise after the two remedials, a certificate will not be awarded.

Firearms Training

Marksmanship is evaluated on a point system. Each student must qualify with a minimum of 70 percent on the practical pistol course. A student who does not achieve a satisfactory level of proficiency in the practical pistol course (210 points out of 300 points—70 percent) will be offered the opportunity to participate in remedial training to correct the deficiency. The total amount of scheduled firearms remedial training offered to a student will not exceed eight hours and two retests. Failure to qualify on this course will preclude the student from successful completion of the training program.

Distinguished Graduate Designation

To be designated a Distinguished Graduate, a student must achieve an overall average of 95 percent on the written examinations, a rating of satisfactory with no remediation on all practical exercises, and a satisfactory score on the required firearms qualification courses.

Course Information

Responsibility for the supervision and delivery of course material to students in the Criminal Investigator Training Program rests with the Office of General Training and the Office of Special Training. The Office of General Training is comprised of five specialized divisions as follows: Behavioral Science, Enforcement Operations, Enforcement Techniques, Legal, and Security Specialties. The Office of Special Training is comprised of four specialized divisions as follows: Driver and Marine, Financial Fraud Institute, Firearms, and Physical Techniques.

Just as laws, kinds and patterns of offenses, and techniques of investigation, enforcement, and prosecution are all subject to change, so the course of study in the Criminal Investigator Training Program is constantly revised and refined to meet current needs. The full program of instruction in the criminal investigator training program that follows is based upon the program in use in 1999. The narrative descriptions of the individual divisions and the individual, in-depth course descriptions are based on the program in an earlier year. You will note some lack of correspondence between information abstracted from course syllabi of different years. Precise format and specific content of courses might have evolved, but the information in these pages should provide you with a good introduction to the training program.

The course descriptions and objectives that follow are presented by instructional division groupings in this format: course title, length and method of presentation, description, objectives, and method of evaluation. The length of the course is shown in hour and minute notations. The three methods of presentation listed in this format are described as follows:

- **Lecture/classroom:** A training situation, indoors or outdoors, in which instructional material is being presented by an instructor.
- **Laboratory:** A training situation, indoors or outdoors, in which students are practicing skills under the guidance of an instructor(s).
- **Practical Exercise:** A training situation, indoors or outdoors, in which students, under the supervision/evaluation of an instructor(s), are participating in a law enforcement-related scenario or performing a law enforcement-related skill that will be graded.

FULL PROGRAM OF INSTRUCTION
CRIMINAL INVESTIGATOR TRAINING PROGRAM

Office of General Training

Course	Hours of Instruction			
	Lecture	Laboratory	Practical Exercise	Total
Behavioral Science				
Ethics and Conduct	2:00			2:00
Interviewing	6:00	4:00	8:00	18:00
Victim/Witness Awareness	2:00			2:00
Subtotal	10:00	4:00	8:00	22:00
Enforcement Operations				
Continuous Case Investigation	1:00			1:00
Criminal Investigations and Case Management	2:00			2:00
Execution of a Search Warrant	4:00	4:00	6:00	14:00
Federal Firearms Violations	2:00			2:00
Firearms Policy		2:00		2:00
Informants	2:00			2:00
Investigative				4:00
Report Writing	3:00		1:00	
Investigative Skills Laboratory		4:00		4:00
Organized Crime	4:00			4:00
Orientation to Federal Law Enforcement Agencies	1:00			1:00
Sources of Information	2:00			2:00
Surveillance	4:00	2:00	4:00	10:00
Undercover Operations	2:00			2:00
Subtotal	29:00	11:00	10:00	50:00
Enforcement Techniques				
Crime Scene Investigation	4:00	2:00		6:00
Description and Identification	2:00			2:00
Fingerprinting	2:00		2:00	4:00
Narcotics	4:00	4:00		8:00
Photography	4:00		2:00	6:00

| | Hours of Instruction | | | |
Course	Lecture	Laboratory	Practical Exercise	Total
Questioned Documents	2:00			2:00
Undercover Operations				
Technical Equipment	2:00			2:00
Subtotal	20:00	6:00	4:00	30:00
Legal				
Conspiracy	4:00			4:00
Constitutional Law	2:00			2:00
Court Testimony				
Including Mock Trial	4:00		4:00	8:00
Criminal Law	2:00			2:00
Detention and Arrest	10:00			10:00
Evidence	10:00			10:00
Federal Court Procedures	8:00			8:00
Parties to Criminal Offenses	2:00			2:00
Relevant Federal Statutes	12:00			12:00
Assault	(:30)			
Bribery	(:30)			
Civil Rights	(2:00)			
Electronic Surveillance	(2:00)			
Entrapment	(1:30)			
False Identification	(:30)			
False Statements, 18 USC 1001	(:30)			
Freedom of Information Act/				
Privacy Act	(1:00)			
Mail Fraud, 18 USC 1341	(1:00)			
Obstruction of Justice	(2:00)			
Theft and Embezzlement	(:30)			
Search and Seizure and				
Affidavit Return P.E.	20:00		1:00	21:00
Self-Incrimination	6:00			6:00
Subtotal	80:00		5:00	85:00
Security Specialties				
Bombs and Explosives	2:00			2:00
Building and Room Searches		2:00		2:00
Contemporary Terrorism	2:00			2:00
Introduction to Officer				
Safety and Survival	2:00			2:00
Introduction to Tactics		2:00		2:00
OPSEC	1:00			1:00

	Hours of Instruction			
Course	Lecture	Laboratory	Practical Exercise	Total
Personal Protection	1:00			1:00
Rapid Building Entry and Search Techniques		2:00		2:00
Subtotal	8:00	6:00		14:00
Office of General Training Division Total	147:00	27:00	27:00	201:00

OFFICE OF SPECIAL TRAINING

Course	Lecture	Laboratory	Practical Exercise	Total
Driver and Marine				
Felony Vehicle Stops	1:00	2:00		3:00
Nonemergency Vehicle Operation	1:30	3:30	:30	5:30
Orientation	:30			:30
Subtotal	3:00	5:30	:30	9:00
Financial Fraud Institute				
Computer Training for Investigators	4:00	2:00		6:00
Subtotal	4:00	2:00		6:00
Firearms				
Basic Marksmanship	1:00	6:00		7:00
Firearms Safety Rules	:45			:45
Instinctive Reaction		1:00		1:00
Judgment Pistol Shooting		2:00	1:00	3:00
Practical Pistol Course	1:00	9:00	2:00	12:00
Reduced Light Course of Fire	:30	1:30		2:00
9mm Semiautomatic Pistol	2:00	4:00		6:00
Shotgun Course	2:00	4:00		6:00
Situational Response	1:00	1:00		2:00
Weapons Maintenance and Cleaning	:05	:10		:15
Subtotal	8:20	28:40	3:00	40:00

Course	Hours of Instruction			
	Lecture	Laboratory	Practical Exercise	Total
Physical Techniques				
Cardiopulmonary Resuscitation	2:00	3:30	2:30	8:00
Introduction to				
Physical Techniques	2:00			2:00
Lifestyle Management	2:00			2:00
Mandatory Physical Fitness		28:00		28:00
Non Lethal Control Techniques	7:00	19:00	4:00	30:00
Physical Efficiency Battery		4:00		4:00
Removal and Transport				
of Reluctant Suspects	1:00		2:00	3:00
Subtotal	14:00	56:30	6:30	77:00
Office of Special Training				
Division Total	29:20	92:40	10:00	132:00
All Divisions Total	176:20	119:40	37:00	333:00

Administrative Hours	
Examinations and Review	12:30
Graduation	1:00
Health Screening and Uniform Measure	1:00
Student Feedback System	4:30
Uniform Issue and Return	2:00
Registration and Orientation	3:00
Total	24:00

Total Program Length Hours	
Lecture	176:20
Laboratory	119:40
Practical Exercise	37:00
Administrative	24:00
Total	357:00

Behavioral Science Division

Over the years, the Behavioral Science Division has provided several courses of instruction in the Criminal Investigator Training Program: ethics and conduct, interpersonal stress, interviewing, and victim/witness awareness.

Unlike the worker in many occupations, a criminal investigator is placed in situations that are without benefit of easily accessible supervision and, often, without any clear written guidelines regarding specific alternatives. Conditions such as these require the investigator to make decisions based on training, instinct, and common sense. For these reasons, a clear understanding of government ethics is necessary—particularly as they are applied to law enforcement activities.

The Behavioral Science Division's course in interpersonal stress management enables students to understand themselves better and to become more effective to their organizations.

A major course taught in the Criminal Investigator Training Program by the Behavioral Science Division is interviewing. In addition to the classroom lectures and exercises, the Division employs professional role-players who confront students with a variety of realistic interviewing scenarios designed to provide a valid test of students' knowledge and skills. Videotape replays are used to critique student performance.

In other center programs, this division teaches a variety of courses designed to enhance law enforcement skills through the development of insight and awareness in human behavior characteristics, with the goal of avoiding or resolving conflicts through improved human relations skills. Included are: authority, communications, conflict management, cross-cultural communications, detection of deception, handling abnormals, hostage situations, hostage-terrorist relationships, post-shooting trauma, roles, values, and on other behavioral topics.

DESCRIPTION OF A TYPICAL COURSE IN THE BEHAVIORAL SCIENCE DIVISION

Course: Interviewing

Length and Method of Presentation:

Lecture	Laboratory	Practical Exercise	Total
6:00	4:00	8:00	18:00

Description: This course is designed to teach the student basic interviewing techniques that utilize a combination of behavioral techniques blended with proven questioning techniques. Students learn to select the proper interview time, place, and environment and learn to formulate interview objectives. The inherent problems, precautions, and benefits in utilizing interpreters during interviews are discussed. The practical exercise includes a series of interview in which the students interview role-players in various situations and are critiqued as to their techniques and performance.

Terminal Performance Objectives: Given a scenario and a comprehensive examination consisting of multiple choice questions, the student will identify and utilize in a simulated interview the principles of the communication system as they apply to interviewing, the essentials in preparation for an interview, and appropriate procedures for conducting an effective interview with an emphasis on conducting the interview in accordance with the principles delineated during the course of instruction to the satisfaction of one or more subject matter experts.

Interim Performance Objectives:

1. Identify and utilize the principles of nonverbal communication as they apply to interview situations.
2. Identify and utilize the principles of verbal, symbolic, and written communications as they apply to interview situations.
3. Identify methods of planning the interview.
4. Identify methods for formulating questions for the interview.
5. Identify factors relative to the physical environment that should be considered when planning the interview.
6. Identify procedures appropriate to follow within the five stages of the interview.
7. Identify procedures appropriate to follow when a team of two persons conducts an interview.
8. Use appropriate measures to plan a simulated interview.
9. Use appropriate procedures to conduct the specific simulated interview as outlined in the P.E. scenario.

Method of Evaluation: Written, multiple-choice examination; demonstrated proficiency.

Enforcement Operations Division

The day-to-day, hands-on, operational aspects of law enforcement are the paramount training concern of the Enforcement Operations Division. In addition to giving classroom presentations, this division conducts extensive practical exercises in vital areas such as: surveillance; executing search warrants; and conducting felony car stops and searches. Realism is the keynote of all practical exercises. This is attained through the employment of professional role-players, appropriate settings, and carefully designed scenarios, as well as transportation, firearms, communications equipment, and other modern implements of the law enforcement profession.

The Enforcement Operations Division is constantly alert to changing procedures, techniques, and operational concepts, and it ensures that course material reflective of such change is incorporated in the program on a timely basis. Courses recently taught by the division in the Criminal Investigator Training Program have included crowd control, dangerous motorcycle gangs, execution of a search warrant, federal firearms violations, felony car stops, firearms policy, informants, orientation to federal law enforcement agencies, report writing, sources of information, surveillance, and undercover operations. Courses taught by this division in other center programs include: case development and informants, orientation to criminal investigations, patrol procedures, radio communications, vehicle search, and V.I.P. protection.

DESCRIPTION OF A TYPICAL COURSE IN THE ENFORCEMENT OPERATIONS DIVISION

Course: Execution of a Search Warrant

Length and Method of Presentation:

Lecture	Laboratory	Practical Exercise	Total
4:00	4:00	6:00	14:00

Description: This course defines the purpose of raids and sets forth procedures for planning a raid, including personnel requirements, equipment needed, raid procedure, the entering detail, the covering detail, the search detail, preventing the escape of violators, minimizing danger, and follow-up procedures. The student will participate in the execution of a search warrant under the direction and supervision of an instructor. The final practical exercise, in which students will execute a second search warrant, is graded.

Terminal Performance Objectives: Given a comprehensive examination consisting of multiple choice questions—some of which may be situations involving the execution of a search warrant—and a practical exercise requiring the simulated execution of a search warrant, the student will identify and, working as a team member, utilize procedures and techniques involved in the execution of a search warrant in accordance with the principles delineated during the course of instruction to the satisfaction of one or more faculty subject matter experts.

Interim Performance Objectives:

1. Identify information to be gathered and disseminated, and define the decisions to be made during the pre-execution of a search warrant investigation.
2. Identify the basic procedures to follow in the pre-execution of a search warrant briefing.
3. Identify factors to consider when selecting ESW team members, including the use of state and local officers.
4. Identify the duties of the entry team and means of carrying out these duties.
5. Identify the duties of the cover team and means of carrying out these duties.
6. Identify the duties of the search team and means of carrying out these duties.
7. Identify means of controlling occupants during the execution of a search warrant.
8. Identify means of offsetting false accusations arising from executions of search warrants.
9. Identify procedures to follow to execute an arrest when executing a search warrant.
10. Identify the basic procedures to follow in the post-ESW critique.
11. Plan a simulated execution of a search warrant, including gathering information, briefing, and selecting team members.
12. Conduct a systematic search of a premises following the principles delineated in the crime scene investigation course.
13. Enter a premises, control the occupants, and conduct a search of the premises.
14. Exhibit proper arrest techniques and search techniques when searching and arresting individuals during the simulated execution of a search warrant according to the principles delineated during physical specialties training.
15. Conduct a post-ESW critique following the simulated execution of a search warrant.

Method of Evaluation: Written, multiple-choice examination; demonstrated proficiency.

Enforcement Techniques Division

The design, development, and conduct of courses relating to contemporary scientific and technological law enforcement knowledge and skills are the prime missions of the Enforcement Techniques Division. Another important division mission is continuing research and exploration into innovative law enforcement methods and techniques to ensure that course content is consistent with state-of-the-art levels.

Classroom lectures—reinforced through various training aids, laboratory, and practical exercise applications—provide meaningful learning experiences for the students. Courses taught by this division in the Criminal Investigator Training Program have included: bombs and explosives, counterfeiting, crime scene investigations, description and identification, fingerprinting, narcotics, officer safety and survival, organized crime, photography, questioned documents, and terrorism. Courses taught in other center programs include: counterfeit currency, crime lab, crime scene search and sketch, defendant processing, introduction to criminalistics, preliminary police investigation, physical security, rape investigation, and violent death investigation.

DESCRIPTION OF A TYPICAL COURSE IN THE ENFORCEMENT TECHNIQUES DIVISION

Course: Officer Safety and Survival

Length and Method of Presentation:

Lecture	Laboratory	Practical Exercise	Total
6:00	2:00		8:00

Description: Through lecture, class discussion, classroom demonstration, and laboratory, this course examines a law enforcement officer's personal weapons system and mistakes made by officers that have been shown to cause injury and death. It will also consider the use of cover and concealment as well as safe methods of foot pursuits and building and room entries. It will also explain the problems faced by officers when working in reduced light. The course will examine proper procedures to be followed if an officer is required to shoot a suspect.

Terminal Performance Objectives: Given a set of facts depicting possible injury to the officer or others on a comprehensive examination consisting of multiple choice questions, the student will identify common errors that might reduce officer safety and determine appropriate means of maintaining maximum officer safety during dangerous situations and after shooting situations, in accordance with the principles delineated during the course of instruction.

Interim Performance Objectives:

1. Identify various errors that could put an officer in danger.
2. Identify the best available cover to use in various types of dangerous situations.
3. Identify various methods of using cover effectively.
4. Identify means of maximizing officer safety and the safety of others when working in reduced light situations.
5. Identify appropriate actions to take in shooting or potential shooting situations.
6. Identify appropriate procedures for maintaining maximum officer safety after a shooting incident, before a back-up arrives.
7. Identify appropriate procedures for maintaining maximum officer safety after a shooting incident, after a back-up arrives.

Method of Evaluation: Written, multiple-choice examination.

Legal Division

The mission of the Legal Division is to provide current and relevant training in the areas of criminal, constitutional, and civil law applicable to law enforcement officers.

In the basic programs, legal training provided in the classroom is reinforced by application of those principles in various practical exercises conducted by the legal staff and other divisions at the center—including in most programs, a realistic mock-trial experience. This is conducted in a courtroom setting and submits the student to strenuous direct and cross examination, as well as to the correct method of introducing various types of evidence.

The Legal Division conducts continuing research and case review and furthers professional development through attendance at programs of the American Bar Association, the Justice Department, and others. Court decisions and other developments impacting on legal aspects of law enforcement are incorporated into lesson plans and classroom presentations on a timely basis. Particular emphasis is placed on criminal and civil sanctions that may be instituted against those officers who act in violation of constitutional rights.

Courses conducted by the Legal Division in the criminal investigator or other center programs include: civil rights, conspiracy, constitutional law, court testimony, detention and arrest, evidence, federal court procedures, parties to criminal offenses, relevant federal statutes, self-incrimination, and search and seizure.

The course titled "Relevant Federal Statutes" covers subjects in: criminal law, theft and embezzlement, The Comprehensive Crime Control Act of 1984, bribery, assault, The Privacy Act, The Freedom of Information Act, The Hobbs Act, entrapment, obstruction of justice, mail fraud, The Travel Act, The Racketeer Influenced and Corrupt Organizations Act (RICO), false identification, and false statements.

EXAMPLE OF A TYPICAL COURSE IN THE LEGAL DIVISION

Course: Federal Court Procedures

Length and Method of Presentation:

Lecture	Laboratory	Practical Exercise	Total
8:00			8:00

Description: This course concentrates on the operation of the federal court system. It emphasizes procedures involved in processing a criminal case from the arrest or indictment of the defendant to the trial. This includes discussion of: the initial appearance, the preliminary examination, the indictment and information, grand jury secrecy, arraignment, pretrial motions, discovery, venue, and other areas of interest to the criminal investigator. The roles of the federal law enforcement officer, the magistrate, the judge, the grand jury, and the trial jury are reviewed.

Terminal Performance Objectives: Given a comprehensive examination consisting of multiple choice questions, the student will identify both rules governing proceedings in criminal cases in the United States Federal Court System and responsibilities of the federal law enforcement officer during these proceedings in accordance with the principles delineated during the course of instruction.

Interim Performance Objectives:

1. Identify the function and structure of the United States District Court System, United States Court of Appeals, and the United States Supreme Court.
2. Identify functions of U.S. magistrates.
3. Identify the federal law enforcement officer's duties in dealing with the U.S. magistrate.
4. Identify legal avenues by which a defendant may be brought before a magistrate.
5. Identify the function and purpose of the initial appearance.
6. Identify the function and purpose of the preliminary examination.
7. Identify the function, structure, and duties of the grand jury.
8. Identify rules governing the secrecy of grand jury proceedings.
9. Identify the federal law enforcement officer's duties in dealing with the grand jury.
10. Identify documents required to formally accuse a defendant and the rules governing their use.
11. Identify the function and purpose of an arraignment.
12. Identify pleas available to a defendant and the rules governing their use.
13. Identify rules governing plea bargaining.
14. Identify rules governing a pretrial motion.
15. Identify the purpose for, and rules governing, a deposition.
16. Identify information subject to discovery and inspection under Rule 16, F.R.C.P.
17. Identify information potentially subject to disclosure to the defense under the Brady Doctrine.
18. Identify information subject to disclosure under The Jencks Act and Rule 26.2, F.R.C.P.
19. Identify rules governing the issuance and use of subpoenas.
20. Identify conditions that determine venue for an offense.
21. Identify rules governing commitment to another district.
22. Identify rules governing the composition, use, and verdicts of jury trials.
23. Identify rules governing the imposition of judgment.
24. Identify rules governing The Speedy Trial Act.
25. Identify rules governing the Statute of Limitations.
26. Identify rules governing extradition.
27. Identify the federal law enforcement officer's duties in dealing with the government attorney.

Method of Evaluation: Written, multiple-choice examination.

Computer and Economic Crime Division

In response to the continuing evolution of complex white collar and computer-related crimes, the Computer and Economic Crime Division (CED), now reconstituted as the Financial Fraud Institute, was established in July, 1984. The CED provides an organizational focal point for the specialized and technical expertise to provide students with the skills necessary to detect and investigate the myriad computer, financial, and other white collar crime schemes. Consistent with FLETC's training philosophy that hands-on experience is one of the best training methodologies, the programs taught by CED blend theory and practical exercises (including simulated case problems) to provide students with specialized skills needed to understand and investigate these sophisticated crimes.

EXAMPLE OF A TYPICAL COURSE IN THE COMPUTER AND ECONOMIC CRIME DIVISION

Course: Introduction to Computers as Investigative Tools

Length and Method of Presentation:

Lecture	Laboratory	Practical Exercise	Total
2:00	2:00		4:00

Description: This course provides the participant with an overview of innovative investigative techniques involving the use of a computer. The emphasis is on various ways in which a computer can be used to assist in an investigation. Discussions of specific and innovative cases in which computers have played major investigative roles are used to stimulate thought relative to creative and innovative means of investigating. This course combines a lecture format with a laboratory exercise to give the student initial hands-on experience with IBM-PC compatible microcomputers. It is designed to provide an exposure to the primary software applications, including a worksheet, a database manager, and a word processor. Several basic features of each application are demonstrated using preconstructed data/text files.

Terminal Performance Objectives: Given a personal computer and associated software, the participant will recognize various ways in which computers can be used in criminal investigations, problems that might be encountered when using computers in investigations, and legal ramifications to consider when using computers for law enforcement investigations. The student will be able to scroll through the files using the video monitor and add, delete, or modify existing data entries in text, database, worksheet and graph files. The student will be able to transfer data from a worksheet application to a graph file according to the principles delineated during the course of instruction.

Interim Performance Objectives:

1. Recognize various means of using the computer to manage investigative information.
2. Recognize various means of using the computer to analyze investigative information and generate leads.
3. Recognize various types of commercial software packages applicable to law enforcement investigations.
4. Recognize various ways the computer can be used in the areas of law enforcement forensics.
5. Use basic word processor commands to erase, insert, move, search/replace, and duplicate text files.
6. Use basic word processor options to set margins and display the screen ruler.
7. Use basic spread sheet commands to duplicate, erase, and define cells.
8. Use basic database manager commands to sort and query a database.

Method of Evaluation: Completion of course.

Driver and Marine Division

The objective of the Driver and Marine Division (DMD) is to train federal law enforcement officers in the safe and efficient operation of motor vehicles. Emphasis is placed on principles and techniques relating to laws of motion, vehicle dynamics, and driver response. Principles and techniques are thoroughly explained in the classroom before students are allowed to participate in laboratory and practical exercises. Under close supervision and guidance, the students train until they recognize their personal limitations, as well as limitations of the vehicle. The DMD training curriculum includes instruction in the following course areas: highway response, defensive driving, skid control, bus operations, four-wheel-drive vehicle operation, transportation of prisoners, vehicle stops (risk and high risk), pursuit driving, evasive maneuver driving techniques, accident investigation, and driver training instructor's course. In the Criminal Investigator Training Program, courses in skid control, defensive driving, and transportation of prisoners and removal of reluctant suspects are provided.

DESCRIPTION OF A TYPICAL COURSE IN THE DRIVER AND MARINE DIVISION

Course: Removal and Transporting Suspects

Length and Method of Presentation:

Lecture	Laboratory	Practical Exercise	Total
1:30	:30		2:00

Description: This unit of instruction provides the student with basic techniques to remove a combative subject from an automobile with minimum injury to the officer and subject. Provides proper seating and restraining of suspect for transportation.

Terminal Performance Objectives: At the conclusion of this unit of instruction, given an actual situation that requires the student to forcibly remove a combative subject from an automobile for transportation, the student will safely and successfully remove the subject and properly restrain the subject, in accordance with the principles delineated during the course of instruction.

Interim Performance Objectives:

1. The student will identify and use various methods of removing a passive or nonpassive subject from a vehicle.
2. The student will identify and use correct techniques to effectively remove a passive or nonpassive subject from a vehicle.
3. The student will properly prepare a subject for transportation.
4. The student will identify and use proper seating positions in the transportation of the subject.

Method of Evaluation: Completion of course.

Firearms Division

The mission of the Firearms Division (FAD) is to train the basic law enforcement officer in the safe handling, proficient employment, and justifiable use of firearms. Additionally, the Firearms Division provides advanced, in-service, refresher, and specialized student training programs designed to enhance firearms proficiency. The division also conducts research and development in weapons technology and training. Ten curricula are offered, ranging from twenty-six hours of training in the five-week basic police programs to fifty-two hours of training in the seventeen-week basic Border Patrol program. The twenty courses that comprise the division's total curriculum are conducted in four phases: Phase I—Basic

Marksmanship, Phase II—Practical Pistol Course, Phase III—PPC Qualification, Phase IV—Realistic/Specialty Courses and Other Weapons. Phase I and II comprise 60 percent of firearms training with the revolver and are designed to develop shooting skills at a progressive pace in double-action, two-handed firing. At the completion of Phase II, students are tested in the Practical Pistol Course, where they must score 70 percent minimum to qualify in firearms. Phase IV offers courses in which reaction time, judgment, and accuracy of fire are tested. Decision reaction, instinctive reaction, reduced light firing, quick point, judgment pistol shooting, and situational response are several of the courses that round out a complete firearms program.

DESCRIPTION OF A TYPICAL COURSE IN THE FIREARMS DIVISION

Course: Judgment Pistol Shooting (JPS)/Instinctive Reaction

Length and Method of Presentation:

Lecture	Laboratory	Practical Exercise	Total
2:00	1:00		3:00

Description: This course introduces judgment situations in which the students must decide whether a shoot situation exists. The videotaped scenarios depict a series of law enforcement encounters typically experienced in field operations. The students incorporate FLETC "use of deadly force" policy as a guideline for their decisions. They must achieve a minimum score of 100 percent on judgment and 70 percent on accuracy. Concurrent training in decision/instinctive reaction is also conducted.

Terminal Performance Objectives: Given a series of filmed shoot/no-shoot situations, the student will be able to:

1. Demonstrate proper judgment to shoot or not to shoot in each taped instance.
2. Demonstrate timely reaction to shoot in each shoot instance.
3. Demonstrate safe revolver handling and proficiency in each shoot situation.
4. Provide a rational explanation to shoot or not to shoot in each instance where judgment is improper.

Interim Performance Objectives: To successfully achieve the requirements of the Terminal Performance Objectives, the student must first be able to:

1. Demonstrate the ability to comprehend and assess moving situations as they develop and respond in accordance with the center's firearms policy and guidelines.
2. Demonstrate the ability to react instinctively and correctly to videotaped moving situations projected onto a screen.
3. Demonstrate safe revolver-handling skills and proficiency learned in Phases I and II of revolver training.

Method of Evaluation: Demonstrated proficiency.

Physical Techniques Division

The Physical Techniques Division has instructional and course development responsibilities for the five major subject matter areas of: arrest techniques, defensive tactics, physical conditioning, survival swimming, CPR, and first aid training.

The eight-week Criminal Investigator Program receives training in arrest techniques, which involves handcuffing and searching procedures; defensive tactics; and American Heart Association CPR Basic Cardiac Life Support certification. Students must successfully complete a practical and/or written exam in each of these subjects.

In addition, students participate in the Physical Efficiency Battery (PEB), which involves assessments of cardiovascular endurance, dynamic upper body strength, body fat composition, agility, and flexibility of the lower back area. Students are evaluated in the PEB both in the beginning and end of the program.

DESCRIPTION OF A TYPICAL COURSE IN THE PHYSICAL TECHNIQUES DIVISION

Course: Arrest Techniques

Length and Method of Presentation:

Lecture	Laboratory	Practical Exercise	Total
2:00	6:00	2:00	10:00

Description: This course provides basic techniques used in effecting the proper custody of a suspect. The techniques include positioning, searching and handcuffing, emphasizing the responsibility of the agent/officer to the arrested subject.

Terminal Performance Objectives: Confronted with three areas of assessment, the student will be able to identify successful or unsuccessful achievement in arrest techniques compared to existing standards. The student must attain a score of 70 percent or better in the arrest techniques evaluation.

Interim Performance Objectives:

1. Correctly handcuff a person.
2. Demonstrate proper searching techniques.
3. Demonstrate the proper release of a handcuffed person.

Method of Evaluation: Demonstrated proficiency.

THREE

The Treasury Enforcement Agent Exam

CONTENTS

Sample Questions: The TEA Exam   59

First Model Examination   67

Second Model Examination   105

SAMPLE QUESTIONS: THE TEA EXAM

The Treasury Enforcement Agent Exam (TEA) is given to candidates for the positions of Internal Security Inspector with the IRS; Secret Service Special Agent; Customs Special Agent; Bureau of Alcohol, Tobacco, and Firearms Special Agent; IRS Special Agent with the Criminal Investigation Division; Deputy U.S. Marshal; and a number of other positions, as well.

The Treasury Enforcement Agent Exam (TEA) is divided into three parts: Part A, verbal reasoning; Part B, arithmetic reasoning; and Part C, problems for investigation. The official sample questions that follow are similar to the questions you will find in the actual test in terms of difficulty and form.

Part A—Verbal Reasoning Questions

In each of these questions you will be given a paragraph that contains all the information necessary to infer the correct answer. Use only the information provided in the paragraph. Do not speculate or make assumptions that go beyond this information. Also, assume that all information given in the paragraph is true, even if it conflicts with some fact known to you. Only one correct answer can be validly inferred from the information contained in the paragraph.

Pay special attention to negated verbs (for example, "are *not*") and negative prefixes (for example, "*in*complete" or "*dis*organized"). Also, pay special attention to quantifiers, such as "all," "none," and "some." For example, from a paragraph in which it is stated that "it is not true that all contracts are legal," one can validly infer that "some contracts are not legal," or that "some contracts are illegal," or that "some illegal things are contracts," but one cannot validly infer that "no contracts are legal," or that "some contracts are legal." Similarly, from a paragraph that states "all contracts are legal" and "all contracts are two-sided agreements," one can infer that "some two-sided agreements are legal," but one cannot validly infer that "all two-sided agreements are legal."

Bear in mind that in some tests, universal quantifiers such as "all" and "none" often give away incorrect response choices. That is not the case in this test. Some correct answers will refer to "all" or "none" of the members of a group.

Be sure to distinguish between essential information and unessential, peripheral information. That is to say, in a real test question, the previous example ("all contracts are legal" and "all contracts are two-sided agreements") would appear in a longer, full-fledged paragraph. It would be up to you to separate the essential information from its context and then to realize that a response choice that states "some two-sided agreements are legal" represents a valid inference and hence the correct answer.

SAMPLE QUESTIONS I AND 2 ARE EXAMPLES OF THE READING QUESTIONS ON THE TEST.

1. Impressions made by the ridges on the ends of the fingers and thumbs are useful means of identification, since no two persons have the same pattern of ridges. If finger patterns from fingerprints are not decipherable, then they cannot be classified by general shape and contour or by pattern type. If they cannot be classified by these characteristics, then it is impossible to identify the person to whom the fingerprints belong.

The paragraph best supports the statement that

(A) if it is impossible to identify the person to whom fingerprints belong, then the fingerprints are not decipherable.

(B) if finger patterns from fingerprints are not decipherable, then it is impossible to identify the person to whom the fingerprints belong.

(C) if fingerprints are decipherable, then it is impossible to identify the person to whom they belong.

(D) if fingerprints can be classified by general shape and contour or by pattern type, then they are not decipherable.

(E) if it is possible to identify the person to whom fingerprints belong, then the fingerprints cannot be classified by general shape and contour or pattern.

The correct answer is response (B). The essential information from which the answer can be inferred is contained in the second and third sentences. These sentences state that "if finger patterns from fingerprints are not decipherable, then they cannot be classified by general shape and contour or by pattern type. If they cannot be classified by these characteristics, then it is impossible to identify the person to whom they belong." Since response (B) refers to a condition in which finger patterns from fingerprints are not decipherable, we know that, in that circumstance, they cannot be classified by general shape and contour or by pattern type. From the paragraph, we can infer that since they cannot be classified by these characteristics, then it is impossible to identify the person to whom the fingerprints belong.

Response (A) cannot be inferred because the paragraph does not give information about all the circumstances under which it is impossible to identify the person to whom the fingerprints belong. It may be that the person is not identifiable for reasons other than the decipherability of the person's fingerprints.

Response (C) is incorrect because the paragraph does not provide enough information to conclude whether or not it would be possible to identify the person to whom the fingerprints belong from the mere fact of the decipherability of the fingerprints.

Response (D) is wrong because it contradicts the information in the second sentence of the paragraph. From that sentence, it can be concluded that if fingerprints can be classified by general shape and contour or by pattern type, then they are decipherable.

Response (E) is incorrect for a similar reason; it contradicts the information presented in the third sentence of the paragraph.

2. Law enforcement agencies use scientific techniques to identify suspects or to establish guilt. One obvious application of such techniques is the examination of a crime scene. Some substances found at a crime scene yield valuable clues under microscopic examination. Clothing fibers, dirt particles, and even pollen grains may reveal important information to the careful investigator. Nothing can be overlooked because all substances found at a crime scene are potential sources of evidence.

The paragraph best supports the statement that

(A) all substances that yield valuable clues under microscopic examination are substances found at a crime scene.

(B) some potential sources of evidence are substances that yield valuable clues under microscopic examination.

(C) some substances found at a crime scene are not potential sources of evidence.

(D) no potential sources of evidence are substances found at a crime scene.

(E) some substances that yield valuable clues under microscopic examination are not substances found at a crime scene.

The correct answer is response (B). The essential information from which the answer can be inferred is contained in the third and fifth sentences. The third sentence tells us that "some substances found at a crime scene yield valuable clues under microscopic examination." The fifth sentence explains that " . . . all substances found at a crime scene are potential sources of evidence." Therefore, we can conclude that "some potential sources of evidence are substances that yield valuable clues under microscopic examination."

Response (A) cannot be inferred because the paragraph does not support the statement that all substances that yield valuable clues are found exclusively at a crime scene. Valuable clues could be found elsewhere.

Responses (C) and (D) are incorrect because they contradict the fifth sentence of the paragraph, which clearly states that "all substances found at a crime scene are potential sources of evidence."

Response (E) is incorrect because the paragraph provides no information about the value of substances found somewhere other than at the crime scene.

Part B—Arithmetic Reasoning Questions

In this part you will have to solve problems formulated in both verbal and numeric form. You will have to analyze a paragraph in order to set up the problem, and then solve it. If the exact answer is not given as one of the response choices, you should select response (E), "none of these." Sample questions 3 and 4 are examples of the arithmetic reasoning questions. The use of calculators will NOT be permitted during the actual testing; therefore, they should not be used to solve these sample questions.

3. A police department purchases badges at $16 each for all the graduates of the police training academy. The last training class graduated 10 new officers. What is the total amount of money the department will spend for badges for these new officers?
   (A) $70
   (B) $116
   (C) $160
   (D) $180
   (E) none of these

The correct response is (C). It can be obtained by computing the following:

$16 \times 10 = 160$

The badges are priced at $16 each. The department must purchase 10 of them for the new officers. Multiplying the price of one badge ($16) by the number of graduates (10) gives the total price for all of the badges.

Responses (A), (B), and (D) are the result of erroneous computations.

4. An investigator rented a car for six days and was charged $450. The car rental company charged $35 per day plus $.30 per mile driven. How many miles did the investigator drive the car?
   (A) 800
   (B) 900
   (C) 1,290
   (D) 1,500
   (E) none of these

The correct answer is (A). It can be obtained by computing the following:

$$6(35) + .30X = 450$$

The investigator rented the car for six days at $35 per day, which is $210; $210 subtracted from the total charge of $450 leaves $240, the portion of the total charge which was expended for the miles driven. This amount divided by the charge per mile ($240 ÷ .30) gives the number of miles (800) driven by the investigator.

Responses (B), (C), and (D) are the result of erroneous computations.

Part C—Problems for Investigation

In this part you will be presented with a paragraph and several related statements. Sample questions 5 through 9 are based on the following paragraph and statements. Read them carefully and then answer questions 5 through 9.

On October 30th, the Belton First National Bank discovered that the $3,000 it had received that morning from the Greenville First National Bank was in counterfeit 10-, 20-, and 50-dollar bills. The genuine $3,000 had been counted by Greenville First National bank clerk Iris Stewart the preceding afternoon. They were packed in eight black leather satchels and stored in the bank vault overnight. Greenville First National clerk Brian Caruthers accompanied carriers James Clark and Howard O'Keefe to Belton in an armored truck. Belton First National clerk Cynthia Randall discovered the counterfeit bills when she examined the serial numbers of the bills.

During the course of the investigation, the following statements were made:

(1) Gerald Hathaway, clerk of the Greenville bank, told investigators that he had found the bank office open when he arrived to work on the morning of October 30th. The only articles that appeared to be missing were eight black leather satchels of the type used to transport large sums of money.

(2) Jon Perkins, head teller of the Greenville bank, told investigators that he did not check the contents of the black leather satchels after locking them in the vault around 4:30 P.M., on October 29th.

(3) Henry Green, janitor of the Greenville bank, said that he noticed Jon Perkins leaving the bank office around 5:30 P.M., one-half hour after the bank closed on October 29th. He said that Perkins locked the door.

(4) A scrap of cloth, identical to the material of the carriers' uniforms, was found caught in the seal of one of the black leather satchels delivered to Belton.

(5) Brian Caruthers, clerk, said he saw James Clark and Howard O'Keefe talking in a secretive manner in the armored truck.

(6)   Thomas Stillman, Greenville bank executive, identified the eight black leather satchels containing the counterfeit money that arrived at the Belton First National Bank as the eight satchels that had disappeared from the bank office. He had noticed a slight difference in the linings of the satchels.

(7)   Virginia Fowler, bank accountant, noticed two 10-dollar bills with the same serial numbers as the lost bills in a bank deposit from Ferdinand's Restaurant of Greenville.

(8)   Vincent Johnson, manager of Ferdinand's Restaurant, told police that Iris Stewart frequently dined there with her boyfriend.

5. Which one of the following statements best indicates that satchels containing the counterfeit bills were substituted for satchels containing genuine bills while they were being transported from Greenville to Belton?
    (A) Statement 1
    (B) Statement 3
    (C) Statement 4
    (D) Statement 5
    (E) Statement 7

   The correct answer is (C). The armor carriers had the greatest opportunity to substitute counterfeit bills for real ones during the transportation procedure. The scrap of material from an armor carrier's uniform caught in the seal of one of the satchels strongly links the carriers to the crime.

6. Which one of the following statements best links the information given in statement (1) with the substitution of the counterfeit bills?
    (A) Statement 2
    (B) Statement 3
    (C) Statement 4
    (D) Statement 5
    (E) Statement 6

   The correct answer is (E). Statement (1) establishes that eight satchels were missing from the Greenville bank. Statement (6) identifies the satchels that arrived at the Belton bank as the missing satchels.

7. Which one of the following statements, along with statement (7), best indicates that the substitution of the counterfeit bills casts suspicion on at least one employee of the Greenville bank?
    (A) Statement 1
    (B) Statement 2
    (C) Statement 3
    (D) Statement 5
    (E) Statement 8

   The correct answer is (E). Statement (7) establishes that two stolen 10-dollar bills were spent at Ferdinand's Restaurant. Statement (8) identifies a bank employee as a frequent diner at Ferdinand's Restaurant. This statement casts suspicion on the bank employee but does not prove complicity.

8. Which one of the following statements would least likely be used in proving a case?
   (A) Statement 1
   (B) Statement 3
   (C) Statement 4
   (D) Statement 5
   (E) Statement 7

The correct answer is (D). The fact that the bank clerk saw the armor carriers talking secretively may cast some suspicion, but would not be useful in proving the case. Men who work together are very likely to exchange private jokes or share personal information.

9. Which one of the following statements best indicates that the substitution of the counterfeit bills could have taken place before the satchels left the Greenville bank?
   (A) Statement 1
   (B) Statement 2
   (C) Statement 3
   (D) Statement 4
   (E) Statement 7

The correct answer is (B). The satchels were locked in the vault at 4:30 p.m. on one day and not delivered until the following morning. Because we learn in statement (2) that the satchels were not checked after they were locked into the vault, the exchange could have taken place in the Greenville bank.

ANSWER SHEET FOR FIRST MODEL EXAMINATION

Part A—Verbal Reasoning Questions

1. Ⓐ Ⓑ Ⓒ Ⓓ Ⓔ   6. Ⓐ Ⓑ Ⓒ Ⓓ Ⓔ   11. Ⓐ Ⓑ Ⓒ Ⓓ Ⓔ   16. Ⓐ Ⓑ Ⓒ Ⓓ Ⓔ   21. Ⓐ Ⓑ Ⓒ Ⓓ Ⓔ

2. Ⓐ Ⓑ Ⓒ Ⓓ Ⓔ   7. Ⓐ Ⓑ Ⓒ Ⓓ Ⓔ   12. Ⓐ Ⓑ Ⓒ Ⓓ Ⓔ   17. Ⓐ Ⓑ Ⓒ Ⓓ Ⓔ   22. Ⓐ Ⓑ Ⓒ Ⓓ Ⓔ

3. Ⓐ Ⓑ Ⓒ Ⓓ Ⓔ   8. Ⓐ Ⓑ Ⓒ Ⓓ Ⓔ   13. Ⓐ Ⓑ Ⓒ Ⓓ Ⓔ   18. Ⓐ Ⓑ Ⓒ Ⓓ Ⓔ   23. Ⓐ Ⓑ Ⓒ Ⓓ Ⓔ

4. Ⓐ Ⓑ Ⓒ Ⓓ Ⓔ   9. Ⓐ Ⓑ Ⓒ Ⓓ Ⓔ   14. Ⓐ Ⓑ Ⓒ Ⓓ Ⓔ   19. Ⓐ Ⓑ Ⓒ Ⓓ Ⓔ   24. Ⓐ Ⓑ Ⓒ Ⓓ Ⓔ

5. Ⓐ Ⓑ Ⓒ Ⓓ Ⓔ   10. Ⓐ Ⓑ Ⓒ Ⓓ Ⓔ   15. Ⓐ Ⓑ Ⓒ Ⓓ Ⓔ   20. Ⓐ Ⓑ Ⓒ Ⓓ Ⓔ   25. Ⓐ Ⓑ Ⓒ Ⓓ Ⓔ

Part B—Arithmetic Reasoning Questions

1. Ⓐ Ⓑ Ⓒ Ⓓ Ⓔ   5. Ⓐ Ⓑ Ⓒ Ⓓ Ⓔ   9. Ⓐ Ⓑ Ⓒ Ⓓ Ⓔ   13. Ⓐ Ⓑ Ⓒ Ⓓ Ⓔ   17. Ⓐ Ⓑ Ⓒ Ⓓ Ⓔ

2. Ⓐ Ⓑ Ⓒ Ⓓ Ⓔ   6. Ⓐ Ⓑ Ⓒ Ⓓ Ⓔ   10. Ⓐ Ⓑ Ⓒ Ⓓ Ⓔ   14. Ⓐ Ⓑ Ⓒ Ⓓ Ⓔ   18. Ⓐ Ⓑ Ⓒ Ⓓ Ⓔ

3. Ⓐ Ⓑ Ⓒ Ⓓ Ⓔ   7. Ⓐ Ⓑ Ⓒ Ⓓ Ⓔ   11. Ⓐ Ⓑ Ⓒ Ⓓ Ⓔ   15. Ⓐ Ⓑ Ⓒ Ⓓ Ⓔ   19. Ⓐ Ⓑ Ⓒ Ⓓ Ⓔ

4. Ⓐ Ⓑ Ⓒ Ⓓ Ⓔ   8. Ⓐ Ⓑ Ⓒ Ⓓ Ⓔ   12. Ⓐ Ⓑ Ⓒ Ⓓ Ⓔ   16. Ⓐ Ⓑ Ⓒ Ⓓ Ⓔ   20. Ⓐ Ⓑ Ⓒ Ⓓ Ⓔ

Part C—Problems for Investigation

1. Ⓐ Ⓑ Ⓒ Ⓓ Ⓔ   7. Ⓐ Ⓑ Ⓒ Ⓓ Ⓔ   13. Ⓐ Ⓑ Ⓒ Ⓓ Ⓔ   19. Ⓐ Ⓑ Ⓒ Ⓓ Ⓔ   25. Ⓐ Ⓑ Ⓒ Ⓓ Ⓔ

2. Ⓐ Ⓑ Ⓒ Ⓓ Ⓔ   8. Ⓐ Ⓑ Ⓒ Ⓓ Ⓔ   14. Ⓐ Ⓑ Ⓒ Ⓓ Ⓔ   20. Ⓐ Ⓑ Ⓒ Ⓓ Ⓔ   26. Ⓐ Ⓑ Ⓒ Ⓓ Ⓔ

3. Ⓐ Ⓑ Ⓒ Ⓓ Ⓔ   9. Ⓐ Ⓑ Ⓒ Ⓓ Ⓔ   15. Ⓐ Ⓑ Ⓒ Ⓓ Ⓔ   21. Ⓐ Ⓑ Ⓒ Ⓓ Ⓔ   27. Ⓐ Ⓑ Ⓒ Ⓓ Ⓔ

4. Ⓐ Ⓑ Ⓒ Ⓓ Ⓔ   10. Ⓐ Ⓑ Ⓒ Ⓓ Ⓔ   16. Ⓐ Ⓑ Ⓒ Ⓓ Ⓔ   22. Ⓐ Ⓑ Ⓒ Ⓓ Ⓔ   28. Ⓐ Ⓑ Ⓒ Ⓓ Ⓔ

5. Ⓐ Ⓑ Ⓒ Ⓓ Ⓔ   11. Ⓐ Ⓑ Ⓒ Ⓓ Ⓔ   17. Ⓐ Ⓑ Ⓒ Ⓓ Ⓔ   23. Ⓐ Ⓑ Ⓒ Ⓓ Ⓔ   29. Ⓐ Ⓑ Ⓒ Ⓓ Ⓔ

6. Ⓐ Ⓑ Ⓒ Ⓓ Ⓔ   12. Ⓐ Ⓑ Ⓒ Ⓓ Ⓔ   18. Ⓐ Ⓑ Ⓒ Ⓓ Ⓔ   24. Ⓐ Ⓑ Ⓒ Ⓓ Ⓔ   30. Ⓐ Ⓑ Ⓒ Ⓓ Ⓔ

FIRST MODEL EXAMINATION

Part A—Verbal Reasoning Questions

Time: 50 minutes. 25 questions.

Directions: For each verbal reasoning question, a paragraph will be given that contains all the information necessary to infer the correct answer. Use only the information provided in the paragraph. Do not speculate or make assumptions that go beyond this information. Also, assume that all information given in the paragraph is true, even if it conflicts with some fact known to you. Only one correct answer can be validly inferred from the information contained in the paragraph. Mark its letter on your answer sheet.

1. A member of the department shall not indulge in liquor while in uniform. A member of the department not required to wear a uniform and a uniformed member while out of uniform shall not indulge in intoxicants to an extent unfitting the member for duty.

   The paragraph best supports the statement that
   (A) an off-duty member, not in uniform, may drink liquor to the extent that it does not unfit the member for duty
   (B) a member not on duty, but in uniform and not unfit for duty, may drink liquor
   (C) an on-duty member, unfit for duty in uniform, may drink intoxicants
   (D) a uniformed member in civilian clothes may not drink intoxicants unless unfit for duty
   (E) a civilian member of the department, in uniform, may drink liquor if fit for duty

2. Tax law specialists may authorize their assistants to sign their names to reports, letters, and papers that are not specially required to be signed personally by the tax law specialist. The signature should be: "Jane Doe, tax law specialist, by Richard Roe, tax technician." The name of the tax law specialist may be written or stamped, but the signature of the tax technician shall be in ink.

   The paragraph best supports the statement that
   (A) if a tax law specialist's assistant signs official papers both by rubber stamp and in ink, the assistant has authority to sign
   (B) if a tax technician does not neglect to include his or her title in ink along with his or her signature following the word "by," the technician may sign papers that are not specially required to be signed personally by the tax law specialist
   (C) no signatory authority delegated to the tax technician by the tax law specialist may be redelegated by the tax technician to an assistant unless so authorized in ink by the tax law specialist
   (D) if a tax law specialist personally signs written requisitions in ink, the technician is not required to identify the source of the order with a rubber stamp
   (E) when a tax technician signs authorized papers for a tax law specialist, the tax technician must write out the tax law specialist's signature in full with pen and ink

67

3. Upon retirement from service, a member shall receive a retirement allowance consisting of an annuity that shall be the actuarial equivalent of his accumulated deductions at the time of retirement, a pension in addition to his annuity that shall be one service-fraction of his final compensation multiplied by the number of years of government service since he last became a member, and a pension that is the actuarial equivalent of the reserve-for-increased-take-home-pay to which he may then be entitled, if any.

    The paragraph best supports the statement that
    (A) a retirement allowance shall consist of an annuity plus a pension plus an actuarial equivalent of a service fraction
    (B) upon retirement from service, a member shall receive an annuity plus a pension plus an actuarial equivalent of reserve-for-increased-take-home-pay, if he is entitled
    (C) a retiring member shall receive an annuity plus reserve-for-increased-take-home-pay, if any, plus final compensation
    (D) a retirement allowance shall consist of a pension plus reserve-for-increased-take-home-pay, if any, plus accumulated deductions
    (E) a retirement allowance shall consist of an annuity that is equal to one service-fraction of final compensation, a pension multiplied by the number of years of government service, and the actuarial equivalent of accumulated deductions from increased take-home-pay

4. If you are in doubt as to whether any matter is legally mailable, you should ask the postmaster. Even though the Postal Service has not expressly declared any matter to be nonmailable, the sender of such matter may be held fully liable for violation of law if he or she does actually send nonmailable matter through the mail.

    The paragraph best supports the statement that
    (A) if the postmaster is in doubt as to whether any matter is legally mailable, the postmaster may be held liable for any sender's sending nonmailable matter through the mail
    (B) if the sender is ignorant of what it is that constitutes nonmailable matter, the sender is relieved of all responsibility for mailing nonmailable matter
    (C) if a sender sends nonmailable matter, the sender is fully liable for law violation even though doubt may have existed about the mailability of the matter
    (D) if the Postal Service has not expressly declared material mailable, it is nonmailable
    (E) if the Postal Service has not expressly declared material nonmailable, it is mailable

5. In evaluating education for a particular position, education in and of itself is of no value except to the degree in which it contributes to knowledge, skills, and abilities needed in the particular job. On its face, such a statement would seem to contend that general educational development need not be considered in evaluating education and training. Much to the contrary, such a proposition favors the consideration of any and all training, but only as it pertains to the position for which the applicant applies.

    The paragraph best supports the statement that
    (A) if general education is supplemented by specialized education, it is of no value
    (B) if a high school education is desirable in any occupation, special training need not be evaluated
    (C) in evaluating education, a contradiction arises in assigning equal weight to general and specialized education
    (D) unless it is supplemented by general education, specialized education is of no value
    (E) education is of value to the degree to which it is needed in the particular position

6.   Statistics tell us that heart disease kills more people than any other illness, and the death rate continues to rise. People over 30 have a fifty-fifty chance of escaping, for heart disease is chiefly an illness of people in late middle age and advanced years. Because there are more people in this age group living today than there were some years ago, heart disease is able to find more victims.

The paragraph best supports the statement that
(A)   if a person has heart disease, there is a 50 percent chance that he or she is over 30 years of age
(B)   according to statistics, more middle-aged and elderly people die of heart disease than of all other causes
(C)   because heart disease is chiefly an illness of people in late middle age, young people are less likely to be the victims of heart disease
(D)   the rising birth rate has increased the possibility that the average person will die of heart disease
(E)   if the stress of modern living were not increasing, there would be a slower increase in the risk of heart disease

7.   Racketeers are primarily concerned with business affairs, legitimate or otherwise, and prefer those that are close to the margin of legitimacy. They get their best opportunities from business organizations that meet the need of large sections of the public for goods or services that are defined as illegitimate by the same public, such as prostitution, gambling, illicit drugs, or liquor. In contrast to the thief, the racketeer and the establishments he or she controls deliver goods and services for money received.

The paragraph best supports the statement that
(A)   since racketeers deliver goods and services for money received, their business affairs are not illegitimate
(B)   since racketeering involves objects of value, it is unlike theft
(C)   victims of racketeers are not guilty of violating the law, therefore racketeering is a victim-less crime
(D)   since many people want services which are not obtainable through legitimate sources, they contribute to the difficulty of suppressing racketeers
(E)   if large sections of the public are engaged in legitimate business with racketeers, the businesses are not illegitimate

8.   The housing authority not only faces every problem of the private developer, it must also assume responsibilities of which private building is free. The authority must account to the community; it must conform to federal regulations; it must provide durable buildings of good standard at low cost; and it must overcome the prejudices of contractors, bankers, and prospective tenants against public operations. These authorities are being watched by antihousing enthusiasts for the first error of judgment or the first evidence of high costs that can be torn to bits before a Congressional committee.

The paragraph best supports the statement that
(A)   since private developers are not accountable to the community, they do not have the opposition of contractors, bankers, and prospective tenants
(B)   if Congressional committees are watched by antihousing enthusiasts, they may discover errors of judgment and high costs on the part of a housing authority
(C)   while a housing authority must deal with all the difficulties encountered by a private builder, it must also deal with antihousing enthusiasts

    (D) if housing authorities are not immune to errors in judgment, they must provide durable buildings of good standard and low cost just like private developers

    (E) if a housing authority is to conform to federal regulations, it must overcome the prejudices of contractors, builders, and prospective tenants

9. Security of tenure in the public service must be viewed in the context of the universal quest for security. If we narrow our application of the term to employment, the problem of security in the public service is seen to differ from that in private industry only in the need to meet the peculiar threats to security in governmental organizations—principally the danger of making employment contingent upon factors other than the performance of the workers.

The paragraph best supports the statement that

    (A) if workers seek security, they should enter public service

    (B) if employment is contingent upon factors other than work performance, workers will feel more secure

    (C) if employees believe that their security is threatened, they are employed in private industry

    (D) the term of employment in public service differs from that in private industry

    (E) the employment status of the public servant with respect to security of tenure differs from that of the private employee by encompassing factors beyond those affecting the private employee

10. The wide use of antibiotics has presented a number of problems. Some patients become allergic to the drugs, so that they cannot be used when they are needed. In other cases, after prolonged treatment with antibiotics, certain organisms no longer respond to them. This is one of the reasons for the constant search for more potent drugs.

The paragraph best supports the statement that

    (A) since a number of problems have been presented by long-term treatment with antibiotics, antibiotics should never be used on a long-term basis

    (B) because some people have developed an allergy to specific drugs, potent antibiotics cannot always be used

    (C) since antibiotics have been used successfully for certain allergies, there must be a constant search for more potent drugs

    (D) if antibiotics are used for a prolonged period of time, certain organisms become allergic to them

    (E) since so many diseases have been successfully treated with antibiotics, there must be a constant search for new drugs

11. The noncompetitive class consists of positions for which there are minimum qualifications but for which no reliable exam has been developed. In the noncompetitive class, every applicant must meet minimum qualifications in terms of education, experience, and medical or physical qualifications. There may even be an examination on a pass/fail basis.

The paragraph best supports the statement that

    (A) if an exam is unreliable, the position is in the noncompetitive class

    (B) if an applicant has met minimum qualifications in terms of education, experience, medical, or physical requirements, the applicant must pass a test

    (C) if an applicant has met minimum qualifications in terms of education, experience, medical or physical requirements, the applicant may fail a test

    (D) if an applicant passes an exam for a noncompetitive position, the applicant must also meet minimum qualifications

    (E) if there are minimum qualifications for a position, the position is in the noncompetitive class

12. Two independent clauses cannot share one sentence without some form of connection. If they do, they form a run-on sentence. Two principal clauses may be joined by a coordinating conjunction, by a comma followed by a coordinating conjunction, or by a semicolon. They may also form two distinct sentences. Two main clauses may never be joined by a comma without a coordinating conjunction. This error is called a comma splice.

The paragraph best supports the statement that

    (A) if the violation is called a comma splice, two main clauses are joined by a comma without a coordinating conjunction

    (B) if two distinct sentences share one sentence and are joined by a coordinating conjunction, the result is a run-on sentence

    (C) when a coordinating conjunction is not followed by a semicolon, the writer has committed an error of punctuation

    (D) while a comma and a semicolon may not be used in the same principal clause, they may be used in the same sentence

    (E) a bad remedy for a run-on sentence is not a comma splice

13. The pay in some job titles is hourly; in others it is annual. Official work weeks vary from 35 hours to $37\frac{1}{2}$ hours to 40 hours. In some positions, overtime is earned for all time worked beyond the set number of hours, and differentials are paid for night, weekend, and holiday work. Other positions offer compensatory time off for overtime or for work during unpopular times. Still other positions require the jobholder to devote as much extra time as needed to do the work without any extra compensation. And in some positions, employees who work overtime are given a meal allowance.

The paragraph best supports the statement that

    (A) if a meal allowance is given, there is compensation for overtime

    (B) if the work week is 35 hours long, the job is unpopular

    (C) if overtime is earned, pay in the job title is hourly

    (D) if a jobholder has earned a weekend differential, the employee has worked beyond the set number of hours

    (E) if compensatory time is offered, it is offered as a substitute for overtime pay

14. All applicants must be of satisfactory character and reputation and must meet all requirements set forth in the Notice of Examination for the position for which they are applying. Applicants may be summoned for the written test prior to investigation of their qualifications and background. Admission to the test does not mean that the applicant has met the qualifications for the position.

The paragraph best supports the statement that

    (A) if an applicant has been admitted to the test, the applicant has not met requirements for the position

    (B) if an applicant has not been investigated, the applicant will not be admired to the written test

    (C) if an applicant has met all requirements for the position, the applicant will be admitted to the test

(D) if an applicant has satisfactory character and reputation, the applicant will not have his or her background investigated

(E) if an applicant has met all the requirements set forth in the Notice of Examination, the applicant will pass the test

15. Although in the past it has been illegal for undocumented aliens to work in the United States, it has not, until now, been unlawful for employers to hire these aliens. With the passage of the new immigration law, employers are now subject to civil penalties and ultimately imprisonment if they "knowingly" hire, recruit, or refer for a fee any unauthorized alien. Similarly, it is also unlawful for employers to continue to employ an undocumented alien who was hired after November 6, 1986, knowing that he or she was or is unauthorized to work.

The paragraph best supports the statement that
(A) under the new immigration law, it is no longer illegal for undocumented aliens to be denied employment in the United States
(B) if an undocumented alien is not remaining on the job illegally, the worker was not hired after November 6, 1986
(C) if a person wishes to avoid the penalties of the new immigration law, the person must not knowingly employ aliens
(D) if an employer inadvertently hires undocumented aliens, the employer may be subject to fine or imprisonment, but not both
(E) if an unauthorized alien is able to find an employer who will hire him or her after November 6, 1986, the alien is welcome to go to work

16. The law requires that the government offer employees, retirees, and their families the opportunity to continue group health and/or welfare fund coverage at 102 percent of the group rate in certain instances where the coverage would otherwise terminate. All group benefits, including optional benefits riders, are available. Welfare fund benefits that can be continued under COBRA are dental, vision, prescription drugs, and other related medical benefits. The period of coverage varies from 18 to 36 months, depending on the reason for continuation.

The paragraph best supports the statement that
(A) the period of coverage continuation varies depending on the reason for termination
(B) upon retirement, welfare fund benefits continue at a 102 percent rate
(C) the law requires employees, retirees, and their families to continue health coverage
(D) COBRA is a program for acquiring welfare fund benefits
(E) if retirees or their families do not desire to terminate them, they can continue group benefits at 102 percent of the group rate

17. Historical records and such rarely constitute an adequate or, more importantly, a reliable basis for estimating earthquake potential. In most regions of the world, recorded history is short relative to the time between the largest earthquakes. Thus, the fact that there have been no historic earthquakes larger than a given size does not make us confident that they will also be absent in the future. It may alternatively be due to the short length of available historical records relative to the long repeat time for large earthquakes.

The paragraph best supports the statement that
(A) if historic earthquakes are no larger than a given size, they are unlikely to recur
(B) potential earthquakes do not inspire confidence in historical records as predictors of time between earthquakes

(C) if the time span between major earthquakes were not longer than the length of available records, history would have greater predictive value

(D) since there have been no historic earthquakes larger than a given size, we are confident that there will be a long time span between major earthquakes

(E) in those regions of the world where recorded history is long, the time between the largest earthquakes is short

18. A language can be thought of as a number of strings or sequences of symbols. The definition of a language defines which strings belong to the language, but since most languages of interest consist of an infinite number of strings; this definition is impossible to accomplish by listing the strings (or sentences). While the number of *sentences* in a language can be infinite, the rules by which they are constructed are not. This may explain why we are able to speak sentences in a language that we have never spoken before, and to understand sentences that we have never heard before.

The paragraph best supports the statement that

(A) if there is an infinite number of sequences of symbols in a language, there is an infinite number of rules for their construction

(B) if we have never spoken a language, we can understand its sentences provided that we know the rules by which they were constructed

(C) a language is defined by its strings

(D) if the number of sentences in an unnatural language were not infinite, we would be able to define it

(E) if sequences of symbols are governed by rules of construction, then the number of sentences can be determined

19. An assumption commonly made in regard to the reliability of testimony is that when a number of persons report the same matter, those details upon which there is an agreement may generally be considered substantiated. Experiments have shown, however, that there is a tendency for the same errors to appear in the testimony of different individuals, and that, apart from any collusion, agreement of testimony is no proof of dependability.

The paragraph best supports the statement that

(A) if details of the testimony are true, all witnesses will agree to it

(B) unless there is collusion, it is impossible for a number of persons to give the same report

(C) if most witnesses do not independently attest to the same facts, the facts cannot be true

(D) if the testimony of a group of people is in substantial agreement, it cannot be ruled out that those witnesses have not all made the same mistake

(E) under experimental conditions, witnesses tend to give reliable testimony

20. In some instances, changes are made in a contract after it has been signed and accepted by both parties. This is done either by inserting a new clause in a contract or by annexing a *rider* to the contract. If a contract is changed by a rider, both parties must sign the rider in order for it to be legal. The basic contract should also note that a rider is attached by inserting new words to the contract, and both parties should also initial and date the new insertion. The same requirement applies if they later change any wording in the contract. What two people agree to do, they can mutually agree not to do—as long as they both agree.

The paragraph best supports the statement that
(A) if two people mutually agree not to do something, they must sign a rider
(B) if both parties to a contract do not agree to attach a rider, they must initial the contract to render it legal
(C) if a rider to a contract is to be legal, that rider must be agreed to and signed by both parties, who must not neglect to initial and date that portion of the contract to which the rider refers
(D) if a party to a contract does not agree to a change, that party should initial the change and annex a rider detailing the disagreement
(E) if the wording of a contract is not to be changed, both parties must initial and date a rider

21. Explosives are substances or devices capable of producing a volume of rapidly expanding gases that exert a sudden pressure on their surroundings. Chemical explosives are the most commonly used explosives, although mechanical and nuclear explosives do exist. All mechanical explosives are devices in which a physical reaction is produced, such as that caused by overloading a container with compressed air. While nuclear explosives are by far the most powerful, all nuclear explosives have been restricted to military weapons.

The paragraph best supports the statement that
(A) all explosives that have been restricted to military weapons are nuclear explosives
(B) no mechanical explosives are devices in which a physical reaction is produced, such as that caused by overloading a container with compressed air
(C) some nuclear explosives have not been restricted to military weapons
(D) all mechanical explosives have been restricted to military weapons
(E) some devices in which a physical reaction is produced, such as that caused by overloading a container with compressed air, are mechanical explosives

22. A sanitizer is an agent, usually chemical in nature, that is used in hospitals to reduce the number of microorganisms to a level that has been officially approved as safe. Frequently, hospitals use stronger antimicrobial agents to ensure that stringent health standards are met. However, if no dangerous microorganisms that must be destroyed are known to be present in a given environment, sanitizers are used.

The paragraph best supports the statement that, in a given hospital environment
(A) if dangerous microorganisms that must be destroyed are known to be present, then sanitizers are used
(B) if sanitizers are used, then some dangerous microorganisms that must be destroyed are known to be present
(C) if sanitizers are not used, then no dangerous microorganisms that must be destroyed are known to be present
(D) if only some dangerous microorganisms are known to be present, then sanitizers are used
(E) if sanitizers are not used, then dangerous microorganisms that must be destroyed are known to be present

23. One use for wild land is the protection of certain species of wild animals or plants in wildlife refuges or in botanical reservations. Some general types of land use are activities that conflict with this stated purpose. All activities that exhibit such conflict are, of course, excluded from refuges and reservations.

The paragraph best supports the statement that
(A) all activities that conflict with the purpose of wildlife refuges or botanical reservations are general types of land use
(B) all activities excluded from wildlife refuges and botanical reservations are those that conflict with the purpose of the refuge or reservation
(C) some activities excluded from wildlife refuges and botanical reservations are general types of land use
(D) no activities that conflict with the purpose of wildlife refuges and botanical reservations are general types of land use
(E) some general types of land use are not excluded from wildlife refuges and botanical reservations

24. Information centers can be categorized according to the primary activity or service they provide. For example, some information centers are document depots. These depots, generally government-sponsored, serve as archives for the acquisition, storage, retrieval, and dissemination of a variety of documents. All documents depots have the capacity to provide a great range of user services, which may include preparing specialized bibliographies; publishing announcements, indexes, and abstracts; and providing copies.

The paragraph best supports the statement that
(A) some information centers are categorized by features other than the primary activity or service they provide
(B) some document depots lack the capacity to provide a great range of user services
(C) no document depot lacks the capacity to provide a great range of user services
(D) all information centers are document depots
(E) some places that provide a great range of user services are not document depots

25. Authorities generally agree that the use of hyphens tends to defy most rules. The best advice that can be given is to consult the dictionary to determine whether a given prefix is joined solidly to a root word or is hyphenated. One reliable rule, however, is that if an expression is a familiar one, such as overtime and hatchback, then it is a nonhyphenated compound.

The paragraph best supports the statement that
(A) if an expression is a familiar one, then it is a hyphenated compound
(B) if an expression is a nonhyphenated compound, then it is a familiar expression
(C) if an expression is not a familiar one, then it is a hyphenated compound
(D) if an expression is a hyphenated compound, containing a suffix rather than a prefix, then it is not a familiar one
(E) if an expression is a hyphenated compound, then it is not a familiar one

STOP

END OF PART A. IF YOU FINISH BEFORE 50 MINUTES IS UP, CHECK OVER YOUR WORK ON PART A. DO NOT TURN TO PART B UNTIL THE SIGNAL IS GIVEN.

Part B—Arithmetic Reasoning Questions

Time: 50 minutes. 20 questions.

Directions: *Analyze each paragraph to set up each problem, then solve it. Mark your answer sheet with the letter of the correct answer. If the correct answer is not given as one of the response choices, you should select response (E), "none of these."*

1. Twelve clerks are assigned to enter certain data on index cards. This number of clerks could perform the task in 18 days. After these clerks have worked on this assignment for 6 days, 4 more clerks are added to the staff to do this work. Assuming that all the clerks work at the same rate of speed, the entire task, instead of taking 18 days, will be performed in
   (A) 9 days
   (B) 12 days
   (C) 15 days
   (D) 16 days
   (E) none of these

2. In a low-cost public-health dental clinic, an adult cleaning costs twice as much as the same treatment for a child. If a family of three children and two adults can visit the clinic for cleanings for a cost of $49, what is the cost for each adult?
   (A) $7
   (B) $10
   (C) $12
   (D) $14
   (E) none of these

3. A government employee is relocated to a new region of the country and purchases a new home. The purchase price of the house is $87,250. Taxes to be paid on this house include: county tax of $424 per year, town tax of $783 per year, and school tax of $466 every six months. The aggregate tax rate is $.132 per $1,000 of assessed value. The assessed value of this house is what percent of the purchase price?
   (A) 14.52%
   (B) 18.57%
   (C) 22.81%
   (D) 29.05%
   (E) none of these

4. The Social Security Administration has ordered an intensive check of 756 SSI payment recipients who are suspected of having above-standard incomes. Four clerical assistants have been assigned to this task. At the end of 6 days at 7 hours each, they have checked on 336 recipients. In order to speed up the investigation, 2 more assistants are assigned at this point. If they work at the same rate, the number of additional 7-hour days it will take to complete the job is, most nearly
   (A) 1
   (B) 2
   (C) 3
   (D) 4
   (E) none of these

5. A family spends 30 percent of its take-home income for food, 8 percent for clothing, 25 percent for shelter, 4 percent for recreation, 13 percent for education, and 5 percent for miscellaneous items. The remainder goes into the family savings account. If the weekly net earnings of this household are $500, how many weeks will it take this family to accumulate $15,000 in savings, before interest?
   (A) 200
   (B) 175
   (C) 150
   (D) 100
   (E) none of these

6. An Internal Revenue Service (IRS) officer is making spot-checks of income reported on income tax returns. A cab driver being audited works on a commission basis, receiving $42 \frac{1}{2}$ percent of fares collected. The IRS allocates that earnings from tips should be valued at 29 percent of commissions. If the cab driver's weekly fare collections average $520, then the IRS projects his reportable monthly earnings to be
   (A) between $900 and $1000
   (B) between $1000 and $1100
   (C) between $1100 and $1200
   (D) between $1200 and $1250
   (E) none of these

7. A department head hired a total of 60 temporary employees to handle a seasonal increase in the department's workload. The following lists the number of temporary employees hired, their rates of pay, and the duration of their employment:

   One-third of the total were hired as clerks, each at the rate of $12,700 a year, for two months.

   30 percent of the total were hired as office machine operators, each at the rate of $13,150 a year, for four months.

   22 stenographers were hired, each at the rate of $13,000 a year, for three months.

   The total amount paid to these temporary employees to the nearest dollar was
   (A) $194,499
   (B) $192,900
   (C) $130,000
   (D) $127,500
   (E) none of these

8. A government worker whose personal car gets 24 miles to the gallon was required to use his own car for government business. He filled the tank before he began, requiring 18 gallons, for which he paid $1.349 per gallon. He drove 336 miles, then filled the tank again at a cost of $1.419 per gallon. The government reimburses him at the rate of $.20 per mile. What was the actual cost of gasoline for this trip?
   (A) $19.87
   (B) $23.05
   (C) $24.28
   (D) $44.15
   (E) none of these

9. The visitors' section of a courtroom seats 105 people. The court is in session 6 hours of the day. On one particular day, 486 people visited the court and were given seats. What is the average length of time spent by each visitor in the court? Assume that as soon as a person leaves a seat it is immediately filled and that at no time during the day is one of the 105 seats vacant. Express your answer in hours and minutes.
   (A) 1 hour 18 minutes
   (B) 1 hour 20 minutes
   (C) 1 hour 30 minutes
   (D) 2 hours
   (E) none of these

10. A worker is paid at the rate of $8.60 per hour for the first 40 hours worked in a week and time-and-a-half for overtime. The FICA (social security) deduction is 7.13 percent, federal tax withholding is 15 percent, state tax withholding is 5 percent, and local tax withholding is $2\frac{1}{2}$ percent. If a worker works 48 hours a week for two consecutive weeks, she will take home
   (A) $314.69
   (B) $580.97
   (C) $629.39
   (D) $693.16
   (E) none of these

11. A court clerk estimates that the untried cases on the docket will occupy the court for 150 trial days. If new cases are accumulating at the rate of 1.6 trial days per day and the court sits five days a week, how many days' business will remain to be heard at the end of 60 trial days?
   (A) 168
   (B) 184
   (C) 185
   (D) 186
   (E) none of these

12. A criminal investigator has an appointment to meet with an important informant at 4 P.M. in a city that is 480 kilometers from his base location. If the investigator estimates that his average speed will be 40 mph, what time must he leave home to make his appointment?
   (A) 8:15 A.M.
   (B) 8:30 A.M.
   (C) 8:45 A.M.
   (D) 9:30 A.M.
   (E) none of these

13. A program analysis office is taking bids for a new office machine. One machine is offered at a list price of $1360 with successive discounts of 20 percent and 10 percent, a delivery charge of $35 and an installation charge of $52. The other machine is offered at a list price of $1385 with a single discount of 30 percent, a delivery charge of $40, and an installation charge of $50. If the office chooses the less expensive machine, the savings will amount to just about
   (A) .6 percent
   (B) 1.9 percent
   (C) 2.0 percent
   (D) 2.6 percent
   (E) none of these

14. An assignment is completed by 32 clerks in 22 days. Assuming that all the clerks work at the same rate of speed, the number of clerks that would be needed to complete this assignment in 16 days is
    (A) 27
    (B) 38
    (C) 44
    (D) 52
    (E) none of these

15. The paralegals in a large legal department have decided to establish a "sunshine fund" for charitable purposes. Paralegal A has proposed that each worker chip in one-half of 1 percent of weekly salary; paralegal B thinks 1 percent would be just right; paralegal C suggests that one-third of 1 percent would be adequate; and paralegal D, who is strapped for funds, argues for one-fifth of 1 percent. The payroll department will cooperate and make an automatic deduction, but the paralegals must agree on a uniform percentage. The average of their suggested contributions is approximately

    (A) $\frac{1}{4}$ percent

    (B) $\frac{1}{3}$ percent

    (C) $\frac{1}{2}$ percent

    (D) $\frac{5}{8}$ percent

    (E) none of these

16. In one Federal office, $\frac{1}{6}$ of the employees favored abandoning a flexible work schedule system. In a second office that had the same number of employees $\frac{1}{4}$ of the workers favored abandoning it. What is the average of the fractions of the workers in the two offices who favored abandoning the system?

    (A) $\frac{1}{10}$

    (B) $\frac{1}{5}$

    (C) $\frac{5}{24}$

    (D) $\frac{5}{12}$

    (E) none of these

17. It costs $60,000 per month to maintain a small medical facility. The basic charge per person for treatment is $40, but 50 percent of those seeking treatment require laboratory work at an additional average charge of $20 per person. How many patients per month would the facility have to serve to cover its costs?
    (A) 1000
    (B) 1200
    (C) 1500
    (D) 2000
    (E) none of these

18. An experimental anti-pollution vehicle powered by electricity traveled 33 kilometers (km) at a constant speed of 110 kilometers per hour (km/h). How many minutes did it take this vehicle to complete its experimental run?
   (A) 3
   (B) 10
   (C) 18
   (D) 20
   (E) none of these

19. It takes two typists three 8-hour workdays to type a report on a word processor. How many typists would be needed to type two reports of the same length in one 8-hour workday?
   (A) 4
   (B) 6
   (C) 8
   (D) 12
   (E) none of these

20. A clerk is able to process 40 unemployment compensation claims in one hour. After deductions of 18 percent for benefits and taxes, the clerk's net pay is $6.97 per hour. If the clerk processed 1,200 claims, how much would the government have to pay for the work, based on the clerk's hourly wage *before* deductions?
   (A) $278.80
   (B) $255.00
   (C) $246.74
   (D) $209.10
   (E) none of these

STOP

END OF PART B. IF YOU FINISH BEFORE 50 MINUTES IS UP, CHECK OVER YOUR WORK IN PART B ONLY. DO NOT RETURN TO PART A NOR GO ON TO PART C.

Part C—Problems for Investigation

Time: 60 minutes. 30 questions.

Directions: Read the paragraph and statements carefully, then answer the questions that follow each investigative situation. Mark the letter of the correct answer on your answer sheet. You may refer to the paragraph and statements as often as needed. Explanations for these questions appear on pages 100 to 102.

Questions 1 to 7 are based upon the following paragraph and statements.

Ellen Bascomb, an Internal Security Inspector with the IRS, received a letter from a citizen, John Riley, alleging misconduct by an IRS agent in the downtown Phoenix, Arizona, office. Riley alleged that his next door neighbor, Ronald Strachan, had "gotten off the hook" after an IRS audit by bribing the agent assigned to the case. Riley did not give the name of the agent.

During the course of the investigation, the following statements were made:

(1)   Ronald Strachan said that his 1983 Federal Income Tax return, which was in perfect order, had been routinely audited by agent Martin Galuski in October 1984.

(2)   John Riley said that Ronald Strachan had purchased an expensive stereo outfit in November and played it loudly at all hours.

(3)   Agent Martin Galuski said that he had audited Ronald Strachan's return and that he had interviewed Strachan in the company of his accountant during the afternoon of October 23, 1984.

(4)   Ronald Strachan's accountant, Barbara Cabrini, said that she had accompanied Strachan to his hearing on the afternoon of October 23, 1984, and that she had not heard Strachan offer a bribe nor Galuski imply that he might accept one.

(5)   Warren Cheung, the IRS agent who occupies the desk next to Galuski's, said that he neither saw nor heard anything out of the ordinary on the afternoon of October 23, 1984.

(6)   Ronald Strachan said that John Riley was an unpleasant neighbor whose house needed painting and that he seldom even said "hello" to him.

(7)   Martin Galuski told Ellen Bascomb that the final disposition of Strachan's case had not yet been made.

(8)   Security guard Harold Henshaw said that he had seen Galuski and Strachan enter the men's room together.

(9)   Bank teller Jesus Ramos said that Warren Cheung had deposited $500 in his savings account on October 24, 1984.

(10)   Mrs. Strachan said that her husband, Ronald, is an honest person who does not lie, cheat, or manipulate.

1. Which of the following statements is most damaging to the accused agent?
   - (A) Statement 3
   - (B) Statement 5
   - (C) Statement 7
   - (D) Statement 8
   - (E) Statement 9

2. Which of the following statements, along with statement (5), indicates that a bribe was not offered during the hearing?
   - (A) Statement 3
   - (B) Statement 4
   - (C) Statement 7
   - (D) Statement 8
   - (E) Statement 10

3. To which of the following statements are the authorities likely to pay LEAST attention in determining guilt or innocence in this case?
   - (A) Statement 4
   - (B) Statement 7
   - (C) Statement 8
   - (D) Statement 9
   - (E) Statement 10

4. Which two of the following statements are likely to make Ellen Bascomb suspicious of the reliability of Riley's information?
   - (A) Statements 2 and 6
   - (B) Statements 1 and 10
   - (C) Statements 3 and 4
   - (D) Statements 4 and 6
   - (E) Statements 5 and 9

5. Which two of the following statements totally corroborate each other?
   - (A) Statements 1 and 3
   - (B) Statements 2 and 6
   - (C) Statements 3 and 7
   - (D) Statements 4 and 10
   - (E) Statements 5 and 10

6. Which of the following statements implies the possibility of collusion?
   - (A) Statement 4
   - (B) Statement 5
   - (C) Statement 8
   - (D) Statement 9
   - (E) Statement 10

7. Which of the following statements presents purely circumstantial evidence?
   (A) Statement 1
   (B) Statement 6
   (C) Statement 7
   (D) Statement 9
   (E) Statement 10

Questions 8 to 15 are based upon the following paragraph and statements.

ATF Special Agent Minna Tharp received an anonymous tip that whiskey was being illegally distilled at $995\frac{1}{2}$ Canal Street and was being sold at the Goodlife Drugstore at 83 Bommel Street. Based on the tip and the strong distillery smell in the neighborhood of $995\frac{1}{2}$ Canal Street, Minna Tharp got a search warrant and discovered a distillery in operation in ground floor apartment A. Sam Mong was found in the apartment where the distillery was operating. Three other apartments of the six in the building were occupied; the rest were vacant. Special Agent Zack Titus purchased a bottle of whiskey that did not have a federal tax seal at the Goodlife Drugstore.

During the course of the investigation, the following statements were made:

(1) Fred Rank, owner and manager of the Goodlife Drugstore, stated that he knew nothing about sales of whiskey at his drugstore.

(2) Alex Skoll, who sold the whiskey to Zack Titus, stated that he did not know that the tax on the whiskey had not been paid and that the whiskey he sold Mr. Titus was the same as the whiskey he had been selling for a long time.

(3) Sam Mong stated that he had just been passing by and entered the apartment in order to get out of the cold. He said he knew nothing about the whiskey.

(4) Natalie Norton, who lives in apartment B directly above apartment A, stated that she had been frightened and knew nothing; however, she knew that the owner of the building, Karl Fitz, was guilty because he had been trying to make her move out.

(5) Jack Sweet, who lives in apartment C, above Natalie Norton, stated that he frequently saw Sam Mong coming in or going out of the building.

(6) Susan Hubble, who lives with her husband and one child in apartment E, stated that she had complained months ago to the janitor, Harvey Stone, about the smell and the activity in apartment A, which was supposed to be empty, but that he hadn't done anything about it.

(7) Harvey Stone stated that he was not paid enough to do anything more than clean and supply heat.

(8) Karl Fitz, owner of the building, stated that he had no knowledge of the use of apartment A. He tried to persuade the remaining tenants to move each month when he collected rent so that he could tear the building down and build a high-rise modern building.

8. Which one of the following statements best indicates that the illegal still had been operating at $995\frac{1}{2}$ Canal Street for months?
   (A) Statement 1
   (B) Statement 2
   (C) Statement 5
   (D) Statement 6
   (E) Statement 7

9. Which of the following statements, along with statement (3), connects Sam Mong with the distillery?
   (A) Statement 4
   (B) Statement 5
   (C) Statement 6
   (D) Statement 7
   (E) Statement 8

10. Which of the following statements, along with statement (8), connects Karl Fitz with knowledge of the distillery?
    (A) Statement 2
    (B) Statement 3
    (C) Statement 4
    (D) Statement 5
    (E) Statement 6

11. Which one of the following statements is LEAST likely to be used in proving a case?
    (A) Statement 4
    (B) Statement 5
    (C) Statement 6
    (D) Statement 7
    (E) Statement 8

12. Which of the following statements best indicates that the illegal sale of whiskey had been going on for months?
    (A) Statement 1
    (B) Statement 2
    (C) Statement 3
    (D) Statement 4
    (E) Statement 5

13. Which of the following statements, along with statement (1), connects Fred Rank with the sale of whiskey without legal tax stamps?
    (A) Statement 2
    (B) Statement 3
    (C) Statement 5
    (D) Statement 6
    (E) Statement 8

14. Of the following, the two statements that appear to provide the most helpful information toward solving this case are
    (A) Statements 1 and 3
    (B) Statements 2 and 5
    (C) Statements 2 and 3
    (D) Statements 3 and 7
    (E) Statements 7 and 8

15. Which single statement presents the most damaging evidence concerning the illegal production of whiskey?
    (A) Statement 2
    (B) Statement 5
    (C) Statement 6
    (D) Statement 7
    (E) Statement 8

Questions 16 to 22 are based upon the following paragraph and statements.

The President's entourage was turning the corner from Hoover Street onto Main Street where the President was to make an address from the court house steps. Secret Service Special Agent Myrna Meyers was among the Special Agents mingling with the crowd lining the route. Agent Meyers was standing in front of a condemned tenement inhabited by down-and-out squatters. Suddenly the air was peppered with short, sharp blasts. Agent Meyers wheeled about, and with Secret Service Special Agent Juan Mendoza at her side, searched for the source of the shot-like sounds. The source was not immediately apparent, and the President continued on his way unharmed.

During the course of the investigation that followed this incident, the following statements were made:

(1) John Doe, a regular police informer, said that Harvey Laveille, an unemployed typesetter residing at 1183 North Hoover Street, was the owner of a shotgun.

(2) Lorraine Brooks, a salesperson at Gregory's Department Store at the corner of Hoover and Main, said that Bill Butlein, a stock-boy, often muttered obscenities about the President.

(3) Takeshi Matsuoka, an artist living at 381 Walnut Street, which runs parallel to Main, said that in the past few days a total stranger—a tall, thin, balding man—had been walking about on the roof of 386 Walnut Street with what appeared to be surveyor's instruments.

(4) Evelyn Bass said that Martina Meadows of 420 Walnut Street had threatened to kill the President if her son Willy were not accepted into the program at the Northside Day Care Center.

(5) George Laveille, brother of Harvey Laveille, said that as the new superintendent of 386 Walnut Street he intended to clear the building of drug dealers and trespassers.

(6)   Ricardo Mancini, owner of the Parkway Diner, said that Bill Butlein and his girlfriend Jody White often talked of their disappointment with the President and of how they would do things differently.

(7)   Bill Butlein said that he held the President directly responsible for the addicts loitering at 1099 North Hoover, but that they were harmless.

(8)   Georgia Delaney of the sporting goods department at Gregory's Department Store said that she had sold rifle ammunition to a tall, thin, balding man whom she did not know.

(9)   Carmella DeAngelis said that she wished the police would stop the group of young boys who often tossed firecrackers at passing cars on High Street behind the diner.

(10)   Sarah Stern, a social worker, said that domestic violence is epidemic among the unemployed.

(11)   Ali Muhamed, who was watching the President from a third-floor window at Gregory's Department Store, said that he did not see anyone running on Hoover or Main.

16. Which of the following statements places an informant in the vicinity of the President at the time of the sounds?
(A) Statement 1
(B) Statement 3
(C) Statement 5
(D) Statement 6
(E) Statement 11

17. Which of the following statements most likely represents an idle threat?
(A) Statement 1
(B) Statement 2
(C) Statement 4
(D) Statement 5
(E) Statement 7

18. Which of the following statements, along with statement (9), might lead Agent Meyers to assume that shots were not aimed at the President?
(A) Statement 3
(B) Statement 4
(C) Statement 5
(D) Statement 10
(E) Statement 11

19. Which of the following statements, along with statement (8), offers a real lead?
(A) Statement 1
(B) Statement 3
(C) Statement 4
(D) Statement 5
(E) Statement 10

20. Which two of the following statements offer another useful lead for Agent Meyers?
   (A) Statements 1 and 5
   (B) Statements 2 and 6
   (C) Statements 6 and 7
   (D) Statements 7 and 10
   (E) Statements 9 and 11

21. Which of the following statements represents social commentary?
   (A) Statement 1
   (B) Statement 6
   (C) Statement 7
   (D) Statement 8
   (E) Statement 9

22. Which of the following statements illustrates cooperation between the local police and Secret Service Special Agents?
   (A) Statement 1
   (B) Statement 4
   (C) Statement 5
   (D) Statement 10
   (E) Statement 11

Questions 23 to 30 are based upon the following paragraph and statements.

There was a crash on the turnpike between two trucks, one of which overturned. The other truck sustained rear end damage. Cartons of cigarettes, some burst open, were found spilled onto the highway. One of the police officers, Ella Twain, who reported to the scene noted that federal tax stamps on some of the cigarette packages were counterfeit. Steven Christian, the driver of the truck that overturned, was injured and had to be taken to the hospital without being questioned. The driver of the other truck, William Cook, stated that he was not carrying cigarettes and knew nothing about the ones on the highway.

During the course of investigation the following statements were made:

(1)   Another police officer who reported to the scene, John Stewart, stated that he had checked the contents of both trucks. He found a quantity of unopened cases marked "cigarettes" in the overturned truck, but he did not open them.

(2)   Sgt. Brian Schwartz who investigated the accident stated that there were 100 boxes of 12 cartons of cigarettes each in the overturned truck and that he had opened three of them at random and found them to contain packages of cigarettes with counterfeit tax stamps.

(3)   Alex Tobin, owner of the overturned truck, stated that the truck contained a full shipment when it left the warehouse, all consigned to L & T Stationery Co. It contained no cigarettes, he stated.

(4)   Mr. Tobin stated that Steven Christian was a liar and that you couldn't trust anything he said.

(5)   Susan Smith, manager of L & T Stationery Co., stated that she was expecting the shipment but did not remember if she had ordered any cigarettes.

(6)   Tom Dunn, salesman for L & T Stationery Co., stated that the stationery store sold a lot of cigarettes because their price was so low.

(7)   William Cook stated that he knew that Steven Christian was a crook from the poor way he drove a truck.

(8)   When Dr. Simon Tate allowed his patient, Steven Christian, to be interviewed, Mr. Christian stated that he was only a truck driver and did not pay any attention to the cargo.

(9)   Dr. Tate stated that Mr. Christian had been badly injured but would recover.

(10)   Packages of cigarettes with counterfeit stamps were found in the L & T Stationery store by local police officer John Temple.

23. Which one of the following statements BEST indicates that there were cigarettes in the overturned truck?
    (A) Statement 1
    (B) Statement 2
    (C) Statement 3
    (D) Statement 4
    (E) Statement 6

24. Which of the following statements, along with statements (2) and (3), throws the greatest suspicion on Alex Tobin as the source of cigarettes with counterfeit stamps?
    (A) Statement 1
    (B) Statement 4
    (C) Statement 6
    (D) Statement 7
    (E) Statement 10

25. Which of the following statements would be LEAST likely to be used in proving the case?
    (A) Statement 1
    (B) Statement 5
    (C) Statement 6
    (D) Statement 7
    (E) Statement 10

26. Which of the following statements is the best indication that William Cook was not involved in using counterfeit cigarette stamps?
    (A) Statement 1
    (B) Statement 4
    (C) Statement 7
    (D) Statement 8
    (E) Statement 10

27. Which of the following statements best indicates that L & T Stationery was selling cigarettes with counterfeit stamps?
    (A) Statement 1
    (B) Statement 2
    (C) Statement 5
    (D) Statement 6
    (E) Statement 10

28. Which of the following two statements are the BEST indication that cigarettes with counterfeit stamps were being transported by truck for sale by L & T Stationery?
    (A) Statements 1 and 4
    (B) Statements 1 and 6
    (C) Statements 2 and 10
    (D) Statements 4 and 6
    (E) Statements 7 and 8

29. Which of the following two statements throws the greatest suspicion on Steven Christian as being involved in the sale of cigarettes with counterfeit stamps?
    (A) Statements 1 and 4
    (B) Statements 2 and 3
    (C) Statements 2 and 5
    (D) Statements 3 and 7
    (E) Statements 4 and 6

30. Which of the following statements, along with statement (6), implies that L & T Stationery Co. was knowingly stocking cigarettes with counterfeit stamps?
    (A) Statement 1
    (B) Statement 3
    (C) Statement 5
    (D) Statement 8
    (E) Statement 10

END OF EXAM

IF YOU HAVE ANY REMAINING TIME, USE IT TO CHECK YOUR WORK ON THIS PART ONLY. YOU MAY NOT RETURN TO ANY PREVIOUS PART.

After Taking the First Model Exam

1. Score yourself. When you have completed the entire examination, check your answers against the correct answers provided on page 91. Give yourself one point for each correct answer. (There is no deduction for wrong answers on the TEA exam.) Then enter your scores in the table below.

SCORE SHEET

Part	Number Correct
Verbal Reasoning	__ ÷ 25 = __ × 100 = __ %
Arithmetic Reasoning	__ ÷ 20 = __ × 100 = __ %
Problems for Investigation	__ ÷ 30 = __ × 100 = __ %
Total	__ ÷ 75 = __ × 100 = __ %

2. Study the answer explanations for *all* questions, even those you answered correctly. The explanations will help you to gain insight into the thinking behind TEA questions.
3. Turn to Part Four. Study the strategies and do all the practice exercises to develop your skill even further.
4. When you feel ready, take the second model examination under actual examination conditions. Set aside three hours so you can work through the entire exam with only a short stretch between sections. Adhere to time limits. Do not peek ahead at the answers.

ANSWER KEY

Part A—Verbal Reasoning Questions

1. A	5. E	8. C	11. D	14. C	17. C	20. C	23. C
2. B	6. C	9. E	12. A	15. B	18. B	21. E	24. C
3. B	7. D	10. B	13. E	16. E	19. D	22. E	25. E
4. C							

Part B—Arithmetic Reasoning Questions

1. C	4. E	7. B	10. C	13. A	15. C	17. B	19. D
2. D	5. A	8. A	11. D	14. C	16. C	18. C	20. B
3. B	6. C	9. A	12. B				

Part C—Problems for Investigation

1. D	5. A	9. B	13. A	17. C	21. C	25. D	28. C
2. B	6. D	10. C	14. B	18. D	22. A	26. A	29. B
3. E	7. D	11. A	15. C	19. B	23. B	27. E	30. C
4. A	8. D	12. B	16. E	20. A	24. E		

EXPLANATIONS

Part A—Verbal Reasoning Questions

1. **(A)** The essential information from which the answer can be inferred is found in the second sentence. Since *a uniformed member while out of uniform* (in other words, an off-duty member) *may not indulge in intoxicants to an extent unfitting the member for duty,* it follows that that same member may drink liquor in moderation. Response (B) is incorrect because it directly contradicts the first sentence. Response (C) is incorrect because it introduces a concept not addressed in the paragraph— that of the uniformed member who reports unfit for duty. Response (D) is wrong because it reverses the meaning of the second sentence—the uniformed member in civilian clothes may drink only to the extent that the member remains fit for duty. Response (E) is incorrect because it raises a topic never mentioned in the paragraph—that of the civilian member of the department in a uniform (what uniform?).

2. **(B)** The paragraph makes the statement that the technician may sign that which it is not required that the specialist personally sign and states the rules that apply to the technician: name and title of tax law specialist followed by "by" and the name and title of the tax technician in ink. Response (B) is incorrect in that the assistant does not have authority to sign all papers. Responses (C) and (D) are incorrect because they address topics not mentioned in the paragraph—redelegation and requisitions. Response (E) is incorrect; the tax law specialist's name may be affixed by rubber stamp.

3. **(B)**   The first clause states that the retiree is entitled to an annuity; the second clause tells of the pension that is the equal of one service-fraction of final compensation multiplied by number of years of government service; and the last clause describes an additional pension that is the actuarial equivalent of any reserve-for-increased-take-home-pay to which the retiree might at that time be entitled. Response (A) is incorrect because it does not complete the explanation of the basis for the second pension. Responses (C), (D), and (E) are all hopelessly garbled misstatements.

4. **(C)**   In effect, the paragraph is saying, "When in doubt, check it out." Ignorance of the nature of the material to be mailed or of how the law pertains to it does not excuse the mailer if the material was indeed subject to a prohibition. Response (A) misinterprets the role of the postmaster. The postmaster is the final authority as to mailability. Response (B) is incorrect in its direct contradiction of the paragraph which states, "Ignorance is no excuse." Responses (D) and (E) both interpret beyond the paragraph. The paragraph places all burden on the mailer.

5. **(E)**   The last sentence makes the point that *any and all training* is valuable, *but only as it pertains to the position for which the applicant applies.* Responses (A) and (D) miss the point. Any training or education is valuable *if it contributes to knowledges, skills, and abilities needed in the particular job.* Responses (B) and (C) make statements not supported by the paragraph.

6. **(C)**   The second sentence tells us that heart disease is an illness of late middle age and old age. Response (A) is totally wrong. Since heart disease is an illness of older people, the odds of a person with heart disease being over 30 are much more than 50 percent. The 50/50 statement refers to the likelihood of persons over 30 sometime developing heart disease. Response (B) confuses death from *all causes* with death from *all other illnesses.* Response (D) makes an unsupported assumption that only the rising birth rate contributes to the number of people above a certain age. Actually, the longevity rate is much more crucial to this figure. Response (E) makes a statement that, whether true or false, is in no way supported by the paragraph.

7. **(D)**   If people want what they can't get through legitimate, entirely legal channels, they will turn to those who supply those products or services. The consumers of less than legitimate products or services are unlikely to betray their suppliers. Response (A) is incorrect. Since racketeers deliver goods and services for money received, they are not engaged in theft, but not all "non- thieves" are engaged in legitimate business. Response (B) is incorrect because both racketeering and theft involve objects of value; the differences are along other dimensions. Response (C) makes no sense at all. Response (E) is unsupported by the paragraph.

8. **(C)**   The first sentence tells us that the problems of the housing authority are numerous, that it faces all the problems of private developers and problems peculiar to a public authority. Being *watched by antihousing enthusiasts* is one of these problems. Response (A) makes an unsupported statement. The paragraph does not enumerate the problems of private developers. Response (B) is incorrect. It is the antihousing authorities who watch for errors and cost overruns and then bring them to the attention of Congressional committees. Responses (D) and (E) make unsupported statements that do not make much sense as statements.

9. **(E)**   *The peculiar threats to security in governmental organizations* to which the paragraph alludes, are factors related to partisan, electoral politics. Other factors—job performance, needs of the marketplace, interpersonal relationships, and internal power plays—affect private and public employees in about equal proportions. Response (A) is unsupported by the paragraph. Response (B) directly contradicts the paragraph. Responses (C) and (D) are entirely unsupported by the paragraph.

10. **(B)**   Some people develop allergies to antibiotics so that when those specific antibiotics might be the drug of choice to counter illness, the antibiotics cannot be used for those people. Response (A) makes a categorical statement that is unsupported by the paragraph. Response (C) is incorrect because antibiotics do not cure allergies; they may cause allergies. Response (D) is incorrect because the organisms do not become allergic to antibiotics (people become allergic). Response (E) is incorrect because there would be no need to search for new drugs if the existing ones were unfailingly effective. We need new drugs precisely because some organisms have become resistant to current ones.

11. **(D)**   The paragraph clearly states that *in the competitive class every applicant must meet minimum qualifications* . . . There may or may not be a pass/fail examination, but there most definitely are minimum qualifications that must be fulfilled. Response (A) is a distortion of the first sentence. The sentence means that there are no reliable exams for noncompetitive positions, not that noncompetitive positions are filled by unreliable exams. Response (B) is incorrect because the paragraph states that there *may* be an exam, not that there *will* be an exam. Response (C) is incorrect because if there is a test, the applicant must pass it. Response (E) goes beyond the scope of the paragraph. The paragraph does not state that *all* positions for which there are minimum qualifications are in the noncompetitive class.

12. **(A)**   The paragraph defines a comma splice as the joining of two main clauses by a comma without a coordinating conjunction. Response (B) is incorrect because a run-on sentence is defined as two independent clauses sharing one sentence with no connective. Response (C) is incorrect because the paragraph suggests that a semicolon used as a connective can stand alone. Response (D) touches on a subject not addressed in the paragraph. Response (E) reverses the intent of the paragraph. A comma splice *is* a bad remedy for a run-on sentence.

13. **(E)**   In *some* positions overtime is earned for time worked beyond the set number of hours; *other* positions offer compensatory time for overtime. Compensatory time is an alternative to overtime pay. Responses (A), (B), and (C) make unsupported statements. Response (D) combines the additional payments for two different classes of services. Overtime pay is for hours in excess of the standard number; weekend differentials are for work on weekends, even if within the standard number of workweek hours.

14. **(C)**   The paragraph makes clear that applicants may take the test before their backgrounds and qualifications have been investigated. If qualification is not even prerequisite to testing, certainly a qualified applicant will not be barred from the exam. Response (A) is incorrect in assuming that all persons admitted to the test are unqualified. The paragraph indicates only that their qualifications need not have yet been verified. Response (B) contradicts the paragraph. Response (D) is incorrect. The investigation is made to verify satisfactory character and reputation. Response (E) is unsupported by the paragraph.

15. **(B)**   Since it is illegal to continue employing an undocumented alien hired after November 6, 1986, it must not be illegal to retain an employee who was hired before that date. Response (A) is incorrect. It never was illegal to *deny* employment to undocumented aliens; it is now illegal to employ them. Response (C) misinterprets the paragraph. The paragraph applies only to undocumented or unauthorized aliens. Aliens who have authorizing documents or "green cards" may be employed legally. Response (D) is incorrect. Penalties are for "knowingly" hiring illegal aliens, not for inadvertent hiring. (You must limit your answers to the material presented in the paragraph, even though you may know of the burden on employers to verify documentation or face penalties.) Response (E) is in contradiction to the paragraph.

16. **(E)** COBRA provides for the continuation of health and welfare benefits upon payment of 102 percent of the group premium. Response (A) misinterprets the variation in the length of continuing coverage to depend upon the reason for termination of coverage rather than upon the reason for continuation of coverage. Response (B) is incorrect because it is the cost to the subscriber that jumps to 102 percent of the group rate, not the extent of the coverage. Response (C) is incorrect because the law requires the employer to offer the opportunity to continue health coverage; it does not require employees, retirees, or their families to continue that coverage. Response (D) is wrong because under COBRA terminated employees and retirees can continue coverage, but they cannot acquire new benefits.

17. **(C)** Recorded history is short relative to the time span between major earthquakes; therefore, history is inadequate as a predictive tool. Either a much longer period of recorded history or a much shorter span between major earthquakes would enhance the predictive value of historical data. Response (A) is not supported by the paragraph. Responses (B) and (D) are not only unsupported, but make no sense. Response (E) makes an assumption that goes beyond the paragraph.

18. **(B)** Basically, the last sentence of the paragraph is saying that if we know the rules of construction of a language, we can understand it. Response (A) contradicts the paragraph. The paragraph states that the number of rules is finite. Response (C) twists the second sentence, which states that definition of a language by listing its strings is impossible because the number of strings is infinite. Response (D) introduces unnatural languages, which is not a subject of the paragraph. Response (E) makes an unsupported statement.

19. **(D)** Just as *agreement of testimony is no proof of dependability,* so agreement of testimony is no proof of undependability. Response (A) is incorrect because the thrust of the paragraph is that people's perceptions are sometimes in error. Response (B) contradicts the paragraph. It is reported that a number of witnesses may report the same erroneous observation even apart from collusion. Response (C) misses the point. Since witnesses can make mistakes, they are just as likely to have not noticed the truth as to have "observed" that which did not happen. Response (E) is a misstatement.

20. **(C)** If a contract is changed by a rider, both parties must sign the rider. The basic contract should note that a rider is being attached, and both parties should initial and date the notice in the basic contract. Response (A) is incorrect in that it creates a rider without necessarily having created a contract. A mutual agreement to refrain from an act may be a first point of agreement and not a change. Responses (B) and (D) are both incorrect because there can be no change unless both parties agree. Response (E) is incorrect because if there is to be no change there is no call for a rider.

21. **(E)** The answer can be validly inferred from the third sentence in the paragraph. This sentence states that *all mechanical explosives are devices in which a physical reaction is produced, such as that caused by overloading a container with compressed air.* From this, we can safely conclude that *some* devices in which a physical reaction is produced, such as that caused by overloading a container with compressed air, are mechanical explosives. Response (A) cannot be inferred because the paragraph does not provide sufficient information to enable the conclusion to be drawn that all explosives that have been restricted to military weapons are nuclear weapons. It may be that other explosives that are not nuclear weapons also have been restricted to military weapons. Responses (B) and (C) are incorrect because they contradict the paragraph. Response (D) is wrong because the paragraph provides no information at all about whether or not mechanical explosives are restricted to military weapons.

22. **(E)** The essential information from which the answer can be inferred is contained in the third sentence of the paragraph. An analysis of this sentence reveals that response (E) is validly inferable because if it were not true that *dangerous microorganisms that must be destroyed are known to be present,* then sanitizers would be used. In (E), we are told that *sanitizers are not used;* therefore, we can conclude that *dangerous microorganisms that must be destroyed are known to be present.* Response (A) is wrong because the paragraph does not definitely state what is done if dangerous microorganisms that must be destroyed are known to be present. It may be that in such cases only stronger antimicrobial agents are used. Responses (B) and (C) are wrong because they run contrary to the information given in the paragraph to the effect that sanitizers are used if no dangerous microorganisms are known to be present. Response (D) is wrong because the information in the paragraph provides no evidence whatsoever about what measures would be adopted if only some (presumably specific) dangerous microorganisms are known not to be present.

23. **(C)** The answer can be inferred from the second and third sentences in the paragraph. The second sentence tells us that *some general types of land use are activities that conflict with* the purpose of wildlife refuges and botanical reservations. The third sentence explains that *all activities that exhibit such conflict are . . . excluded from refuges and reservations.* Therefore, we can conclude that *some activities excluded from refuges and reservations* (the ones that conflict with the purpose of refuges and reservations) *are general types of land use.* Response (A) is wrong because the paragraph does not give any information as to whether all activities that conflict with the purpose of refuges and reservations are general types of land use. The paragraph only says that *all activities that exhibit such conflict are . . . excluded from refuges and reservations.* Response (B) cannot be inferred because the paragraph does not give enough information about *all* activities that are excluded from refuges and reservations. Thus, we must recognize that we only know about *some* excluded activities. Response (D) is incorrect because the paragraph states that *some general types of land use are activities that conflict with the purpose of refuges and reservations.* It follows that *some* activities that conflict with this purpose are general types of land use. Response (E) is incorrect because there is insufficient information to infer whether some general types of land use are *not* excluded from wildlife refuges.

24. **(C)** This answer can be inferred from the information presented in the last sentence of the paragraph, which says in part that *all document depots have the capacity to provide a great range of user services.* In view of this statement, it is clearly the case that *no* document depot lacks such a capacity. Response (A) is incorrect because it goes beyond the information given in the paragraph. While there may be other ways of categorizing information centers, the paragraph only provides information about one method—by the primary activity or service provided. Statements about other methods would be speculation since they could not be inferred from the information in the paragraph. Response (B) is incorrect because it contradicts the information presented in the last sentence of the paragraph. Since all document depots have the capacity to provide a great range of user services, it cannot be true that some document depots lack this capacity. Response (D) is not supported by the paragraph because it draws an overly general conclusion from the information presented. The second sentence states that *some information centers are document depots.* It can be inferred from this that *some* document depots are information centers, but it cannot be inferred that *all* information centers are document depots. Response (E) goes beyond the information that is implicit in the last sentence of the paragraph. That sentence says that *all document depots have the capacity to provide a great range of user services.* From this statement nothing can be inferred about whether or not there are places that provide a great range of user services, but are not document depots.

25. **(E)**   The conclusion expressed in (E) can be derived from the information presented in the last sentence of the paragraph. That sentence says that *if an expression is a familiar one . . . then it is a nonhyphenated compound.* Therefore, if an expression is a hyphenated compound, it cannot be a familiar one. Response (A) is incorrect because it contradicts the information in the paragraph. By stating that a familiar expression is a hyphenated compound, response (A) directly contradicts the last sentence of the paragraph. Response (B) is incorrect because the paragraph does not give us information about *all* non-hyphenated compounds, only those which are familiar expressions. It could be that there are words that are non-hyphenated even though they are not familiar expressions. Response (C) is incorrect because the information in the paragraph is not complete enough to enable one to draw the conclusion that all expressions that are not familiar are hyphenated. The paragraph gives us complete information about familiar expressions (i.e., they are non-hyphenated) but it does not give us enough information about the entire class of expressions that are not familiar. Response (D) is incorrect because it represents an unwarranted inference from the information given in the paragraph. The paragraph provides no information whatsoever about compounds that have suffixes.

Part B—Arithmetic Reasoning Questions

1.   **(C)**   The first 12 clerks complete $\frac{6}{18}$, or $\frac{1}{3}$ of the job in 6 days, leaving $\frac{2}{3}$ of the job to be completed.

One clerk would require $12 \times 18 = 216$ days to complete the job, working alone. Sixteen clerks require $216 \div 16$, or $13\frac{1}{2}$ days for the entire job. But only $\frac{2}{3}$ of the job remains. To do $\frac{2}{3}$ of the job, 16 clerks require

$$\frac{2}{3} \times 13\frac{1}{2} = \frac{2}{3} \times \frac{27}{2} = 9 \text{ days}$$

The entire job takes 6 days + 9 days = 15 days.

2.   **(D)**   Let x = cost of a child's cleaning.

Then $2x$ = cost of an adult's cleaning.

$$2(2x) + 3(x) = \$49$$
$$4x + 3x = \$49$$
$$7x = \$49$$
$$x = \$7$$

$7 is the cost of a child's cleaning; $2 \times \$7$ or $14 is the cost of an adult's cleaning.

3.   **(B)**   First determine the total annual tax:

$424 + \$783 + (2)\$466 = \$424 + \$783 + \$932 = \$2139$

Divide the total taxes by the tax rate to find the assessed valuation.

$2139 \div .132 = \$16,204$

To find what percent one number is of another, create a fraction by putting the part over the whole and convert to a decimal by dividing.

$\frac{\$16,204}{\$87,250} = \$16,204 \div \$87,250 = 18.57\%$

4. **(E)** The correct answer, not given, is 5 additional days. Four assistants completed 336 cases in 42 hours (6 days at 7 hours per day). Therefore, each assistant completed 336 ÷ 4, or 84 cases in 42 hours, for a rate of 2 cases per hour per assistant.

After the first 6 days, the number of cases remaining is

756 – 336 = 420

It will take 6 assistants, working at the rate of 2 cases per hour per assistant 420 ÷ 12 or 35 hours to complete the work. If each workday has 7 hours, then 35 ÷ 7 or 5 days are needed.

5. **(A)** Add what the family spends.

30% + 8% + 25% + 4% + 13% + 5% = 85%

Since it spends 85 percent, it has 100 percent – 85 percent = 15 percent remaining for savings.

15% of $500 = .15 × $500 = $75 per week

$15,000 ÷ $75 = 200 weeks

6. **(C)** Commission = $42\frac{1}{2}$% of fares

$$42\frac{1}{2}\% \text{ of } \$520 = .425 \times \$520$$

$$= \$221 \text{ commission}$$

$$\text{Tips} = 29\% \text{ of commission}$$

$$29\% \text{ of } \$221 = .29 \times \$221$$

$$= \$64.09 \text{ tips}$$

Weekly earnings:

$221.00
+ 64.09
$285.09

Monthly earnings, based on four-week month:

$285.09
× 4
$1140.36

Earnings in a month a few days longer than four weeks clearly fall between $1100 and $1200.

7. **(B)** Take this problem one step at a time. Of the 60 employees, one-third, or 20, were clerks. 30 percent, or 18, were machine operators. 22 were stenographers.

The clerks earned $12,750 ÷ 12 = $1,062.50 per month

Machine operators earned $13,150 ÷ 12 = $1,095.83 per month

Stenographers earned $13,000 ÷ 12 = $1,083.33 per month

20 clerks × $1,062.50 × 2 months =$42,500.00

18 machine operators × $1,095.83 × 4 months = $78,899.76

22 stenographers × $1,083.33 × 3 months= $71,499.78

$42,500.00 + $78,889.76 + $71,499.78 = $192,899.54 total cost

8. **(A)**   The government worker drove 336 miles and his car got 24 miles per gallon; so he used 336 ÷ 24 = 14 gallons for which he paid $1.419 per gallon or $1.419 × 14 = $19.87. All other information is irrelevant; disregard it.

9. **(A)**   There are 360 minutes in a 6-hour day. If each seat is occupied all day there are 105 × 360 = 37,800 minutes of seating time to be divided among 486 people. 37,800 ÷ 486 = 77.77 minutes of seating time per person = 1 hour 17.7 minutes per person.

10. **(C)**   The worker earns $8.60 per hour for two 40-hour weeks or $8.60 × 80 hours = $688 and $12.90 per hour for an additional 16 hours ($12.90 × 16 hours = $206.40), so her gross pay is $688 + $206.40 = $894.40. From this are deducted: FICA at 7.13 percent = $63.77 and the three withholding taxes at the combined rate of 22.5% = $201.24. Add the deductions: $63.77 + $201.24 = $265.01, and subtract the sum from the gross pay: $894.40 – $265.01 = $629.39.

11. **(D)**   Since the court does one day's work per day, at the end of 60 days there will be 150 – 60 = 90 trial days of old cases remaining. New cases are accumulating at the rate of 1.6 trial days per day; therefore, there will be 60 × 1.6 = 96 trial days of new cases at the end of 60 days. 96 new trial days added to the backlog of 90 trial days would make the total backlog 186 trial days.

12. **(B)**   A kilometer is $\frac{5}{8}$ of a mile.

480 km × $\frac{5}{8}$ = 300 miles;

300 miles ÷ 40 mph = 7.5 hours

Subtract 7.5 hours from the required arrival time of 4 P.M. to find that he must leave at 8:30 A.M. (noon to 4 P.M. is 4 hours + 8:30 to noon is $3\frac{1}{2}$ hours).

13. **(A)**   Calculate the cost of the first machine.

$1360 – 20% = $1360 × 80% = $1088 then

$1088 – 10% = $1088 × 90% = $979.20 + $35 + $52 = $1066.20

Calculate the cost of the second machine.

$1385 – 30% = $1385 × 70% = $969.50 + $40 + $50 = $1059.50

The second machine is less expensive ($1066.20 – $1059.50 = $6.70); $6.70 ÷ $1066.20 = .6% savings by buying the second machine.

14. **(C)**   The proportion is 32 × 22 = X × 16

$$16X = 704$$

$$X = 704 ÷ 16 = 44$$

15. **(C)** Add the suggested contributions and divide by the number of paralegals to get the average.

$$\frac{1}{2}\% = \frac{15}{30}\%$$

$$1\% = \frac{30}{30}\%$$

$$\frac{1}{3}\% = \frac{10}{30}\%$$

$$+\frac{1}{5}\% = \frac{6}{30}\%$$

$$\frac{61}{30}\% = 2\% + 4 \text{ paralegals} = \frac{1}{2}\%$$

16. **(C)** Compute the following:

$$(\frac{1}{6} + \frac{1}{4}) \div 2 = X$$

This simple arithmetic averaging of two fractions can be accomplished by first finding their lowest common denominator:

$$\frac{1}{6} = \frac{2}{12} \text{ and } \frac{1}{4} = \frac{3}{12}$$

The sum of $\frac{2}{12}$ and $\frac{3}{12}$ is $\frac{5}{12}$. This fraction, when multiplied by $\frac{1}{2}$ (which is the same as dividing by 2) gives the correct answer.

$$\frac{5}{12} \times \frac{1}{2} = \frac{5}{24}$$

17. **(B)** Compute the following:

$$40X + 20(.5X) = 60,000$$

$$X = 60,000 \div 50 = 1200$$

The basic charge of $40 applies to *all* patients (X); the additional average charge of $20 applies to only 50 percent (or one-half) of them (.5X). The combined charges—$40 times the total number of patients (40X) plus $20 times one-half the total number of patients (20(.5X) or 10X)—must equal $60,000, the cost of maintaining the medical facility. Solving for X gives the result 1200, the number of patients who must be served per month for the facility to cover its costs.

18. **(C)** Set up a simple proportion.

$$\frac{110 \text{ km}}{60 \text{ min.}} = \frac{33 \text{ km}}{X \text{ min.}}$$

Solving this proportion we obtain 110X = 1980; X = 1980 ÷ 110 = 18.

19. **(D)** Compute the following:

$$3 \times 2 \times 2 = X$$

The left side of the equation represents the total number of 8-hour workdays of typing required for the two reports: three days times two typists times two reports equals twelve 8-hour workdays of typing. If all of this had to be accomplished in one 8-hour workday, twelve typists would be needed to do the job.

20. **(B)**   Compute the following:

(1) $.82S = 6.97$

and

(2) $1200 \div 40 \times S = Y$

The clerk's net pay of $6.97 per hour represents .82 of his or her gross pay (100% − 18% = 82% or .82). Solving equation 1 we find that the clerk's hourly salary (*S*) before deductions is $8.50. Substituting this figure in equation (2), we compute the total number of hours of work involved (1200 forms divided by 40 forms per hour equals 30 hours of work), and then multiply 30 hours by an hourly wage of $8.50 to get $255.00, the amount the government would have to pay for the work.

Part C—Problems for Investigation

1. **(D)**   The fact that the agent, Galuski, was seen entering the men's room with the individual whose return he was inspecting offers circumstantial evidence against him. While no one can prove that Galuski asked for a bribe nor that Strachan offered one, this statement suggests that there was an opportunity for this to happen.

2. **(B)**   Strachan's accountant, Barbara Cabrini, stated that a bribe was not offered in her presence. This statement corroborates that of Warren Cheung, who stated that he did not hear a bribe being offered.

3. **(E)**   Character reference by a spouse is inadmissible in court except under very special specified conditions.

4. **(A)**   The fact that Strachan and Riley evidently do not like each other must make the agent suspect that Riley is just trying to make trouble for his neighbor. Furthermore, if the two men do not speak to each other, Riley must either have fabricated the information or have acquired it from an unnamed third party.

5. **(A)**   The information as to time of inspection and inspecting agent given by Strachan is confirmed by the agent.

6. **(D)**   The implication of statement (9) is that Cheung did indeed overhear a bribe offer and that he was given money to keep him quiet.

7. **(D)**   The fact that Cheung happened to make a deposit into his savings account the day after Galuski interviewed Strachan is purely circumstantial evidence.

8. **(D)**   If Susan Hubble had complained months ago to the janitor about the smell, chances are pretty good that the still had been operating for some months.

9. **(B)**   Since a resident of the building saw Sam Mong coming in and out frequently, it is reasonable to assume that Mong had something to do with the distillery.

10. **(C)**   No proof is offered, but if Karl Fitz was trying to get tenants out it is entirely possible that he was aware of the distillery and did not want tenants who might become aware and mention the fact to the authorities.

11. **(A)** The fact that a building owner asks a tenant to move out is, in itself, no indication that the owner of the building is involved in illegal activity.

12. **(B)** Alex Skoll said that he had been selling the same whiskey for a long time.

13. **(A)** The untaxed whiskey had been sold at Goodlife Drugstore for quite some time. It is most unlikely that Rank, owner and manager of the drugstore, who ordered, stocked, and inventoried, would be unaware of the illegal source of whiskey sold in his store.

14. **(B)** There might be other, more useful, statements, but of the choices offered, statement (2), which indicates the extended nature of the sale of illegal whiskey, and statement (5), which implicates Sam Mong, are the most useful.

15. **(C)** Statement (6), in which activity and smell are cited, presents the clearest evidence of the existence of the illegal distillery in apartment A.

16. **(E)** Ali Muhamed stated that he was on the third floor of Gregory's Department Store when the President passed.

17. **(C)** Martina Meadows might have been concerned about her son's placement for the following year, but her statement has the ring of complaint rather than true threat.

18. **(D)** Sarah Stern's statement suggests that the shots might have been fired by and at residents in one of the condemned tenements. Statement (9) implies that there were no shots at all, that the noise was the sound of firecrackers.

19. **(B)** In statement (8), Georgia Delaney tells of selling rifle ammunition to a tall, thin, balding stranger. In statement (3) Takeshi Matsuoka tells of seeing a tall, thin, balding stranger on the roof of a building along the parade route.

20. **(A)** Statement (1) tells of an unhappy man who happens to be a gun owner. Statement (5) tells us that the brother of the gun owner lives in a building with convenient sight lines and within shotgun range of the parade route.

21. **(C)** The comment about the policies of the President being responsible for drug addiction is nothing more than social commentary.

22. **(A)** The services of a regular local police informer were offered to assist the Secret Service.

23. **(B)** Sergeant Schwartz opened boxes on the truck and found them to contain cigarettes with counterfeit tax stamps. Statement (1) implies that there were cigarettes on the truck since cases were so marked, but the opening of the boxes in statement (2) offers more certain proof.

24. **(E)** Statement (3) establishes Alex Tobin as the owner of the truck and the truck's destination as L & T Stationery. Statement (2) establishes that cigarettes with counterfeit stamps were carried on Alex Tobin's truck. Statement (10) establishes that cigarettes with counterfeit tax stamps were sold in L & T Stationery, which was supplied by Alex Tobin.

25. **(D)** Driving ability has nothing to do with honesty.

26. **(A)** The police officer makes no mention of cigarettes on William Cook's truck.

27. **(E)** This is straightforward. Packages of cigarettes with counterfeit tax stamps were found in L & T Stationery store.

28. **(C)** Cigarettes with counterfeit tax stamps were found on a truck bound for L & T Stationery store, and cigarettes with counterfeit tax stamps were found in L & T Stationery store.

29. **(B)** Steven Christian was the driver of a truck carrying cigarettes with counterfeit tax stamps. As such, he was involved in the sale of cigarettes with counterfeit tax stamps, knowingly or unwittingly.

30. **(C)** It does seem unlikely that the manager of the store did not remember whether or not she had ordered cigarettes. Surely she kept records, so her "not remembering" was by nature an attempted cover-up. The price of cigarettes at L & T Stationery store was probably so low because nonpayment of tax kept the cost low.

ANSWER SHEET FOR SECOND MODEL EXAMINATION

Part A—Verbal Reasoning Questions

1. Ⓐ Ⓑ Ⓒ Ⓓ Ⓔ	6. Ⓐ Ⓑ Ⓒ Ⓓ Ⓔ	11. Ⓐ Ⓑ Ⓒ Ⓓ Ⓔ	16. Ⓐ Ⓑ Ⓒ Ⓓ Ⓔ	21. Ⓐ Ⓑ Ⓒ Ⓓ Ⓔ
2. Ⓐ Ⓑ Ⓒ Ⓓ Ⓔ	7. Ⓐ Ⓑ Ⓒ Ⓓ Ⓔ	12. Ⓐ Ⓑ Ⓒ Ⓓ Ⓔ	17. Ⓐ Ⓑ Ⓒ Ⓓ Ⓔ	22. Ⓐ Ⓑ Ⓒ Ⓓ Ⓔ
3. Ⓐ Ⓑ Ⓒ Ⓓ Ⓔ	8. Ⓐ Ⓑ Ⓒ Ⓓ Ⓔ	13. Ⓐ Ⓑ Ⓒ Ⓓ Ⓔ	18. Ⓐ Ⓑ Ⓒ Ⓓ Ⓔ	23. Ⓐ Ⓑ Ⓒ Ⓓ Ⓔ
4. Ⓐ Ⓑ Ⓒ Ⓓ Ⓔ	9. Ⓐ Ⓑ Ⓒ Ⓓ Ⓔ	14. Ⓐ Ⓑ Ⓒ Ⓓ Ⓔ	19. Ⓐ Ⓑ Ⓒ Ⓓ Ⓔ	24. Ⓐ Ⓑ Ⓒ Ⓓ Ⓔ
5. Ⓐ Ⓑ Ⓒ Ⓓ Ⓔ	10. Ⓐ Ⓑ Ⓒ Ⓓ Ⓔ	15. Ⓐ Ⓑ Ⓒ Ⓓ Ⓔ	20. Ⓐ Ⓑ Ⓒ Ⓓ Ⓔ	25. Ⓐ Ⓑ Ⓒ Ⓓ Ⓔ

Part B—Arithmetic Reasoning Questions

1. Ⓐ Ⓑ Ⓒ Ⓓ Ⓔ	5. Ⓐ Ⓑ Ⓒ Ⓓ Ⓔ	9. Ⓐ Ⓑ Ⓒ Ⓓ Ⓔ	13. Ⓐ Ⓑ Ⓒ Ⓓ Ⓔ	17. Ⓐ Ⓑ Ⓒ Ⓓ Ⓔ
2. Ⓐ Ⓑ Ⓒ Ⓓ Ⓔ	6. Ⓐ Ⓑ Ⓒ Ⓓ Ⓔ	10. Ⓐ Ⓑ Ⓒ Ⓓ Ⓔ	14. Ⓐ Ⓑ Ⓒ Ⓓ Ⓔ	18. Ⓐ Ⓑ Ⓒ Ⓓ Ⓔ
3. Ⓐ Ⓑ Ⓒ Ⓓ Ⓔ	7. Ⓐ Ⓑ Ⓒ Ⓓ Ⓔ	11. Ⓐ Ⓑ Ⓒ Ⓓ Ⓔ	15. Ⓐ Ⓑ Ⓒ Ⓓ Ⓔ	19. Ⓐ Ⓑ Ⓒ Ⓓ Ⓔ
4. Ⓐ Ⓑ Ⓒ Ⓓ Ⓔ	8. Ⓐ Ⓑ Ⓒ Ⓓ Ⓔ	12. Ⓐ Ⓑ Ⓒ Ⓓ Ⓔ	16. Ⓐ Ⓑ Ⓒ Ⓓ Ⓔ	20. Ⓐ Ⓑ Ⓒ Ⓓ Ⓔ

Part C—Problems for Investigation

1. Ⓐ Ⓑ Ⓒ Ⓓ Ⓔ	7. Ⓐ Ⓑ Ⓒ Ⓓ Ⓔ	13. Ⓐ Ⓑ Ⓒ Ⓓ Ⓔ	19. Ⓐ Ⓑ Ⓒ Ⓓ Ⓔ	25. Ⓐ Ⓑ Ⓒ Ⓓ Ⓔ
2. Ⓐ Ⓑ Ⓒ Ⓓ Ⓔ	8. Ⓐ Ⓑ Ⓒ Ⓓ Ⓔ	14. Ⓐ Ⓑ Ⓒ Ⓓ Ⓔ	20. Ⓐ Ⓑ Ⓒ Ⓓ Ⓔ	26. Ⓐ Ⓑ Ⓒ Ⓓ Ⓔ
3. Ⓐ Ⓑ Ⓒ Ⓓ Ⓔ	9. Ⓐ Ⓑ Ⓒ Ⓓ Ⓔ	15. Ⓐ Ⓑ Ⓒ Ⓓ Ⓔ	21. Ⓐ Ⓑ Ⓒ Ⓓ Ⓔ	27. Ⓐ Ⓑ Ⓒ Ⓓ Ⓔ
4. Ⓐ Ⓑ Ⓒ Ⓓ Ⓔ	10. Ⓐ Ⓑ Ⓒ Ⓓ Ⓔ	16. Ⓐ Ⓑ Ⓒ Ⓓ Ⓔ	22. Ⓐ Ⓑ Ⓒ Ⓓ Ⓔ	28. Ⓐ Ⓑ Ⓒ Ⓓ Ⓔ
5. Ⓐ Ⓑ Ⓒ Ⓓ Ⓔ	11. Ⓐ Ⓑ Ⓒ Ⓓ Ⓔ	17. Ⓐ Ⓑ Ⓒ Ⓓ Ⓔ	23. Ⓐ Ⓑ Ⓒ Ⓓ Ⓔ	29. Ⓐ Ⓑ Ⓒ Ⓓ Ⓔ
6. Ⓐ Ⓑ Ⓒ Ⓓ Ⓔ	12. Ⓐ Ⓑ Ⓒ Ⓓ Ⓔ	18. Ⓐ Ⓑ Ⓒ Ⓓ Ⓔ	24. Ⓐ Ⓑ Ⓒ Ⓓ Ⓔ	30. Ⓐ Ⓑ Ⓒ Ⓓ Ⓔ

Part A—Verbal Reasoning Questions

Time: 50 minutes. 25 questions.

Directions: *For each verbal reasoning question you will be given a paragraph that contains all the information necessary to infer the correct answer. Use only the information provided in the paragraph. Do no speculate or make assumptions that go beyond this information. Also, assume that all information given in the paragraph is true, even if it conflicts with some fact known to you. Only one correct answer can be validly inferred from the information contained in the paragraph. Mark its letter on your answer sheet.*

1. The modern conception of the economic role of the public sector (government), as distinct from the private sector, is that every level of government is a link in the economic process. Government's contribution to political and economic welfare must, however, be evaluated not merely in terms of its technical efficiency, but also in the light of its acceptability to a particular society at a particular state of political and economic development. Even in a dictatorship, this principle is formally observed, although the authorities usually destroy the substance by presuming to interpret to the public its collective desires.

   The paragraph best supports the statement that
   (A) it is not true that some levels of government are not links in the economic process
   (B) all dictatorships observe the same economic principles as other governments
   (C) all links in the economic process are levels of government
   (D) the contributions of some levels of government do not need to be evaluated for technical efficiency and acceptability to society
   (E) no links in the economic process are institutions other than levels of government

2. All property is classified as either personal or real property, but not both. In general, if something is classified as personal property, it is transient and transportable in nature, while real property is not. Things such as leaseholds, animals, money, and intangible and other moveable goods are examples of personal property. Permanent buildings and land, on the other hand, are fixed in nature and are not transportable.

   The paragraph best supports the statement that
   (A) if something is classified as personal property, it is not transient and transportable in nature
   (B) some forms of property are considered to be both personal property and real property
   (C) permanent buildings and land are real property
   (D) permanent buildings and land are personal property
   (E) tangible goods are considered to be real property

3. Personnel administration begins with the process of defining the quantities of people needed to do the job. Thereafter, people must be recruited, selected, trained, directed, rewarded, transferred, promoted, and perhaps released or retired. However, it is not true that all organizations are structured so that workers can be dealt with as individuals. In some organizations, employees are represented by unions, and managers bargain directly only with these associations.

The paragraph best supports the statement that
(A) no organizations are structured so that workers cannot be dealt with as individuals
(B) some working environments other than organizations are structured so that workers can be dealt with as individuals
(C) all organizations are structured so that employees are represented by unions
(D) no organizations are structured so that managers bargain with unions
(E) some organizations are not structured so that workers can be dealt with as individuals

4. Many kinds of computer programming languages have been developed over the years. Initially, programmers had to write instructions in machine language. If a computer programming language is a machine language, then it is a code that can be read directly by a computer. Most high-level computer programming languages, such as Fortran and Cobol, use strings of common English phrases that communicate with the computer only after being converted or translated into a machine code.

The paragraph best supports the statement that
(A) all high-level computer programming languages use strings of common English phrases that are converted to a machine code
(B) if a computer programming language is a machine language, then it is not a code that can be read directly by a computer
(C) if a computer programming language is a code that can be read directly by a computer, then it is not a machine language
(D) if a computer programming language is not a code that can be read directly by a computer, then it is not a machine language
(E) if a computer programming language is not a machine language, then it is a code that can be read directly by a computer

5. The Supreme Court's power to invalidate legislation that violates the Constitution is a strong restriction on the powers of Congress. If an Act of Congress is deemed unconstitutional by the Supreme Court, then the Act is voided. Unlike a presidential veto, which can be overridden by a two-thirds vote of the House and the Senate, a constitutional ruling by the Supreme Court must be accepted by the Congress.

The paragraph best supports the statement that
(A) if an Act of Congress is voided, then it has been deemed unconstitutional by the Supreme Court
(B) if an Act of Congress has not been voided, then it has not been deemed unconstitutional by the Supreme Court
(C) if an Act of Congress has not been deemed unconstitutional by the Supreme Court, then it is voided
(D) if an Act of Congress is deemed unconstitutional by the Supreme Court, then it is not voided
(E) if an Act of Congress has not been voided, then it has been deemed unconstitutional by the Supreme Court

6. All child-welfare agencies are organizations that seek to promote the healthy growth and development of children. Supplying or supplementing family income so that parents can maintain a home for their children is usually the first such service to be provided. In addition to programs of general family relief, some special programs for broken families are offered when parental care is temporarily or permanently unavailable.

   The paragraph best supports the statement that
   (A) it is not true that some organizations that seek to promote the healthy growth and development of children are child-welfare agencies
   (B) some programs offered when parental care is temporarily or permanently unavailable are not special programs for broken families
   (C) it is not true that no special programs for broken families are offered when temporary or permanent parental care is unavailable
   (D) all programs offered when parental care is temporarily or permanently unavailable are special programs for broken families
   (E) some organizations that seek to promote the healthy growth and development of children are not child-welfare agencies

7. In its 1964 decision in the case of *The New York Times v. Sullivan,* the Supreme Court said that notwithstanding the press was inaccurate, even negligent, and the inaccuracy substantially damaged a public figure, there would be no liability on the part of the press. Only if the press were guilty of actual malice—that is a deliberate falsification, or conduct that evinced a reckless disregard—could there be a recovery.

   The paragraph best supports the statement that
   (A) if the press is not liable, there can be no malice
   (B) substantial damage to a public figure may be caused by negligence
   (C) the press was not inaccurate in its treatment of Sullivan
   (D) if the press is guilty of deliberate falsification, it can recover
   (E) the press is not liable if it damages a public figure

8. The purpose of elections in which both candidates have the same ideological outlook is three-fold. First, elections give the people a chance to pick the candidate who is the most technically qualified and politically astute. Second, elections insure that legislators keep in touch with their constituencies. Finally, competitive elections prevent the establishment of a firmly entrenched party elite who would develop their own interests and not remain accountable to the people. Thus, elections tend to clamp down on corruption by party and government officials.

   The paragraph best supports the statement that
   (A) there are three good reasons for both candidates to have the same ideological outlook
   (B) if there are elections, the candidates should have the same ideological outlook
   (C) if both candidates do not have the same ideological outlook, there is no reason for elections
   (D) elections offer the party an opportunity to clamp down on corruption
   (E) elections promote accountability to the electorate by those elected

9. The commonsense character of the merit system seems so natural to most Americans that many people wonder why it should ever have been inoperative. After all, the American economic system, the most phenomenal the world has ever known, is also founded on a rugged selective process that emphasizes the personal qualities of capacity, industriousness, and productivity. The criteria may not have always been appropriate and competition has not always been fair, but competition there was, and the responsibilities and the rewards—with exceptions, of course—have gone to those who could measure up in terms of intelligence, knowledge, or perseverance. This has been true not only in the economic area, in the moneymaking process, but also in achievement in the professions and other walks of life.

The paragraph best supports the statement that
(A) a merit system is based on the same principles as the American economic system
(B) competition, both fair and unfair, is unique to the American way of life
(C) the American economic system has led to phenomenal achievement in the professions
(D) common sense is a natural American trait
(E) capacity, industriousness, and productivity are not unfair criteria in competition

10. The popular view of war is that war is uncontrolled violence and barbarism, near the bottom in the annals of man's inhumanity to man. Actually, war is a political act, usually undertaken only when it appears that all other alternatives have failed. The laws of war are those portions of international law that deal with the inception of war, the conduct of war, and the cessation of war. They regulate the relations between states at war and the relationships of those states that claim to be neutral powers. The laws of war apply whether the war is declared or undeclared.

The paragraph best supports the statement that
(A) if a war is undeclared, it is not according to law
(B) war, defined as uncontrolled violence and barbarism, is popular rather than political
(C) a state that claims to be a neutral power should not have relationships with warring states outside of the regulation of the laws of war
(D) cessation of war can only occur under mandate of international law
(E) when all other alternatives have failed, the laws of war may be invoked so that states may conduct war

11. An important function of IRS Special Agents involves investigations of organized crime activities. Under federal law, income from illegal sources such as bootlegging, prostitution, and narcotics sales is subject to tax. Such income is used by members of organized crime to support other illegal activities or to infiltrate legitimate businesses. As a result of IRS investigations, many crime figures have been prosecuted and convicted of tax evasion, resulting in substantial blows to the financial resources of criminal groups. As part of this effort, the Internal Revenue Service participates in the Federal Organized Crime Strike Force Program and works on a cooperating basis with other law enforcement agencies at all levels of government.

The paragraph best supports the statement that
(A) the Federal Organized Crime Strike Force Program cooperates with other law enforcement agencies in governing the country
(B) although income is derived from illegal activities, it is illegal to not pay income tax on such income
(C) members of organized crime use reserved tax monies to infiltrate legitimate businesses

(D) IRS Special Agents prosecute and convict members of organized crime

(E) as a result of conviction of tax evasion, criminal groups apply their financial resources to cooperation with law enforcement agencies

12. The terms of trade have historically favored manufacturing. Commodity prices change quickly in response to supply and demand, just as classical price theory describes. But prices of manufactured goods are more sticky because they are usually set on a "cost-plus" basis, at least in the short run. It stands to reason that erratic prices lead to uncertainty. Even if the terms of trade on balance favor commodities, industrial exporting countries still benefit from a more stable price trend. Investment decisions can be made with greater confidence when prices are reasonably predictable. This means that total investment will be higher.

The paragraph best supports the statement that

(A) classical price theory describes quick changes in supply of and demand for commodities

(B) while industrial exporting countries may benefit from a more stable price trend, the terms of trade, on balance, still favor commodities

(C) total investment is higher when prices are reasonably predictable, allowing for investment decisions to be made with greater confidence

(D) prices on sticky manufactured goods tend to be set on a cost-plus basis

(E) unreasonable prices are erratic and are consequently uncertain

13. Proper firearms training is one phase of law enforcement that cannot be ignored. No part of the training of a law officer is more important or more valuable. The officer's life, and often the lives of his or her fellow officers, depend directly upon skill with the weapon he or she is carrying. Proficiency with the revolver is not attained exclusively by the volume of ammunition used and the number of hours spent on the firing line. Supervised practice and the use of training aids and techniques help make the shooter. It is essential to have a good firing range where new officers are trained and older personnel practice in scheduled firearms sessions. The fundamental points to be stressed are grip, stance, breathing, sight alignment, and trigger squeeze. Coordination of thought, vision, and motion must be achieved before the officer gains confidence in shooting ability. Attaining this ability will make the student a better officer and enhance his or her value to the force.

The paragraph best supports the statement that

(A) the volume of ammunition used and the number of hours spent on the firing range are the exclusive keys to proficiency with the revolver

(B) skill with weapons is a phase of law enforcement training that is too often ignored

(C) the value of an officer to the force is enhanced by the officer's self-confidence and coordination

(D) the most useful and essential single factor in the training of a law officer is proper firearms training

(E) the lives of law enforcement officers always depend directly upon the skill with weapons displayed by fellow officers

14. Revolutions have tended to result in authoritarian regimes. In fact, in European history since 1789, the more involved the people became in a change of governments, the more likely the new government was to be an authoritarian one, oppressive and dismissive of human and civil rights. When the change in government was controlled by the middle class, a relatively peaceful coup d'état took place and a regime no more authoritarian than the one before it came into power. However, when the masses rioted and staged a violent revolution, the new government ended by being extremely authoritarian.

    The paragraph best supports the statement that
    (A) it has not been observed that the government following a coup d'état by the middle class is no more authoritarian than the one in power before it
    (B) a violent coup d'état staged by military officers and troops loyal to them usually leads to imposition of a highly authoritarian military government
    (C) it is a fact that since 1789 European masses have frequently rioted and led revolutions for the purpose of deposing authoritarian governments
    (D) if a change of government follows a relatively peaceful rebellion by the middle class, the ensuing government will be less authoritarian than the government it replaces
    (E) a new government that is highly arbitrary and restrictive generally develops after a bloody revolution fomented by an angry populace that was rebelling against a similarly, though slightly less, authoritarian regime

15. Self-contained diving suits have made it possible for a diver to explore the depths without the local authorities' knowing very much about it. Should the diver be lucky enough to discover a wreck, he or she can recover the less cumbersome fragments—bronzes, marble, or bits of statuary—without attracting official attention. Today, one can indulge in a secret treasure hunt right down to the seabed with the added advantage that it is harder to keep a watch on sunken treasure than it is to protect excavations on shore. So the modem despoiler, as those robbers who in Egypt and Syria have deprived us of invaluable data, is becoming as great a pest to the serious archeologist at sea as on land. The archeological scavenger nearly always ransacks his objective to take away some portable trophy which appears to be valuable. He keeps his treasure house a secret, and we must blame him for the subsequent out-of-context appearance of various objects which prove impossible to date or catalogue.

    The paragraph best supports the statement that
    (A) divers in Egypt and Syria have stripped shipwrecks of sunken treasure and artifacts
    (B) everything salvaged from an ancient shipwreck is valuable
    (C) it is not impossible to date and catalogue objects recovered by responsible archeologists
    (D) before the development of self-contained diving suits, seabed treasure hunters presented less problem to archeologists than did land-based explorers
    (E) local authorities are charged with protecting excavations on shore

16. A percentile score is the rank expressed in percentage terms and indicates what proportion of the group received lower composite raw scores. A person at the 50th percentile would be the "typical" individual. The 50th percentile is known as the median and indicates a score exactly in the middle of the test group. The higher the percentile, the better the individual's standing; the lower the percentile, the poorer the individual's standing. Percentiles above 50 indicate above-average performance; percentiles below 50 indicate below-average performance.

The paragraph best supports the statement that

(A) a percentile is a percentage of composite raw scores

(B) the score of a person at the 50th percentile is the average of all scores of persons taking the examination

(C) the ranking of a person at the 49th percentile is not higher than the ranking of a person at the median

(D) a "typical" person achieves a percentage score of 50 which places that person at the 50th percentile

(E) it is not true that half of the people taking an examination will score below the median

17. For a number of years, a group of scientists has been attempting to make fortunes by breeding "bugs"—micro-oganisms that will manufacture valuable chemicals and drugs. This budding industry is called genetic engineering, and out of this young program, at least one company has induced a lowly bacterium to manufacture human interferon, a rare and costly substance that fights virus infections by "splicing" human genes into their natural hereditary material. But there are dangers in this activity, including the accidental development of a mutant bacterium that may change the whole life pattern on earth. There are also legal questions about whether a living organism can be patented and what new products can be marketed from living matter. The Congressional agency that oversees these new developments says that it will be several more years before any new product developed by genetic engineering will be allowed to be placed on the market.

The paragraph best supports the statement that

(A) human interferon is not a mutant bacterium that splices human genes into their natural hereditary material thereby changing the whole life pattern on earth

(B) the danger of breeding "bugs" is that this activity raises legal questions about the patenting of living organisms and marketing of new products derived from living matter

(C) the genetic engineering industry is operated by micro-organisms that manufacture valuable chemicals and drugs

(D) scientists have earned fortunes by breeding a rare and costly substance that fights viral infections

(E) it is not true that Congress plays a part in regulating scientific inquiry

18. The success or failure of a criminal prosecution usually depends upon the evidence presented to the court. Evidence may be divided into three major classifications: direct evidence, circumstantial evidence, and real evidence. Evidence must also be admissible, that is, material and relevant. An eyewitness account of a criminal act is direct evidence. Where an eyewitness does not have immediate experience, but reasonably infers what happened, circumstantial evidence is offered. Real evidence comprises objects introduced at a trial to prove or disprove a fact. For example, a gun, fingerprints, or bloodstains are real evidence. Real evidence may be direct or circumstantial. Evidence is immaterial if it is unimportant to the trial. For example, if someone is being tried for larceny of a crate of oranges, it is immaterial that the oranges were yellow in color. Evidence is irrelevant or immaterial if it does not prove the truth of a fact at issue. For example, if a murder had been committed with a bow and arrow, it is irrelevant to show that the defendant was well-acquainted with firearms.

The paragraph best supports the statement that
(A) if circumstantial evidence is not real it cannot be immaterial
(B) no evidence offered by an eyewitness can be circumstantial
(C) it is not impossible for real, direct evidence to be inadmissible
(D) direct circumstantial evidence is immaterial if it is not relevant
(E) if a criminal prosecution fails, the failure cannot be attributed to the nature of the evidence

19. After examining a document and comparing the characters with specimens of other handwritings, the laboratory technician may conclude that a certain individual definitely did write the questioned document. This opinion could be based on a large number of similar, as well as a small number of dissimilar but explainable, characteristics. On the other hand, if the laboratory technician concludes that the person in question did not write the questioned document, such an opinion could be based on the large number of characteristics that are dissimilar, or even on a small number that are dissimilar, provided that these are of overriding significance, and despite the presence of explainable similarities. The laboratory expert is not always able to give a positive opinion. He may state that a certain individual probably did or did not write the questioned document. Such an opinion is usually the result of insufficient material, either in the questioned document or in the specimens submitted for comparison. Finally, the expert may be unable to come to any conclusion at all because of insufficient material submitted for comparison or because of improper specimens.

The paragraph best supports the statement that
(A) if there are a number of explainable similarities between two specimens of handwriting, it is not possible for the laboratory technician to not give a positive opinion
(B) if there is a small number of dissimilar characteristics of overriding significance and the specimens submitted for comparison are insufficient, the laboratory technician may state that the individual probably did not write the questioned document
(C) if the specimens are improper, the laboratory technician may give a positive opinion only that the certain individual definitely did not write the document in question, hut not that the individual did write the document
(D) a positive opinion that the person did write the questioned document may be based on the presence of a large number of similar characteristics and a small number of unexplainable dissimilar characteristics
(E) if there are explainable similarities in two writing specimens, a laboratory expert may give a positive opinion that the same person wrote both specimens even if there are many characteristics that are dissimilar

20. A person who intends to effect or facilitate the escape of a prisoner, whether the escape is effected or attempted or not, and who enters a prison, or conveys to a prisoner any information, or sends into a prison any disguise, instrument, weapon, or other thing, is guilty of felony if the prisoner is held upon a charge, arrest, commitment, or conviction for a felony. The person is guilty of a misdemeanor if the prisoner is held upon a charge, arrest, commitment, or conviction of a misdemeanor.

The paragraph best supports the statement that
(A) a person who enters a prison as a visitor and conveys to a prisoner a weapon for the prisoner to use in escape is guilty of a misdemeanor even if the prisoner is unsuccessful in the escape attempt

(B) if a visitor to a prison brings into the prison an escape weapon and conveys same to a prisoner who was convicted on a misdemeanor charge and that prisoner seriously injures a guard in the course of the escape, the visitor will be guilty of a felony

(C) a visitor to a prison who carries for delivery to a prisoner imprisoned on a murder charge a sealed envelope containing detailed plans for escape without knowledge of the contents of the envelope is guilty of a felony

(D) a person who enters a prison in disguise is guilty of a misdemeanor if visiting a prisoner being held on a misdemeanor charge and of a felony if visiting a prisoner who is being held on a felony charge

(E) a person who attempts to help a prisoner to escape is guilty of the same level of offense as that on which prisoner is being held even if the prisoner has not been convicted

21. German scientists synthesized methadone during World War II because of a shortage of morphine. Although chemically unlike morphine or heroin, it produces many of the same effects. Introduced into the United States in 1947 as an analgesic and distributed under such brand names as Amidone, Dolophine, and Methadone, it became widely used in the 1960s in the treatment of narcotic addicts. The effects of Methadone differ from morphine-based drugs in that they have a longer duration of action, lasting up to 24 hours, thereby permitting administration only once a day in heroin detoxification and maintenance programs. Moreover, Methadone is almost as effective when administered orally as it is by injection. But tolerance and dependence may develop, and withdrawal symptoms, though they develop more slowly and are less severe, are more prolonged. Ironically, Methadone, designed to control narcotic addiction, has emerged in some metropolitan area as a major cause of overdose deaths.

The paragraph best supports the statement that
(A) it is not true that Methadone may lead to fatal addiction
(B) Methadone is a synthetic narcotic developed to mimic morphine in its chemical composition and in its analgesic effects
(C) a disadvantage of Methadone is that its effects last only 24 hours when the drug is administered orally
(D) while Methadone was originally synthesized to replace morphine, more recently Methadone has been used as a substitute for heroin
(E) Methadone was an effective component of the German war effort during the Second World War

22. If the second or third felony is such that, upon a first conviction, the offender would be punishable by imprisonment for any term less than his or her natural life, then such person must be sentenced to imprisonment for an indeterminate term, the minimum of which shall be not less than one-half of the longest term prescribed upon a first conviction, and the maximum of which shall be not longer than twice such longest term; provided, however, that the minimum sentence imposed hereunder upon such second or third felony offender shall in no case be less than five years; except that where the maximum punishment for a second or third felony offender hereunder is five years or less, the minimum sentence must be not less than two years.

The paragraph best supports the statement that a person who has a second felony conviction shall receive as a sentence for that second felony an indeterminate term
(A) not less than twice the minimum term prescribed upon a first conviction as a maximum
(B) not less than one-half the maximum term of the first conviction as a minimum
(C) not more than twice the minimum term prescribed upon a first conviction as a minimum

(D) with a maximum of not more than twice the longest term prescribed for a first conviction for this crime

(E) in no case to be less than five years

23. There are two kinds of leaders, born leaders and developed leaders. Born leaders always find themselves in the forefront, even during their years of development. People naturally look up to them and are willing to follow them. Very often the "captain" of an athletic team is not the best athlete but rather an individual whom team members will follow in difficult situations and whose advice they tend to accept. The other kind of leader is not by nature a born leader, one who possesses natural qualifies of leadership, but instead one whose ambitions are directed towards assuming responsibility and leading others in an effort to achieve desired objectives. This kind of leader must develop himself in such a way that ultimately the possesses the same qualities that the born leader is endowed with naturally.

The paragraph best supports the statement that
(A) it is not true that the advice of the captain of an athletic team is not likely to be accepted by members of the team
(B) a person who is not a natural-born leader may ultimately channel his or her ambitions into development of leadership qualities
(C) during their years of development, born leaders can concentrate on expanding their athletic talents
(D) despite all best efforts, the kind of leader who must develop himself cannot ultimately possess the same qualities that the born leader is endowed with naturally
(E) if the best athlete on the team is not the captain of the team it is because the best athlete is not a born leader

24. Occasionally one encounters a rigid, protectionist division chief in a government agency who wishes to restrict promotions to supervisory positions in his division exclusively to employees in his division. Such a division chief may develop staunch loyalties among his employees, but critics outside his agency are likely to describe his attitude as being as provincial as an isolationist country's unwillingness to engage in any international trade whatsoever on the ground that it will be required to buy something from outsiders that could possibly be produced by local talent, even though not as well and not as cheaply.

The paragraph best supports the statement that
(A) because the products of local talent are always competitive with foreign goods, a protectionist division chief will not engage in international trade
(B) since loyal employees are likely to be the staunchest critics of a rigid division chief, they are unlikely to be promoted to supervisory positions
(C) it is not possible to deny attitudinal similarities between protective government officials and isolationist countries
(D) regardless of intermediate effects, the final result of a provincial attitude is positive and beneficial
(E) the fact is that division chiefs in provincial, isolationist countries are loyal, rigid, and protectionist and will not buy goods from outsiders

25. Automobile tire tracks found at the scene of a crime constitute an important link in the chain of physical evidence. In many cases, these are the only clues available. In some areas, unpaved ground adjoins the highway or paved streets. A suspect will often park his or her car off the

paved portion of the street when committing a crime, sometimes leaving excellent tire tracks. Comparison of the tire track impressions with the tires is possible only when the vehicle has been found. However, the initial problem facing the police is the task of determining what kind of car probably made the impressions found at the scene of the crime. If the make, model, and year of the car that made the impressions can be determined, it is obvious that the task of elimination is greatly lessened.

The paragraph best supports the statement that
(A) it is not true that when searching for clear signs left by the car used in the commission of a crime the most likely place for agents to search would be the highway adjoining unpaved streets
(B) the make, model, and year of a car can be determined by the kind of tire tracks it has left at the scene of a crime
(C) automobile tire tracks found at the scene of a crime are of little value as evidence in that they are circumstantial rather than direct
(D) it is true that an automobile with chains leaves important physical evidence
(E) tire track impressions can be made only when the ground adjacent to the scene of the crime is unpaved and near a highway

STOP

END OF PART A. IF YOU FINISH BEFORE 50 MINUTES IS UP, CHECK OVER YOUR WORK ON PART A. DO NOT TURN TO PART B UNTIL THE SIGNAL IS GIVEN.

Part B—Arithmetic Reasoning Questions

Time: 50 minutes. 20 questions.

Direction: Analyze each paragraph to set up each problem; then solve it. Mark your answer sheet with the letter of the correct answer. If the correct answer is not given as one of the response choices, you should select response (E), "none of these."

1. A federal agency had a personal computer repaired at a cost of $49.20. This amount included a charge of $22 per hour for labor and a charge for a new switch that cost $18 before a 10 percent government discount was applied. How long did the repair job take?
    (A) 1 hour, 6 minutes
    (B) 1 hour, 11 minutes
    (C) 1 hour, 22 minutes
    (D) 1 hour, 30 minutes
    (E) none of these

2. In a large agency where mail is delivered in motorized carts, two tires were replaced on a cart at a cost of $34 per tire. If the agency had expected to pay $80 for a pair of tires, what percent of its expected cost did it save?
    (A) 7.5 percent
    (B) 17.6 percent
    (C) 57.5 percent
    (D) 75.0 percent
    (E) none of these

3. An interagency task force has representatives from three different agencies. Half of the task force members represent Agency A, one-third represent Agency B, and three represent Agency C. How many people are on the task force?
    (A) 12
    (B) 15
    (C) 18
    (D) 24
    (E) none of these

4. It has been established in recent productivity studies that, on the average, it takes a filing clerk 2 hours and 12 minutes to fill 4 drawers of a filing cabinet. At this rate, how long would it take 2 clerks to fill 16 drawers?
    (A) 4 hours
    (B) 4 hours, 20 minutes
    (C) 8 hours
    (D) 8 hours, 40 minutes
    (E) none of these

5. In a class of 36 students, 28 passed an examination, 4 failed the test, and the remainder did not take the test because they were absent. Approximately what percentage of the class was absent?
   (A) 22%
   (B) $14\frac{2}{7}\%$
   (C) $11\frac{1}{9}\%$
   (D) 75%
   (E) none of these

6. Mr. A. paid $90 a share for stock and bought 100 shares. The stock paid a quarterly dividend of $2.25 a share. What rate of interest did Mr. A. make on his stock in one year?
   (A) 7.5%
   (B) 9%
   (C) 14.5%
   (D) 16.5%
   (E) none of these

7. A tower casts a shadow of 40 feet at the same time that a yardstick casts a shadow of 2 feet. Assuming that both are in the same general location, how high would you expect the tower to be?
   (A) 40 feet
   (B) 60 feet
   (C) 80 feet
   (D) 100 feet
   (E) none of these

8. The scale of a map is $\frac{3}{8}$ inch = 100 miles. Approximately how far apart are two cities that are 2.25 inches apart on the map?
   (A) 1200 miles
   (B) 300 miles
   (C) 600 miles
   (D) 150 miles
   (E) none of these

9. The daily almanac report for one day during the summer stated that the sun rose at 6:14 A.M. and set at 6:06 P.M. Find the number of hours and minutes in the time between the rising and setting of the sun on the day.
   (A) 12 hours, 8 minutes
   (B) 11 hours, 2 minutes
   (C) 12 hours, 48 minutes
   (D) 11 hours, 42 minutes
   (E) none of these

10. Two cars are 550 miles apart, both traveling on the same road. If one travels at 50 miles per hour, the other at 60 miles per hour, and they both leave at 1:00 P.M., what time will they meet?
    (A) 4:00 P.M.
    (B) 4:30 P.M.
    (C) 5:45 P.M.
    (D) 6:00 P.M.
    (E) none of these

11. Assume that there are 2,300 employees in a federal agency. Also assume that 5 percent of these employees are accountants, that 80 percent of the accountants have college degrees, and that one-half of the accountants who have college degrees have 5 years of experience. Then the number of employees in the agency who are accountants with college degrees and 5 years of experience is
    (A) 46
    (B) 51
    (C) 460
    (D) 920
    (E) none of these

12. A snapshot measures $2\frac{1}{2}$ inches by $1\frac{7}{8}$ inches. It is to be enlarged so that the longer dimension will be 4 inches. The length of the enlarged shorter dimension will be
    (A) $2\frac{1}{2}$ inches
    (B) 3 inches
    (C) $3\frac{3}{8}$ inches
    (D) $2\frac{5}{8}$ inches
    (E) none of these

13. The value of shares on the New York Stock Exchange rose an estimated 35 cents, 40 cents, 25 cents, and 50 cents on four successive days. If an average daily gain of 30 cents is to be achieved that week, how much must the average gain be on the fifth day?
    (A) 10 cents
    (B) 25 cents
    (C) zero
    (D) 35 cents
    (E) none of these

14. In a major Midwestern state, 128,896 adults were arrested for robbery last year. Of these, 106,090 actually came to trial. Of those who came to trial, 46% were found guilty and imprisoned. How many were acquitted?
    (A) 46,083
    (B) 51,844
    (C) 56,792
    (D) 57,288
    (E) none of these

15. The price of an airplane trip between New York and Chicago rose as follows:
    • November 1979: $105.00
    • February 1980: $122.50
    • June 1980: $175.00
    • November 1980: $195.00
    • February 1981: $205.00

    What was the percentage of change in the cost of a trip between New York and Chicago between February 1980 and February 1981?

(A) 60%

(B) 67%

(C) 75%

(D) 80%

(E) none of these

16. A typist uses lengthwise a sheet of paper 9 inches by 12 inches. He leaves a 1-inch margin on each side and a $1\frac{1}{2}$-inch margin on top and bottom. What fractional part of the page is used for typing?

(A) $\frac{21}{22}$

(B) $\frac{7}{12}$

(C) $\frac{5}{9}$

(D) $\frac{3}{4}$

(E) none of these

17. A person owned $\frac{5}{6}$ of a piece of property and sold $\frac{3}{4}$ of his share for $1,800. What was the value of the property?

(A) $2,808.00

(B) $2,880.00

(C) $2,088.00

(D) $2,880.80

(E) none of these

18. A parade is marching up an avenue for 60 city blocks. A sample count of the number of people watching the parade is taken, first in a block near the end of the parade, and then in a block at the middle. The former count is 4,000, the latter is 6,000. If the average for the entire parade is assumed to be the average of the two samples, then the estimated number of persons watching the entire parade is most nearly

(A) 240,000

(B) 300,000

(C) 480,000

(D) 600,000

(E) none of these

19. Village A has a population of 6,800, which is decreasing at a rate of 120 per year. Village B has a population of 4,200, which is increasing at a rate of 80 per year. In how many years will the population of the two villages be equal?

(A) 9

(B) 11

(C) 13

(D) 14

(E) none of these

20. One wheel has a diameter of 30 inches and a second wheel has a diameter of 20 inches. The first wheel travels a certain distance in 240 revolutions. In how many revolutions does the second wheel travel the same distance?
    (A) 120
    (B) 160
    (C) 360
    (D) 420
    (E) none of these

STOP

END OF PART B. IF YOU FINISH BEFORE 50 MINUTES IS UP, CHECK OVER YOUR WORK IN PART B ONLY. DO NOT RETURN TO PART A, NOR GO ON TO PART C.

Part C—Problems for Investigation

Time: 60 minutes. 30 questions.

Directions: Read the paragraph and statements carefully. Then answer the questions which follow each investigative situation. Mark the letter of the correct answer on your sheet. You may refer to the paragraph and statements as often as needed. Explanations for these questions appear on pages 141 to 143.

Questions 1 to 7 are based upon the following paragraph and statements.

Customs Inspector Kerry McDevitt was suspicious. The shipment was clearly labeled, "500 lbs., rayon acetate fabric, 30 inches wide." The valuation seemed reasonable for such a shipment. The place of origin of the shipment was Korea. Yet, somehow, the crates appeared to be too securely fastened, and the addressee appeared too eager to claim his shipment in a hurry. So Inspector McDevitt sent for Customs Special Agent Sam Lazarus. Lazarus opened one crate and reached inside. The fabric on top of the pile was obviously rayon acetate, but as he reached farther in he felt a finer, silkier fabric. Customs Chemist Maria Martinez was called in and confirmed that the bulk of the shipment was pure silk.

In the course of the investigation, the following statements were made:

(1) Sun Ehee from the Seoul office of Hwang Trading Corp. said that he had sold 500 pounds of rayon acetate to Charmaine Fabrics, Inc. of New York City and had ordered shipment of same to Charmaine.

(2) Charles Kim, who went to the pier to pick up the shipment for Charmaine Fabrics, Inc., said that his instructions were to pick up 500 pounds of rayon acetate packed in three crates.

(3) Warren Park of the New York office of Hwang Trading Corp. said that the more usual procedure was for shipments to be made to the New York office for local delivery, but that direct shipments to customers were sometimes made.

(4) Myung Suh of the Seoul office of Hwang Trading Corp. said that Sun Ehee had personally supervised packing and shipment of this particular order, which was not his usual custom.

(5) Sun Ehee said that he occasionally involved himself physically in preparation of a shipment because he felt it was good for morale within the company.

(6) George Bruling, guard at Pier 31 where the shipment had come in, said that he had noticed a couple of Asians with a partly loaded truck hanging around the pier from early in the morning of the day the shipment arrived, and off and on until the following afternoon when Charles Kim arrived to meet the crates as they passed through Customs.

(7) Thomas Hardy, night watchman at Pier 31, said that people with trucks were always hanging around the pier but that he was alert for hijackers and never left his post until relieved.

(8) Charles Kim stated that Charmaine Fabrics, Inc. deals only in synthetics and not in natural fibers.

(9) Helen Lim of the New York office of Hwang Trading Corp. said that Warren Park and Charles Kim had discussed this particular shipment in Korean though both are fluent and often do business in English. Helen Lira stated that she does not feel competent to report on conversations she has overheard in Korean.

1. Which of the following statements appears to indicate that Charmaine Fabrics, Inc. was not involved in the importation of silk labeled as rayon?
   (A) Statement 1
   (B) Statement 2
   (C) Statement 4
   (D) Statement 8
   (E) Statement 9

2. Which of the following statements casts suspicion on Charles Kim as being involved with the nature of the shipment?
   (A) Statement 2
   (B) Statement 3
   (C) Statement 6
   (D) Statement 8
   (E) Statement 9

3. Which of the following statements suggests that this was not the first time Hwang Trading Corp. sent a shipment mislabeled to avoid high import duties?
   (A) Statement 3
   (B) Statement 4
   (C) Statement 6
   (D) Statement 7
   (E) Statement 9

4. Which of the following statements suggests that attempts are sometimes made to substitute legitimate goods for contraband before cargo passes through Customs?
   (A) Statement 3
   (B) Statement 4
   (C) Statement 6
   (D) Statement 7
   (E) Statement 8

5. By which two of the following statements does Sun Ehee attempt to establish his own innocence in the case?
   (A) Statements 1 and 2
   (B) Statements 1 and 4
   (C) Statements 1 and 5
   (D) Statements 1 and 8
   (E) Statements 4 and 5

6. Which of the following statements suggests that port security serves more than one purpose?
   (A) Statement 2
   (B) Statement 3
   (C) Statement 5
   (D) Statement 6
   (E) Statement 7

7. Which of the following statements, along with statement (8), does NOT implicate Charles Kim in an attempt to defraud the United States of duties on imported silk?
   (A) Statement 2
   (B) Statement 4
   (C) Statement 6
   (D) Statement 7
   (E) Statement 9

Questions 8 to 15 are based upon the following paragraph and statements.

Ted Green visited an office of the Bureau of Alcohol, Tobacco, and Firearms and informed them that he had been fired from his job as a porter in the Jan Star Warehouse after having been accused of stealing a typewriter by Sam Opit, who rents a storage room in the warehouse. Mr. Green stated that he had stolen nothing but was fired because he saw that Sam Opit had four boxes of machine guns that were marked "Bathtubs." One of the boxes had broken open and Green had seen what it really contained. ATF Agent Ralph Cohen secured a search warrant and verified the presence of the machine guns. He asked the warehouse manager, John Stem, *not* to reveal that he had been there. ATF Agent Sarah Swift determined that Sam Opit had no license to have machine guns. The next day Sam Opit arrived at the warehouse with a truck and loaded on to it four boxes marked "Bathtubs." He then drove away followed by ATF Agents Joyce Guyst and Jan Chen. With the assistance of police officer Will Suggs, the truck was stopped when it went through a red light and was found to contain only boxes of bathtubs. Ralph Cohen thereupon re-entered the warehouse and discovered that the room rented by Sam Opit was empty. However, he noted a faint line of grease leading from the room. He followed the line to another room where he discovered the machine guns. This latter room is rented by Agness Heft.

During the course of the investigation, the following statements were made:

(1) Sam Opit stated that he knew nothing about machine guns; that he owned only bathtubs that he had stored in the warehouse.

(2) Agness Heft said that the room that she rented was temporarily vacant. She had not authorized anyone to use the room.

(3) John Stern stated that he had talked to no one about the machine guns.

(4) Joyce Guyst stated that Sam Opit's driving made her believe that he knew that the truck was being followed when he went through the red light.

(5) Police Officer Will Suggs stated that he knew other people like Sam Opit and that they were all crooks.

(6) A check on the background of Ted Green disclosed that his police record consisted of having been twice convicted of speeding, once when driving at 90 miles per hour.

(7) Sam Opit stated that he had not sold the bathtubs but that he was carrying them around in the truck to try to find someone to buy them.

(8) Agness Hert said that Ted Green had been very helpful to her when she moved her garden ornaments from the warehouse to a showroom three blocks away.

(9) John Stern said that Ted Green was a better porter than the new man, Jim York, who left grease slicks on the floor. Stem said that he was sorry he had to fire Ted Green for stealing Sam Opit's typewriter.

8. Which of the following statements casts the most suspicion on Sam Opit?
   (A) Statement 1
   (B) Statement 4
   (C) Statement 5
   (D) Statement 7
   (E) Statement 9

9. Which of the following statements indicates that Opit may have been tipped off about the ATF investigation?
   (A) Statement 1
   (B) Statement 2
   (C) Statement 3
   (D) Statement 4
   (E) Statement 7

10. Which of the following statements gives credence to the fact that Sam Opit was a bathtub salesman?
    (A) Statement 1
    (B) Statement 4
    (C) Statement 5
    (D) Statement 7
    (E) Statement 9

11. Which of the following statements, along with statement (8), indicates that Agness Hert knew nothing about the machine guns in her room?
    (A) Statement 2
    (B) Statement 3
    (C) Statement 6
    (D) Statement 7
    (E) Statement 9

12. Which of the following statements should NOT be used against Ted Green in determining the truth of his allegations?
    (A) Statement 3
    (B) Statement 5

    (C) Statement 6
    (D) Statement 8
    (E) Statement 9

13. Which of the following statements is likely to be of LEAST use in solving this case?
    (A) Statement 2
    (B) Statement 3
    (C) Statement 4
    (D) Statement 5
    (E) Statement 6

14. Which of the following statements leads one to have questions about the warehouse owner's relationship with his employees and with his tenants?
    (A) Statement 2
    (B) Statement 3
    (C) Statement 6
    (D) Statement 8
    (E) Statement 9

15. Which of the following statements is a statement of opinion and not a statement of fact?
    (A) Statement 1
    (B) Statement 2
    (C) Statement 4
    (D) Statement 6
    (E) Statement 9

Questions 16 to 23 are based upon the following paragraph and statements.

The Treasury Department has become aware of a problem with U.S. Savings Bonds apparently sold by a branch of the Swanee Savings Bank. Several different people have recently attempted to cash in savings bonds with certificate numbers of bonds that have already been cashed in. In each case, the original bond that had been cashed in and the counterfeit bond that had been presented for payment carried the same date of purchase. The dates of purchase were all in the year before last. Each of the original bonds was found to have been redeemed in February or March of last year in the name of Frank Watts.

During the course of the investigation, the following statements were made:

  (1)   John Zinn, who presented one of the counterfeit bonds for redemption at the Swanee Savings Bank, stated that he had been a regular depositor at the bank for years, had bought the bond at the bank but now needed the money. He said he liked to buy bonds when he had the money because it is patriotic and the process takes only a few minutes.

  (2)   Sheila Tredd, who presented one of the counterfeit bonds for redemption at Pioneer State Bank of Swanee, stated that she had bought the bond at the Swanee Savings Bank when she was a depositor there before she moved across town. She now needs the money to buy furniture.

(3)   Shirley Bristol who, with her daughter Ann, presented one of the counterfeit bonds for redemption at the Montgomery National Bank, stated that Ann had received the bond as a gift from a relative living in Swanee but that she wanted the money to buy a computer.

(4)   Bank Teller Lola Capone of the Barstow National Bank stated that she had cashed several bonds for Frank Watts, who had had an account at the bank for a short period of time. Watts had opened his account with a small amount of cash and had identified himself with a driver's license and on the basis of an account with the Swanee Savings Bank.

(5)   Jean Scott, assistant manager for special services of this branch of the Swanee Savings Bank, stated that during the period in question and up to January of last year either she or teller Graham Murphy handled almost all sales of bonds. She stated that Graham Murphy had left the bank's employ to return to his hometown and care for his ill mother.

(6)   Special Agent Edith McCarthy stated that she had been unable to locate the whereabouts of either Graham Murphy or Frank Watts.

(7)   Bank Manager Paul Mead stated that he had full confidence in Jean Scott since her father belongs to the same social clubs that he does and Mead knows the father to be a perfect gentleman.

(8)   Teller Robert Conyer, who replaced Graham Murphy at the Swanee Bank branch, stated that the counterfeit bonds that he had seen do not appear to have been sold by Graham Murphy. Murphy had cautioned Conyer to initial his work so that "you can't be blamed for someone else's mistakes."

(9)   Wesley Adams, who had been a teller at the Swanee Savings Bank branch that sold the bonds and now works at another branch of the bank, stated that he had once been called upon to sell a bond when neither Graham Murphy nor Jean Scott was in the bank and had come across two bonds in a bottom drawer. These two bonds were not filled out and showed no indication of having been sold. However, they had the same certificate numbers as bonds that the tally sheet showed as having been sold three days before. Since he did not understand the sales process very well, he left the bonds where he found them. A couple of days later they were gone, so he forgot about the matter.

16. Which of the following statements indicates that Frank Watts was a real person and not a creation of the counterfeiter's imagination?
(A) Statement 3
(B) Statement 4
(C) Statement 5
(D) Statement 6
(E) Statement 9

17. Which two of the following statements indicate that the counterfeit bonds were sold at Swanee Savings Bank?
(A) Statements 1 and 2
(B) Statements 1 and 3
(C) Statements 1 and 4
(D) Statements 2 and 3
(E) Statements 5 and 8

18. Which of the following statements indicates that both the legitimate and the counterfeit bonds were sold at Swanee Savings Bank?
    (A) Statement 4
    (B) Statement 5
    (C) Statement 6
    (D) Statement 8
    (E) Statement 9

19. Which of the following statements indicates that the Treasury Department will have difficulty with this investigation?
    (A) Statement 4
    (B) Statement 5
    (C) Statement 6
    (D) Statement 8
    (E) Statement 9

20. Which of the following statements, along with statement (5), casts most suspicion on Jean Scott as having knowledge of the counterfeiting operation?
    (A) Statement 4
    (B) Statement 6
    (C) Statement 7
    (D) Statement 8
    (E) Statement 9

21. Which of the following statements along with statement (5) casts most suspicion on Graham Murphy in this case?
    (A) Statement 1
    (B) Statement 6
    (C) Statement 7
    (D) Statement 8
    (E) Statement 9

22. Which of the following statements appears to be a reasonable alibi for another teller?
    (A) Statement 4
    (B) Statement 5
    (C) Statement 6
    (D) Statement 7
    (E) Statement 8

23. Which of the following statements is LEAST likely to be helpful in solving this case?
    (A) Statement 4
    (B) Statement 5
    (C) Statement 6
    (D) Statement 7
    (E) Statement 8

Questions 24 to 30 are based upon the following paragraph and statements.

Patrolman Myron Friedman was approached by Beatrice Brown on the 400 block of Cedar Road. Ms. Brown was quite agitated and said, "There's been a murder in my building." Ms. Brown led Patrolman Friedman to apartment 6B of 421 Cedar Road, where the lifeless body of Claude LeClair lay facedown on the floor with a gaping gunshot wound at the back of the head. On the wall was a floor plan of the Haitian embassy and beside it a map blow-up showing all the streets and alleys surrounding the embassy. In a green wooden box in one corner of the room was a small arsenal of pistols, revolvers, and submachine guns. Containers of gasoline and black powder sat tightly closed on the kitchen counter.

During the course of the investigation, the following statements were made.

(1) Beatrice Brown said that she is the occupant of apartment 6A at 421 Cedar Road and that she did not know Claude LeClair.

(2) Hector Jones, manager of 421 Cedar Road, said that LeClair was a Haitian immigrant who had lived with two other men in apartment 6B for eight months and who always paid his rent on time.

(3) Matilda DePaso of apartment 5B said that there were often late-night meetings in 6B with lots of stomping around and loud talk in a foreign language that she assumed to be French.

(4) Beatrice Brown said that she did not really know that a murder had been committed but assumed there had been one since she had heard a shot and had seen a man with a gun running down the stairs.

(5) Luis Sanchez, the Secret Service Special Agent who was called into the case because of the apparent threat to the Haitian embassy, said that Claude LeClair had been a known opponent of the Haitian regime.

(6) Robert Levasseur, one of LeClair's roommates in apartment 6B, said that although LeClair was opposed to the Haitian regime, he was far less inclined toward violence than were some of his friends.

(7) From an album of pictures of Haitians in the area who were considered by the Secret Service to be potential troublemakers, Hubert Horan of apartment 1D identified either Alphonse St. Jacque or Pierre Monet as the man with the gun who had run past his windows.

(8) Pierre Monet's employer, William Bell, produced Monet's time card to show that Monet had been at work at the Mavis Tire Center at the time of the murder.

(9) Alphonse St. Jacque's wife, Monique, said that St. Jacque was ill at home on the day of the murder.

(10) Robert Levasseur said that both St. Jacque and Monet were among the group that often met with LeClair in his apartment.

24. Which of the following statements appears to offer a motive for the killing?
    (A) Statement 2
    (B) Statement 3
    (C) Statement 5
    (D) Statement 6
    (E) Statement 7

25. Which of the following statements implicates St. Jacque in the murder?
    (A) Statement 5
    (B) Statement 6
    (C) Statement 7
    (D) Statement 9
    (E) Statement 10

26. Which of the following statements, along with statement (10), identifies Monet as a member of a Haitian dissident group?
    (A) Statement 3
    (B) Statement 5
    (C) Statement 6
    (D) Statement 7
    (E) Statement 8

27. Which of the following statements represents the best alibi in this case?
    (A) Statement 1
    (B) Statement 4
    (C) Statement 6
    (D) Statement 8
    (E) Statement 9

28. Which two of the following statements indicate that the Secret Service was aware of a potential danger to the Haitian embassy?
    (A) Statements 2 and 5
    (B) Statements 5 and 6
    (C) Statements 5 and 7
    (D) Statements 6 and 7
    (E) Statements 7 and 10

29. Which of the following statements is likely to be LEAST helpful in solving this case?
    (A) Statement 2
    (B) Statement 3
    (C) Statement 4
    (D) Statement 6
    (E) Statement 9

30. Which of the following statements represents LeClair as an upstanding citizen?
   (A) Statement 2
   (B) Statement 3
   (C) Statement 5
   (D) Statement 6
   (E) Statement 10

END OF EXAM

IF YOU HAVE ANY REMAINING TIME, USE IT TO CHECK YOUR WORK ON THIS PART ONLY. YOU MAY NOT RETURN TO ANY PREVIOUS PART.

After Taking the Second Model Exam

SCORE SHEET

Part	Number Correct
Verbal Reasoning	___ ÷ 25 = ___ × 100 = ___%
Arithmetic Reasoning	___ ÷ 20 = ___ × 100 = ___%
Problems for Investigation	___ ÷ 30 = ___ × 100 = ___ %
Total	___ ÷ 75 = ___ × 100 = ___ %

Compare these scores with the scores you achieved on the First Model Examination. The two exams are of comparable difficulty, so with familiarity with the question styles, practice, and concentration, you should have raised your scores. If you are still not confident of your ability to score well on the TEA exam, review answer explanations and Part Four once more.

Part	First Model Exam	Second Model Exam
Verbal Reasoning	___ %	___ %
Arithmetic Reasoning	___ %	___ %
Problems for Investigation	___ %	___ %
Total	___ %	___ %

ANSWER KEY

Part A—Verbal Reasoning Questions

1. A	5. B	8. E	11. B	14. E	17. A	20. E	23. B
2. C	6. C	9. A	12. C	15. D	18. C	21. D	24. C
3. E	7. B	10. C	13. D	16. C	19. B	22. D	25. A
4. D							

Part B—Arithmetic Reasoning Questions

1. D	4. E	7. B	10. D	13. C	15. B	17. B	19. C
2. E	5. C	8. C	11. A	14. D	16. B	18. B	20. C
3. C	6. E	9. E	12. B				

Part C—Problems for Investigation

1. D	5. C	9. C	13. D	17. A	21. B	25. C	28. C
2. E	6. E	10. D	14. E	18. E	22. E	26. D	29. E
3. A	7. A	11. A	15. C	19. C	23. D	27. D	30. A
4. C	8. B	12. C	16. B	20. E	24. D		

EXPLANATIONS

Part A—Verbal Reasoning Questions

1. **(A)** This answer can be inferred from the first sentence of the paragraph, which states that *every level of government is a link in the economic process.* It can be deduced that its contradictory statement, *some levels of government are not links in the economic process,* cannot be true. Response (B) is not supported by the paragraph because it goes beyond the information given. The third sentence of the paragraph states that a dictatorship observes (at least formally) *one* of the same principles as other governments. It cannot be concluded from this that dictatorships observe more than this one principle in common with other governments. Responses (C) and (E) represent incorrect interpretations of the information given in the first sentence, which states that *every level of government is a link in the economic process.* It cannot be inferred from this statement that *all links in the economic process are levels of government,* only that some are. We know that the category "all levels of government" is contained in the category "links in the economic process," but we do not know if other links in the economic process exist that are not levels of government. In regard to response (E), it cannot be inferred that *no links in the economic process are institutions other than levels of government,* because that would be the same as saying that all links in the economic process are levels of government. Response (D) is not supported by the passage because the second sentence implies that the contributions of *all* levels of government must be evaluated for technical efficiency

and acceptability to society. There is nothing to suggest that the contributions of some levels of society do *not* need to be evaluated.

2. **(C)** The answer can be inferred from information contained in the first, second, and fourth sentences. The first sentence is a disjunction; that is, it presents two mutually exclusive alternatives—*all property is classified as either personal property or real property, but not both.* The second sentence states that *if something is classified as personal property, it is transient and transportable in nature.* The fourth sentence states that *permanent buildings and land . . . are fixed in nature and are not transportable.* From this it can be concluded that, since permanent buildings and land are not transient and transportable in nature, they are not personal property. In view of the disjunction in the first sentence, it can be seen that they must be real property. Response (A) is incorrect because it contradicts the information presented in the second sentence of the paragraph. Response (B) is incorrect because it contradicts the first sentence, which states that *all property is classified as either personal property or real property, but not both.* Response (D) contradicts the information presented in the second and fourth sentences. The second sentence states that if something is classified as personal property, it is transient and transportable in nature. The fourth sentence indicates that permanent buildings and land do not have these qualities. Therefore, it can be concluded that they are not personal property. Response (E) seems to be derived from the third sentence, which says that intangible goods are examples of personal property. However, it cannot be concluded from this statement that tangible goods are real property. In fact, the third sentence gives examples of tangible goods that are personal property.

3. **(E)** This conclusion can be derived from information contained in the third sentence of the paragraph, which states that *it is not true that all organizations are structured so that workers can be dealt with as individuals.* From this statement, it can be inferred that *some organizations are not structured so that workers can be dealt with as individuals.* Response (A) is incorrect because it contradicts the information in the third and fourth sentences of the paragraph. With its double negation, response (A) is in effect saying that all organizations are structured so that workers can be dealt with as individuals. This flatly contradicts the third sentence and also contradicts the fourth sentence, which says that *in some organizations, employees are represented by unions, and managers bargain with these associations.* Response (B) is not supported by the paragraph because the paragraph gives no information about working environments other than organizations. Response (C) is not supported by the paragraph because the paragraph says only that employees are represented by unions in *some* organizations. One cannot generalize from this to say that employees are represented by unions in *all* organizations. Response (D) is incorrect because it contradicts the fourth sentence, which says that managers bargain with unions in some organizations.

4. **(D)** The answer can be derived from the information presented in the third sentence. That sentence states that *if a computer programming language is a machine language, then it is a code that can be read directly by a computer.* From this statement it can be seen that all machine languages are codes that can be read directly by a computer and that if a computer programming language is not such a code, then it is not a machine language. Response (A) goes beyond the information presented in the paragraph, which states only that *most* high level computer programming languages use strings of common English phrases. Response (B) represents a complete contradiction of the third sentence of the paragraph. Response (C) contradicts the paragraph. We know from the paragraph that at least some coded languages that can be read directly by a computer are machine languages. Response (E) is incorrect because the paragraph does not say whether or not computer languages that are *not* machine languages are codes that can be read directly by a computer.

5. **(B)** The essential information from which the answer is to be inferred is contained in the second sentence, which states that if an Act of Congress has been deemed unconstitutional, then it is voided. In (B), we are told that an Act of Congress is not voided; therefore, we can conclude that *it has not been deemed unconstitutional by the Supreme Court*. Response (A) is not supported by the paragraph because the paragraph does not indicate whether an Act of Congress is voided *only* when it has been deemed unconstitutional or if it could be voided for other reasons. Response (C), like response (A), cannot be inferred from the paragraph because the paragraph does not indicate whether or not an Act of Congress would be voided if the Supreme Court did not declare it to be unconstitutional. Responses (D) and (E) are incorrect because they both contradict the paragraph.

6. **(C)** The answer can be inferred from the last sentence in the paragraph, which states that *some special programs for broken families are offered when parental care is temporarily or permanently unavailable*. If this statement is true, then its negation, *no special programs for broken families are offered when temporary or permanent parental care is unavailable* cannot be true. Response (A) is incorrect because it contradicts the first sentence of the paragraph. Responses (B) and (D) cannot be validly inferred because the paragraph does not provide sufficient information to support the inferences made. Specifically, for response (B), there is insufficient information to determine whether some programs offered when parental care is temporarily or permanently unavailable are *not* special programs for families. As far as response (D) is concerned, the paragraph does not state that *all* programs offered when parental care is temporarily or permanently unavailable are special programs for broken families. Response (E) is wrong because the paragraph states that *all child-welfare agencies are organizations that seek to promote the healthy growth and development of children*. There is no way of knowing from this statement whether or not there are organizations, other than child-welfare agencies, that seek to promote the healthy growth and welfare of children.

7. **(B)** This answer may be inferred from the "notwithstanding" clause. This clause makes it clear that Sullivan was substantially damaged by the negligence of the press, but that even so the press was not liable to pay for the damages. The second sentence clarifies that liability stems from malice, not from mere damage to the public figure. Response (A) cannot be supported. It is possible that malice that caused no damage would not lead to liability. Response (C) is directly contradicted by the first sentence. Response (D) is a nonsense statement. Response (E) is inaccurate in that it is based upon only a part of the paragraph.

8. **(E)** This is the point of the third justification for competitive elections even where there is no real difference in ideology between the candidates. Response (D) is a misinterpretation: elections eliminate party corruption because voters have the opportunity to vote out corrupt officials. Responses (A), (B), and (C) are all way off the mark.

9. **(A)** This is the whole point of the paragraph. The paragraph claims that the success of the American economic system, as well as financial and professional success of American individuals, have all been based upon rugged competition and rewarding of the most capable competitors. A merit system, that is, a competitive civil service, is based on the same meritocracy. Response (B) makes an unsupported statement; nowhere does the paragraph claim that competition is a uniquely American trait. Response (C) misinterprets the paragraph to claim that the American economic system is responsible for individuals' professional success; actually is it the competitive excellence of the individuals that has led to their personal successes. Responses (D) and (E) represent ridiculous statements made by combining single words out of context.

10. **(C)** Since the laws of war regulate the relations of those states that claim to be neutral powers and states at war, such relationships should not be maintained outside of this regulation. Of course, there are no guarantees that all parties will adhere to all laws. Response (A) is contradicted by the last sentence. Responses (B), (D), and (E) are ridiculous misinterpretations of the paragraph.

11. **(B)** The second sentence states explicitly that *under federal law, income from illegal sources such as bootlegging, prostitution, and narcotics sales is subject to tax.* Response (A) overstates the last sentence. The Federal Organized Crime Strike Force Program does indeed cooperate with other law enforcement agencies at all levels of government, but the cooperation has to do with law enforcement and not with governing the country. Response (C) is incorrect because members of organized crime use the income from illegal activities to support other illegal activities and to infiltrate legitimate businesses. Their use of reserved tax monies for this purpose is only incidental. Response (D) is also a misinterpretation. IRS Special Agents investigate; federal prosecutors prosecute; juries convict. Response (E) is a non sequitur.

12. **(C)** The last two sentences make the point that investment decisions can be made with greater confidence when prices are reasonably predictable and that therefore, under such circumstances, total investment will be higher. Response (A) is incorrect because classical *price* theory describes the changes in price in response to changes in supply and demand, not the change in supply and demand itself. Response (B) totally twists the meaning of the sentence that states that regardless of a possible temporary favoring of the price of commodities, the stable price trend of industrial exports is more important. The word "sticky" as used in the paragraph refers to the fact that the same price tends to stick to the manufactured good over time; it has nothing to do with the texture of the product as implied by Response (D). Response (E) may make a true statement, but it is not supported by the paragraph.

13. **(D)** If no part of the training of a law officer is more important or more valuable, then clearly the most useful and essential single factor in the training of a law officer is proper firearms training. Response (A) directly contradicts the paragraph wherein it is stated, "Proficiency with the revolver is not attained exclusively by the volume of ammunition used and the number of hours spent on the firing line." Response (B) is incorrect because the first sentence of the paragraph says only that firearms training *cannot* be ignored not that it *is* ignored. Response (C) combines a number of incomplete thoughts to make an inadequate statement. Response (E) is an overstatement; the lives of law enforcement officers often depend directly upon the weapons skills of their fellow officers, but not always.

14. **(E)** This is precisely the meaning of the last sentence. Response (A) is a direct contradiction of the third sentence, which states that a change in government controlled by the middle class results in a regime no more authoritarian than the one that came before it. In Response (C), the word "frequently" is not supported by the paragraph. Response (D) is incorrect because the phrase "no more authoritarian" of the paragraph does not necessarily imply "less authoritarian."

15. **(D)** The paragraph describes underwater exploration as a fairly recent development in treasure hunting. It then goes on to describe modern despoilers—that is divers—as persons who are becoming pests similar to those who earlier ransacked archeological sites on land. Response (A) is incorrect because the modern despoilers, the divers, are being compared to earlier tomb robbers of land sites in Egypt and Syria. Response (B) overstates the case. Everything salvaged from an ancient shipwreck may be interesting, but not everything is valuable. The paragraph makes this clear with the statement,

" . . . ransacks his objective to take away some portable trophy which *appears* to be valuable." Response (C) misinterprets the last sentence. Responsible archeologists keep careful notes and records. Scavengers introduce their "treasures" at a later time and without documentation; this makes it difficult or impossible to date and catalogue them. Response (E) makes an assumption that is not implied by the paragraph. Local authorities try to keep track of what is going on in their jurisdictions, but the paragraph does not say that they are charged with guard duty.

16. **(C)** The median is the middle, which is the 50th percentile. A person ranked at the 49th percentile is ranked lower than, not higher than, a person at the median. Response (A) is entirely wrong. A percentile is a ranking expressed in percentage terms, but it is *not* a percent nor is it a score. A percentile merely expresses the point at which a person's score appears among all the scores of all persons taking the same test. Response (B) is incorrect because a median is not an average. The median is the middle. This means that half the scores are higher and half are lower. The average, also called the mean, is quite different. The mean may be higher or lower than the median depending upon the number of very high or very low scores. Response (D) again misinterprets. The "typical" person is indeed at the 50th percentile, but that person's percentage score is simply the score at which half of the test takers scored above and half below. No percentage score automatically accompanies the 50th percentile. Response (E) is just wrong. Half of the people taking an examination will indeed score below the median, for the median is based upon the score at which half of the test takers score below.

17. **(A)** You can easily infer this answer. Since the paragraph states that human interferon is *a rare and costly substance that fights virus infections by "splicing" human genes into their natural hereditary material* it is obviously not a mutant bacterium that will change the whole life pattern on earth. Response (B) is incorrect because the raising of legal questions is a concern but not a danger and surely not a danger created by the breeding of "bugs." The true danger lies in the accidental development of deadly mutant bacteria. Response (C) is confused. The genetic engineering *industry* is operated by scientists; the microorganisms harnessed by this industry in turn manufacture valuable chemicals and drugs. Response (D) misinterprets. The scientists have been attempting to make fortunes, as stated in the first sentence, but surely have not yet made these fortunes since, as stated in the last sentence, their products have not yet been allowed to reach the market. Response (E) is incorrect because, to the extent that a Congressional agency oversees new developments and can control their marketing, Congress does indeed have a hand in regulating scientific inquiry.

18. **(C)** Real, direct evidence is evidence of the most reliable kind and carries the greatest weight, but if that real, direct evidence has no bearing on the case under consideration, then it is irrelevant to the case and is inadmissible. Response (A) is a nonsense statement. Evidence, whether direct or circumstantial, is immaterial if it is not relevant. Whether or not evidence is real evidence, it is material if relevant and immate. Response (D) is incorrect because "direct circumstantial evidence" is not possible. Evidence may be direct or circumstantial but not both. Response (E) contradicts the first sentence of the paragraph.

19. **(B)** The correct answer is based upon two separate elements of the paragraph. A conclusion that the person in question did not write the questioned document may be based on even a small number of characteristics which are dissimilar provided that these are of overriding significance. On the other hand, the expert may state an opinion that the individual probably did not write the questioned document if there is insufficient material for comparison. Response (A) negates the paragraph. Response (C) makes a statement that is simply not supported by the paragraph. Responses (D) and (E) both contradict the information in the paragraph.

20. **(E)** Whether the prisoner is being held on charge of felony or misdemeanor, the person who attempts to assist in the escape is guilty of the same level of offense as the person who *is held upon a charge, arrest, commitment, or conviction.* Response (A) is incorrect because while the person who assists the attempt to escape is indeed guilty whether or not the escape is successful, he or she is guilty of the same level of offense as the prisoner—misdemeanor if the prisoner is being held as a misdemeanant, felony if as a felon. The fact that the attempt fails does not reduce the offense to a misdemeanor. Likewise in response (B), the outcome of the escape attempt does not change the guilt of the person assisting the escape; that guilt is based upon the original reason that the prisoner was being held. The first sentence of the paragraph refers specifically to *intent.* The unknowing carrier of the plans in response (C) is not guilty because there is clearly no intent. Response (D) represents a misreading of the paragraph. There is no suggestion that the person who intends to assist in the escape has come in disguise.

21. **(D)** The Germans developed Methadone to replace *morphine* for use in easing the pain of severely wounded soldiers during the war. In the United States, Methadone has been used in *heroin* detoxification and maintenance programs. Response (A) is incorrect because Methadone can become addictive, and addicts can overdose, leading to their own deaths. Response (B) is contradicted by the second sentence that specifically states that methadone is *chemically* unlike morphine or heroin. Response (C) is incorrect because the fact that the effects of methadone last 24 hours is considered an advantage and these effects are similar whether the drug is administered orally or by injection. Response (E) makes an unwarranted assumption not supported by the paragraph.

22. **(D)** This answer is directly stated in the last clause before the first semicolon: . . . *the maximum of which shall be not longer than twice such longest term; . . .* Responses (A), (B), and (C) are somewhat incoherent sentences composed of words and phrases lifted from the paragraph and combined indiscriminately. Response (E) accepts a phrase from the paragraph without considering the exception that follows it, namely that where the maximum punishment is five years or less, the minimum must be not less than *two* years.

23. **(B)** The last sentence of the paragraph implies that the individual who aspires toward leadership, even though not a born leader, may ultimately develop leadership qualities similar to those that the born leader is endowed with naturally. Responses (A) and (D) both directly contradict information stated in the paragraph. Response (C) makes an unsupported statement. Response (E) makes a statement beyond the sense of the paragraph. Lack of born leadership qualities is only one of many possible reasons—lack of desire springs easily to mind—why the best athlete on the team might not be the captain.

24. **(C)** This is the precise implication of the statement that *critics outside his agency are likely to describe his attitude as being as provincial as an isolationist country's unwillingness to engage in any international trade . . .* Response (A) misses the point that the isolationist country is unwilling to engage in international trade *even though* local talent cannot produce the goods as well nor as cheaply. Response (B) makes a self-contradictory statement. Loyal employees are not likely to be the staunchest critics; loyal employees are, rather, those most likely to be promoted to supervisory positions. Following the remainder of the analogy, those loyal divisional employees may not be the best qualified for the supervisory positions. Response (D) may be countered with the explanation of response (B). If the loyal employees who are promoted are not the best qualified, the final result is not the most positive nor beneficial. Response (E) is a garbled statement.

25. **(A)**   *A suspect will often park his or her car off the paved portion of the street when committing a crime, sometimes leaving excellent tire tracks.* Obviously, the place to search is this unpaved area, not the highway adjoining it. Response (B) reflects wishful thinking. Tire tracks are helpful, but not determining. Response (C) is not supported by the paragraph because the question of direct versus circumstantial evidence is nowhere addressed. Response (D) represents a misreading. The chain of physical evidence is simply the totality of evidence that is amassed; it does not refer to tire chains at all. Response (E) makes an unsupported absolute statement. Excellent tire track evidence is left on the unpaved area adjacent to paved roadway, but tire track evidence may be left on the paved portion as well and surely the paved roadway need not be an identified highway.

Part B—Arithmetic Reasoning Questions

1. **(D)**   Compute the following:

$$\frac{49.20 - \left(18 - \left(18 \times .10\right)\right)}{22} = X$$

$X = \frac{33}{22} = 1.5$ hours or 1 hour 30 minutes

The cost of the switch after the government discount of 10% is applied is $18 - (18 \times .10)$ or $16.20. This amount, when subtracted from the total charge of $49.20, leaves $33, which represents the charge for labor. A charge of $33 at the rate of $22 per hour represents 1.5 hours, or 1 hour and 30 minutes, of work.

2. **(E)**   The correct answer is not given as one of the response choices. The answer can be obtained by computing the following:

$$\frac{\frac{80}{2} - 34}{40} = X$$

$$X = \frac{6}{40} = .15$$

$$.15 \times 100 = 15\%$$

The expected $80 cost for a pair of tires would make the cost of a single tire $40. The difference between the actual cost of $34 per tire and the expected cost of $40 per tire is $6, which is 15 percent of the $40 expected cost.

3. **(C)**   Compute the following:

$$\frac{1}{2}X + \frac{1}{3}X + 3 = X$$

X is equal to the total number of task force members; $\frac{1}{2}X$ represents the number from Agency A; $\frac{1}{3}X$ represents the number from Agency B; and 3 is the number from Agency C. The first two terms on the left side of the equation can be combined by computing their lowest common denominator, which is 6. Therefore:

$$\frac{1}{2}X = \frac{3}{6}X \text{ and } \frac{1}{3}X = \frac{2}{6}X$$

The sum of $\frac{3}{6}X$ and $\frac{2}{6}X$ is $\frac{5}{6}X$, which, when subtracted from X (or $\frac{6}{6}X$), yields the results:

$$\frac{1}{6}X = 3 \text{ and } X = 18$$

4. **(E)** The correct answer is not given as one of the response choices. The answer can be obtained by first converting 12 minutes to .2 hour, and then setting up a simple proportion:

$$\frac{2.2}{4} = \frac{X}{16}$$

Solving this proportion, we obtain $4X = 35.2$; $X = 8.8$. This, however, is the number of hours that it would take one filing clerk to do the job. If two clerks are filling the 16 drawers, the job would be completed in half that time or in 4.4 hours, which is 4 hours, 24 minutes.

5. **(C)** The number absent is the difference between the total class and the number present; $36 - (28 + 4) = 36 - 32 = 4$.

This result, 4, is then divided by the total class to get the fraction $\frac{4}{36}$ or $\frac{1}{9}$, which is approximately 11%. (To convert a fraction to a percent, divide the numerator by the denominator and multiply the result by 100. $(1 \div 9 = .11 \times 100 = 11\%.)$

6. **(E)** The correct answer is not given.

The answer is 10%. The annual dividend is 2.25×4, or \$9.00 a year per share. Based on the purchase price of \$90 per share, the dividend is equal to 10% of the purchase price of a share. The fact that 100 shares were purchased is irrelevant.

7. **(B)** You know that a yardstick is the same as 3 feet. If a 3-foot item casts a shadow of 2 feet, then a tower casting a shadow in the same proportions would fit into the equation:

$$\frac{3}{2} = \frac{x}{40}$$

$$2x = 120$$

$$x = 60 \text{ feet}$$

8. **(C)** Since $\frac{3}{8}$ inch = .375 inches $(3 \div 8 = .375)$, then the following equation can be derived to solve the problem:

$$.375x = 225$$

$$x = 600$$

9. **(E)** The correct answer is not given.

The answer is 11 hours 52 minutes. You do not need to do complicated calculations to answer this question. $14 - 6 = 8$. The sun was above the horizon for 8 minutes less than 12 hours. $60 - 8 = 52$.

10. **(D)** The cars are traveling toward each other, so the distance between them is being reduced at $60 + 50$ or 110 miles per hour. At a rate of 110 mph, 550 miles will be covered in 5 hours. If both cars left at 1:00 P.M., they should meet at 6:00 P.M.

11. **(A)** This is a progressive problem. If 5% of $2,300 = 115$ accountants and 80% of $115 = 92$ with college degrees, then $\frac{1}{2}$ of $92 = 46$ accountants with college degrees and five years of experience.

12. **(B)** This is a proportion problem. Set up the proportion as follows:

$$\frac{2\frac{1}{2}}{4} = \frac{1\frac{7}{8}}{?}$$

Substitute x for?

$$\frac{2\frac{1}{2}}{4} = \frac{1\frac{7}{8}}{x}$$

Cross-multiply

$$\frac{2\frac{1}{2}}{4} \times \frac{1\frac{7}{8}}{x}$$

$$= 2\frac{1}{2}x = 4 \cdot 1\frac{7}{8}$$

Divide both sides by the coefficient of x and calculate:

$$\frac{5}{2}x = \frac{4}{1} \cdot \frac{15}{8}$$

$$\frac{5}{2}x = \frac{15}{2}$$

$$x = \frac{15}{2} \div \frac{5}{2}$$

$$x = \frac{15}{2} \times \frac{2}{5} = 3$$

13. **(C)** The average gain equals the sum of all the gains $(35 + 40 + 25 + 50 + x = 150 + x)$ divided by the number of gains:

$$\frac{150 + x}{5} = 30$$

$$150 + x = 150$$

$$x = 0$$

14. **(D)** If 46% of those who came to trial were found guilty, then $100 - 46 = 54\%$ were acquitted. To find the number who were acquitted, multiply 106,090 by .54. The result is 57,288.

15. **(B)** The difference in cost between February 1980 and February 1981 was $82.50. Divide that figure by the base year and convert to a percentage.

$$\frac{82.50}{122.50} \times 100 = 67\%$$

16. **(B)** Typing space is $12 - 3 = 9$ inches long and $9 - 2 = 7$ inches wide.

$$\text{Part used} = \frac{9 \times 7}{9 \times 12} = \frac{7}{12}$$

17. **(B)** To solve this problem, perform the following:

$\frac{3}{4}$ of $\frac{5}{6} = \frac{5}{8}$, which is the amount of property the individual sold. If $\frac{5}{8} = \$1,800$, the price received upon selling the property, then $\frac{1}{8} = \$360$. Therefore, the entire piece of property or $\frac{8}{8} = \$2880$, which is the value of the property.

18. **(B)** Average is $\frac{4000 + 6000}{2} = 5000$ per block.

    If there are 60 blocks, there are

    $60 \times 5000 = 300,000$ people

19. **(C)** Let x = number of years for the two populations to become equal

    Then $6800 - 12x = 4200 + 80x$

    $2600 = 200x$

    $x = 13$

20. **(C)** The number of revolutions is inversely proportional to the size of the wheel. Thus $\frac{30}{20} = \frac{n}{240}$ where n = number of revolutions for second wheel.

    $2n = 720$

    $n = 360$

Part C—Problems for Investigation

1. **(D)** If Charmaine Fabrics deals only in synthetics, then there should be no reason for the company to import silk.

2. **(E)** Conversations carried on in a foreign language in the presence of a person who is not fluent in that language always lead to suspicion.

3. **(A)** Shipping of an order directly to the customer instead of to the New York office was not the usual procedure, but it had been done before. Statement (4) is not the correct answer because there is no mention in it that Sun Ehee had personally packed previous orders.

4. **(C)** Statement (6) implies that one method of smuggling is to spirit away contraband before it passes through Customs, substituting in its place legitimate cargo.

5. **(C)** Sun Ehee says that he ordered the shipment of rayon acetate and that he worked with the packers of this shipment for the sole purpose of building worker morale.

6. **(E)** Hijacking is another peril of the piers.

7. **(A)** The fact that Charles Kim said that he went to the pier to pick up 500 pounds of rayon acetate does not automatically exonerate him, but it certainly does not implicate him in the attempt to defraud.

8. **(B)** Of all the statements, only the statement that Sam Opit drove as if to elude someone following him casts any suspicion on him.

9. **(C)** John Stern said that he had not talked to anyone about machine guns, but he did not say that he had not talked about the ATF investigation.

10. **(D)**   Sam Opit had a truck full of bathtubs.

11. **(A)**   Agness Hert stated that her room was vacant, said that no one had permission to use it, and described the merchandise that she had kept in the room.

12. **(C)**   Ted Green's speeding convictions have nothing to do with his being accused of stealing a typewriter nor with his allegations of illegal activity by Sam Opit.

13. **(D)**   Gratuitous statements by police officers or others have no bearing on any investigations and are, in fact, out of order.

14. **(E)**   John Stern's firing of Ted Green upon allegations of his stealing even when he was satisfied with his work leads one to wonder if he may have been in some collusion with Sam Opit.

15. **(C)**   Joyce Guyst thought that Opit's driving through a red light stemmed from the fact that he suspected he was being followed, but he may indeed have simply been a poor driver.

16. **(B)**   Frank Watts presented himself to Lola Capone with his driver's license and savings book.

17. **(A)**   John Zinn said that he had bought his bond at Swanee Savings Bank. Sheila Tredd also said that she had bought her bond at Swanee Savings Bank. Shirley Bristol only said that Ann's bond had come from relatives in Swanee, but not that the bond had been bought at Swanee Savings Bank.

18. **(E)**   When Wesley Adams was filling in, he discovered blank bonds in the drawer with the same serial numbers as bonds listed as having been sold in Swanee Savings Bank three days before.

19. **(C)**   Since both Graham Murphy and Frank Watts have disappeared, the Treasury Department must put on a diligent search and must, in the meantime, proceed without two very important witnesses.

20. **(E)**   Jean Scott was one of two persons with major responsibility for selling bonds. Since unsold bonds with the same serial numbers as sold bonds were kept in a drawer that she presumably used, one must suspect that Scott had knowledge of the counterfeiting operation.

21. **(B)**   Graham Murphy left the bank to care for his ill mother, he should be easy to locate through his mother or through others in his home town.

22. **(E)**   Conyer initials his bonds.

23. **(D)**   Jean Scott's father's club affiliations and character are irrelevant.

24. **(D)**   The implication is that LeClair was attempting to thwart plans of his more violent cohorts.

25. **(C)**   Hubert Horan identified St. Jacque as likely to have been the man with the gun.

26. **(D)**   Monet was in the Secret Service album of potential troublemakers among Haitians in the area.

27. **(D)**   Monet's time card indicating that he was at work at the time of the shooting represents a good alibi.

28. **(C)**   The Secret Service kept lists and photographs of Haitian dissidents active in the area.

29. **(E)**   A wife can be expected to cover for her husband. Her statement is likely to be discounted, especially if it is without corroboration.

30. **(A)**   LeClair was reasonably stable, having lived at the same address for eight months, and paid his rent promptly.

FOUR

Skills and Strategies for the TEA Exam

CONTENTS

Verbal Reasoning   147

Arithmetic Reasoning   165

Problems for Investigation   225

Test-Taking Techniques   241

Self-Descriptive Inventories   243

The Interview   251

VERBAL REASONING

The verbal reasoning questions on the TEA are similar to reading questions, but they include a twist. The passages are short, but the questions are tricky. The questions require that you read and reread with careful consideration to what each is really asking. You must be aware that two negatives make a positive and that the third negative in the same sentence makes it negative again. Fortunately, you have 50 minutes to read, interpret, and answer 25 questions.

TEA verbal reasoning questions demand logical reasoning ability as much as they require reading proficiency. A formal logic course is not necessary, but practice reasoning from your reading can be helpful. On the following pages you will find three short exercises in logical thinking. Although the questions in these exercises are not as complex as the questions on the TEA, the practice will sharpen your reasoning skill. As you approach each question in these exercises, read carefully, think carefully, then circle the letter of the answer you choose. When you have completed an exercise, study the answers and explanations beginning on page 159.

Exercise 1

Example:

The black horse jumped over more hurdles than the spotted horse. The white horse jumped over more hurdles than the spotted horse. The white horse jumped over more hurdles than the black horse. If the first two statements are true, the third statement is

(A) true
(B) false
(C) uncertain

Explanation:

From the first two statements, we know that both the black horse and the white horse jumped over more hurdles than the spotted horse. This is all we know. The first two statements do not give us any information about the comparative achievements of the black horse and white horse. The answer, therefore, is (C). The third statement can be neither affirmed nor denied on the basis of the first two statements.

1. George is older than Bob. Fred is younger than George. Bob is older than Fred. If the first two statements are true, the third statement is
   (A) true
   (B) false
   (C) uncertain

2. Group A sings higher than Group C. Group B sings lower than Group C. Group A sings higher than Group B. If the first two statements are true, the third statement is
   (A) true
   (B) false
   (C) uncertain

3. Percolator coffee is weaker than electric drip coffee. Extractor coffee is stronger than percolator coffee. Electric drip coffee is stronger than extractor coffee. If the first two statements are true, the third statement is
   (A) true
   (B) false
   (C) uncertain

4. Red kites fly higher than yellow kites. Yellow balloons fly higher than red kites. Yellow kites fly higher than yellow balloons. If the first two statements are true, the third statement is
   (A) true
   (B) false
   (C) uncertain

5. The New York team lost fewer games than the Boston team. The Boston team won more games than the Baltimore team but not as many games as the New York team. The Baltimore team lost the fewest games. If the first two statements are true, the third statement is
   (A) true
   (B) false
   (C) uncertain

6. The history book has more pages than the poetry book but fewer pages than the math book. The math book has more pages than the science book but fewer pages than the English book. The poetry book has the fewest pages. If the first two statements are true, the third statement is
   (A) true
   (B) false
   (C) uncertain

7. Bill runs faster than Mike. Jeff runs faster than Bill. Jeff is not as fast as Mike. If the first two statements are true, the third statement is
   (A) true
   (B) false
   (C) uncertain

8. Ann reads faster than Sue. Karen reads faster than Ann. Karen reads more slowly than Sue. If the first two statements are true, the third statement is
   (A) true
   (B) false
   (C) uncertain

9. Paul is taller than Peter. Peter is shorter than John. Paul is taller than John. If the first two statements are true, the third statement is
   - (A) true
   - (B) false
   - (C) uncertain

10. Harry is more intelligent than George. Sam is more intelligent than Ralph. Harry is more intelligent than Ralph. If the first two statements are true, the third statement is
    - (A) true
    - (B) false
    - (C) uncertain

11. A is north of B. B is north of C. C is south of A. If the first two statements are true, the third statement is
    - (A) true
    - (B) false
    - (C) uncertain

12. All tumps are winged boscs. No blue boscs have wings. No blue boscs have wings. No tumps are blue. If the first two statements are true, the third statement is
    - (A) true
    - (B) false
    - (C) uncertain

13. River A is wider than River B. River B is narrower than River C. River A is wider than River C. If the first two statements are true, the third statement is
    - (A) true
    - (B) false
    - (C) uncertain

14. Grapes cost more than apples but less than pineapples. Oranges cost more than apples but less than lemons. Apples cost the least of the fruits. If the first two statements are true, the third statement is
    - (A) true
    - (B) false
    - (C) uncertain

15. A is northeast of B. C is southwest of D, but northwest of A. C is north of B. If the first two statements are true, the third statement is
    - (A) true
    - (B) false
    - (C) uncertain

16. Jay's batting average is better than Michael's. Michael's batting average is higher than Tom's. Jay's batting average is lower than Tom's. If the first two statements are true, the third statement is
    - (A) true
    - (B) false
    - (C) uncertain

17. Jon ran faster than Carl. Ron ran faster than George, but not as fast as Jon. Carl was the fastest runner. If the first two statements are true, the third statement is
    (A) true
    (B) false
    (C) uncertain

18. All Blips are Bleeps. No Bleeps are Blops. No Blops are definitely Blips. If the first two statements are true, the third statement is
    (A) true
    (B) false
    (C) uncertain

Exercise 2

For each question, find the statement that must be true according to the given information.

Example:

The little red house on our block is very old. It was once used as a church, and Abraham Lincoln may have worshipped there. It also served as a schoolhouse.

(A) At one time schools were used for worship.

(B) Abraham Lincoln prayed in school.

(C) The house has an interesting history.

(D) Red is a popular color for schools.

Explanation:

Take one statement at a time. Choice (A) cannot be supported by the paragraph. The paragraph states that the house was once used as a church, not that it was used as a church and a school at the same time. Choice B also cannot be supported by the paragraph. If Abraham Lincoln worshipped in the house, he did so when it was a church. While Abraham Lincoln may have prayed in a school as a child, such information is extraneous to the paragraph. Choice (C) is clearly correct. The house does have a long and interesting history dating back to or before the Civil War and having been at various times a church, a school, and a house. Chances are that (C) is the correct answer, but check out choice (D) before choosing your answer. Choice (D) makes a statement of fact that is true in its own right, but one that is not supported by the information in the passage. You must therefore choose (C).

1. Mr. Stonehill worked in the corporate headquarters of a large corporation. Another company acquired Mr. Stonehill's company and sold off the operating divisions one by one. There can be no corporate headquarters without any operating divisions. Mr. Stonehill is

    (A) unemployed

    (B) working for one of the operating divisions

    (C) no longer working in corporate headquarters

    (D) working for the new company

2. Mr. Moffitt is a high school chemistry teacher. As a young man, Mr. Moffitt worked in the textile dyes division of a chemical company. Besides teaching chemistry, Mr. Moffitt operates a business cleaning Oriental carpets.

    (A) Mr. Moffitt changes jobs often.

    (B) Mr. Moffitt teaches students how to clean carpets.

    (C) Mr. Moffitt is a wealthy man.

    (D) Mr. Moffitt is well qualified for the work he does.

3. Sally and Susie are twins. Sally lives near her parents in a Chicago suburb with her husband and children. Susie lives in a remote area of Alaska and raises dogs.

    (A) Susie does not get along with her parents.

    (B) Twins may have different interests and tastes.

    (C) Sally does not like dogs.

    (D) There are special bonds between twins.

4. The baby woke and cried in the middle of the night. Molly Davis changed the baby's diaper, gave him a warm bottle, and put him back to bed.
   (A) The baby woke because it was time for his bottle.
   (B) The baby's mother's name is Molly Davis.
   (C) The baby woke with a wet diaper.
   (D) After his bottle, the baby went back to sleep.

5. Eight children went trick-or-treating together on Halloween. Each child carried a lighted flashlight and a big bag. Jill and Mary did not wear masks.
   (A) The children went trick-or-treating at night.
   (B) Six children wore masks.
   (C) The bags were heavy.
   (D) The youngest children were Jill and Mary.

6. Julie is in second grade. Laura is in third grade. Julie's sister Anne rides a tricycle.
   (A) Laura is smarter than Julie.
   (B) Anne is physically handicapped.
   (C) Julie is behind Laura in school.
   (D) Julie and Laura are sisters.

7. Jeffrey is a law student. On Monday evenings he plays the violin in an orchestra. On Tuesdays and Thursdays he goes square dancing. On Friday afternoon Jeffrey fiddles for a children's folk dancing group.
   (A) Jeffrey plays the violin at least twice a week.
   (B) Jeffrey likes music better than the law.
   (C) Jeffrey dances three times a week.
   (D) Musicians are good dancers.

8. Debbie took the written Foreign Service Officer examination in December. Today Debbie received an appointment date for her Oral Assessment. Debbie is very happy.
   (A) Debbie failed the written exam.
   (B) Debbie is now a Foreign Service officer.
   (C) Everyone who takes the Foreign Service Officer exam must take an oral exam as well.
   (D) Debbie is still under consideration for appointment as a Foreign Service officer.

9. Bill and Dan were exploring an abandoned house. The windows swung loose, the floorboards creaked, and dust and cobwebs filled the air. Suddenly, the two boys ran from the house.
   (A) The house was haunted.
   (B) Something frightened the boys.
   (C) There were bats flying about.
   (D) Someone told the boys to get out.

10. Mr. and Mrs. Chen drive a blue Chevrolet station wagon that they keep in their driveway. Their son Warren has a red Toyota that he puts in the garage each night.
    (A) Blue cars are less susceptible to ravages of weather than are red cars.
    (B) The Chens have a one-car garage.
    (C) Warren has a new car.
    (D) Warren's car is garaged regularly.

11. Mark was distracted by his dog while jumping on the trampoline; he slipped and broke his right arm. That same afternoon the dog chased the cat up a tree. Another time when Mark was walking his dog, the dog pulled Mark too fast and Mark fell and broke his right arm.
    (A) Mark's dog is dangerous.
    (B) Mark should let his sister walk the dog.
    (C) Mark is left-handed.
    (D) Mark is accident-prone.

12. There was a crash on the turnpike between two trucks, one of which overturned. The other truck sustained rear end damage. Cartons of cigarettes, some burst open, were found spilled onto the highway. One of the police officers, who reported to the scene noted that federal tax stamps on some of the cigarette packages were counterfeit. Steven Christian, the driver of the truck that overturned, was injured and had to be taken to the hospital without being questioned. The driver of the other truck, William Cook, stated that he was not carrying cigarettes and knew nothing about the ones on the highway.
    (A) Federal tax stamps are affixed to cigarette cartons.
    (B) The driver of the damaged truck made a false statement.
    (C) The driver of the overturned truck did not admit to guilt.
    (D) William Cook's truck hit that driven by Steven Christian.

Exercise 3

The questions that follow look like ordinary reading questions, but be careful; there is a twist to each.

1. Life is very complicated, and it is art's business to simplify it. The artist must find the common denominator, that which is similar among all of us, and draw upon that to produce a work that not only unites us but also separates us. Each of us must be able to see something different in the work, although the underlying thing we grasp in it is the same.

   With which of the following statements is the author most likely to agree?
   (A) All art imitates nature.
   (B) Every man is an artist.
   (C) Because we cannot see it, music is not art.
   (D) The artist must simplify and then complicate.
   (E) No great art was ever created without tears.

2. Through advertising, manufacturers exercise a high degree of control over consumers' desires. However, the manufacturer assumes enormous risks in attempting to predict what consumers will want and in producing goods in quantity and distributing them in advance of final selection by the consumers.

   The paragraph best supports the statement that manufacturers
   (A) can eliminate the risk of overproduction by advertising
   (B) distribute goods directly to the consumers
   (C) must depend on the final consumers for the success of their undertakings
   (D) can predict with great accuracy the success of any product they put on the market
   (E) are more concerned with advertising than with the production of goods

3. For a society to function properly, everyone must function with everyone else. Individual effort is great—for the individual. Social scientists should devote less time to figuring out how and why the individual does what he or she does and should spend more time figuring out how to get people to do more of what everybody should do—cooperate.

   The author of this statement would probably approve most of
   (A) a psychological study of the determinants of behavior
   (B) a sociologic study of why people go to war
   (C) a historical study of the communes that have failed
   (D) an increase in the number of social scientists
   (E) a psychological study of what makes people cooperative or antisocial

4. For the United States, Canada has become the most important country in the world, yet there are few countries about which Americans know less. Canada is the third largest country in the world; only Russia and China are larger. The area of Canada is more than a quarter of the whole British Commonwealth.

   The paragraph best supports the statement that
   (A) the British Commonwealth is smaller than Russia or China
   (B) the territory of China is greater than that of Canada
   (C) Americans know more about Canada than about China or Russia

     (D) the United States is the most important nation in the world as far as Canada is concerned

     (E) Americans know less about Canada than about China or Russia

5. Since the government can spend only what it obtains from the people, and this amount is ultimately limited by their capacity and willingness to pay taxes, it is very important that the people be given full information about the work of the government.

    The paragraph best supports the statement that

     (A) governmental employees should be trained not only in their own work, but also in how to perform the duties of other employees in their agency

     (B) taxation by the government rests on the consent of the people

     (C) the release of full information on the work of the government will increase the efficiency of governmental operations

     (D) the work of the government, in recent years, has been restricted because of reduced tax collections

     (E) the foundation of our government is abhorence of the principle of taxation without representation

6. With the exception of earth, all of the planets in our solar system are named for gods and goddesses in Greek or Roman legends. This is because the other planets were thought to be in heaven like the gods and our planet lay beneath, like the ground.

    The paragraph best supports the statement that all the planets except earth

     (A) were part of Greek and Roman legends

     (B) were thought to be in heaven

     (C) are part of the same solar system

     (D) were thought to be gods

     (E) were worshipped as gods

7. The game of Monopoly is a frustrated capitalist's delight. One rushes around a board trying to amass property and drive one's competitors into bankruptcy. I think it is no wonder that the game was invented by an unemployed man during the Depression, and that the game immediately caught the fancy of poverty-stricken America.

    The author would probably agree that

     (A) poor people enjoy Monopoly more than middle-class people do

     (B) Monopoly's popularity declines in more prosperous times

     (C) unemployed people are more creative than employed people

     (D) when Monopoly was invented, it was played more often by unemployed than by employed people

     (E) Monopoly was more likely to have been a success when it was introduced than it would have been during prosperous times

8. It's dangerous to change the weather and the climate. We do not know enough about how such changes will affect the earth. What may seem good for one area may be bad for another. If you change a grassland into a vegetable farm, where will the cattle in that area graze? Before we tinker with our natural environment, we should be very sure of what we are doing.

The writer believes that
(A) changes in climate and weather may be harmful
(B) changing climate and weather will improve the earth's surface
(C) man should never meddle with his natural environment
(D) it's easy to figure out what will happen when you change the weather
(E) steady, unchanging weather is better for cattle

9. Without innovation, society cannot progress. Yet without an intellectual tradition to follow, real innovation is not possible. A free-thinking society with no cultural heritage will flounder just as surely as will a tradition-bound society with no independent thought.

The author would be most likely to oppose a philosophy that
(A) advocates building a new society upon the ashes of the old one
(B) advocates remedying historical wrongs by overturning the existing social order
(C) holds imagination to be more valuable than tradition
(D) venerates ancestors
(E) does not venerate ancestors

10. Restlessness such as ours, success such as ours, do not make for beauty. Other things must come first: good cookery; cottages that are homes, not playthings; gardens; repose. These are first-rate things, and out of first-rate stuff art is made. It is possible that machinery has finished us as far as this is concerned. Nobody stays at home any more; nobody makes anything beautiful any more.

The author's argument is predicated on the assumption that
(A) an artist must be a gourmet
(B) beauty depends on utility
(C) there are no successful artists any more
(D) the true artist can never know peace
(E) industrialization is inimical to excellence

11. Only about one-tenth of an iceberg is visible above the water. Eight to nine times as much ice is hidden below the water line. In the Antarctic Ocean, near the South Pole, there are icebergs that rise as high as 300 feet above the water.

The paragraph best supports the statement that icebergs in the Antarctic Ocean
(A) are usually 300 feet high
(B) can be as much as 3,000 feet in total height
(C) are difficult to spot
(D) are a hazard to navigation
(E) are near the South Pole

12. The existence of a vacuum is impossible. For there to be a vacuum, for example, in a container, nothing material must be present in it. But if nothing material is in the container, then there is nothing between any pair of opposite points on the inner surface of the container. Consequently, no distance separates these two points, so that the two points would be one. This, of course, is absurd.

The best summary of the above argument is:

(A) Because a container must contain something, no vacuum can exist.
(B) Since, on the assumption that a vacuum exists in a container, the nonexistence of the container logically follows, there can be no vacuum.
(C) Since it has been shown logically that, if a vacuum exists, there can be no containers, a vacuum must exist outside a container.
(D) If we carefully examine a container by observing its contents, we will see that it is never really empty.
(E) Since nothing can be removed from a container if the parts of its inner surface are not separated from each other, no vacuum can be produced.

13. In response to those who say that the introduction of nuclear weapons into the area would destabilize conditions and lead to greater danger for its inhabitants, I say that the best defense is the capability for a strong offense; and I remind you that no one ever won a football game without scoring any points.

The speaker apparently believes that
(A) football games should be played with atomic weapons
(B) nuclear weapons are good things
(C) the introduction of nuclear weapons would not destabilize conditions in the area under discussion
(D) relations between countries are analogous to a game
(E) all inhabitants of the area would be safer if nuclear weapons were produced there.

14. Psychology has a lot to say, but sometimes it says too much. In one experiment with dogs, a mild shock applied to the left leg caused a response in the right leg. The observers then claimed that a stimulation of one side of the body would cause a response on the opposite side, and these results were generalized to people. But when a researcher later applied the same mild shock to the right legs of the dogs, their left legs did not respond!

Which of the following best sums up the author's attitude?
(A) All psychologists draw unjustified conclusions from their data.
(B) Psychologists who repeat the experiments of others only cause trouble.
(C) Scientists must be careful not to draw unsupported inferences.
(D) Dogs' right legs are less sensitive to shocks than are their left legs.
(E) Animal studies should not be applied to people; only studies on people are relevant to people.

15. Not only do nice guys finish last in sports, but they don't do so well in real life. It's the bad guys I know who get the girls, the good jobs, and the respect of society. The nice, good guys are praised but not respected, are liked by women and employers but are passed up by both in favor of the more aggressive, ambitious guy who doesn't care what people think of him just so long as he gets what he wants. Nice guys finish last and are dopes.

The author's description of nice guys and bad guys suggests that he believes
(A) that many people are neither nice nor bad
(B) it is good to be a bad guy
(C) that success in sports is a good predictor of success in other aspects of life
(D) aggressiveness and ambition are associated more with bad than with nice guys
(E) nice guys are bachelors

16. If the United States keeps on crusading for human rights around the world, it will wind up with a lot of sympathizers, none of whom will be in power.

Which of the following represents an assumption of the author?
(A) The United States should stop crusading for human rights.
(B) No political leader is at present sympathetic to the United States' human rights crusade.
(C) The United States' stand on human rights is approved of by many people.
(D) Any political leader now sympathetic to the United States' human rights stand is certain to fall from power.
(E) Countries should act in their own self-interest.

ANSWER KEY

Exercise 1

1. C	4. B	7. B	9. C	11. A	13. C	15. A	17. B
2. A	5. C	8. B	10. C	12. A	14. A	16. B	18. A
3. B	6. C						

Exercise 2

1. C	3. B	5. A	7. A	9. B	11. D
2. D	4. C	6. C	8. D	10. D	12. C

Exercise 3

1. D	3. E	5. B	7. E	9. A	11. B	13. D	15. D
2. C	4. B	6. B	8. A	10. E	12. B	14. C	16. C

EXPLANATIONS

Exercise 1

1. **(C)** We know only that George is the oldest. There is no way to tell whether Bob is older than Fred or Fred than Bob.

2. **(A)** Group A sings the highest of the three.

3. **(B)** Extractor coffee is the strongest, electric drip comes next, and percolator coffee is the weakest.

4. **(B)** Balloons appear to fly higher than kites.

5. **(C)** We know for certain that Baltimore *won* the fewest games, but without information about how many games were played, we have no knowledge of how many games Baltimore *lost*.

6. **(C)** The English book has the most pages, followed by the math book. The history book has more pages than the poetry book. However, we do not have enough information to rank the science book; it may have more or fewer pages than the poetry book.

7. **(B)** If the first two statements are true, Jeff runs faster than both Bill and Mike.

8. **(B)** Because the first two statements are true and Karen reads faster than Ann, she must also read faster than Sue.

9. **(C)** From the first two statements it is only certain that Peter is the shortest of the three boys. The relationship between Paul and John cannot be determined.

10. **(C)** The first two statements indicate no relationship between Harry and Ralph; therefore, the third statement is uncertain.

11. **(A)** From the first two statements it is known that B is south of A. Because C is south of B, it must also be south of A.

12. **(A)** Because the first two statements are true, all tumps are a part of a larger set of boscs with wings. Blue boscs have no wings, therefore they cannot be tumps, nor can tumps be blue.

13. **(C)** Though the first two statements are considered true, they do not provide any information as to the direct relationship between rivers A and C.

14. **(A)** Because the first two statements are true and all the other fruits cost more than apples, apples must cost the least.

15. **(A)** Because the first two statements are true and C is north of A, it must also be north of B.

16. **(B)** Because the first two statements are true, Jay's batting average must be higher than Tom's.

17. **(B)** Because the first two statements are true and the third statement is in direct opposition to the first, it cannot be true.

18. **(A)** In fact, no Blops could possibly be Blips. Blipdom and Blopdom are mutually exclusive occurrences. If the nonsense words confuse you, substitute real words, thus: If all robins are birds and no birds are fish, then no fish are definitely robins.

Exercise 2

1. **(C)** There is no information as to whether or not Mr. Stonehill is now working, nor for whom. However, if the operating divisions have been sold, there is no corporate headquarters. If there is no corporate headquarters, most certainly Mr. Stonehill does not work there.

2. **(D)** With the credentials required of all schoolteachers and with his specialized experience in a chemical company, Mr. Moffitt is clearly qualified to teach high school chemistry. The training that Mr. Moffitt received working in the textile dyes division applies beautifully to his sideline occupation, cleaning Oriental carpets. The other choices, while all possible, are in no way supported by the paragraph.

3. **(B)** The only statement definitely supported by the paragraph is that twins may have different interests and tastes.

4. **(C)** Nobody changes a dry diaper in the middle of the night. The other choices are possibilities but not certainties. The baby might have wakened for any number of reasons; Molly Davis might be a baby-sitter; the baby might have played happily in his crib once dry and fed.

5. **(A)**   If all eight children carried *lighted* flashlights, we might be pretty sure that it was dark. The information that Jill and Mary did not wear masks implies that the other children did, but does not prove it. Some of the others might also have not worn masks or might have worn sheets over their heads. Sometimes the youngest children wear masks while older youngsters apply complicated makeup. Jill and Mary were not necessarily the youngest.

6. **(C)**   The only certainty is that Julie is behind Laura in school. The fact that Laura is ahead in school does not necessarily mean that she is smarter, possibly only older. Anne might well be a normal, healthy two-year-old. Julie and Anne are sisters, but Laura's relationship to them is not given.

7. **(A)**   Jeffrey definitely plays the violin at least twice a week, on Monday and Friday. While we know that Jeffrey enjoys both music and dancing, we have no way of knowing if he prefers either of these activities to the study of law. From this paragraph, you cannot tell how often Jeffrey dances.

8. **(D)**   Chances are that Debbie did not fail the written exam since she is about to go for an Oral Assessment. Surely the person who failed the first step would not be called for the second. Likewise, we can assume that only people who pass the written exam take the oral exam. Otherwise, both exams could be scheduled in advance. If Debbie were already a Foreign Service officer, she would not need to go for an Oral Assessment. You may assume from this paragraph that Debbie is happy because she passed the exam and is still under consideration for appointment as a Foreign Service Officer.

9. **(B)**   The only certainty is that something frightened the boys, and they got out in a hurry.

10. **(D)**   All of the choices could be true, but the only fact of which you may be certain is that Warren's car is garaged regularly.

11. **(D)**   Clearly, Mark is accident-prone and breaks his right arm easily. His dog is not dangerous; we do not even know if Mark has a sister; he may be learning to use his left hand out of necessity, but we do not know if he is left- or right-handed.

12. **(C)**   The driver of the overturned truck was injured and was taken directly to the hospital without questioning. Obviously, he made no statement and did not admit to guilt. If you read carefully, you will note that the counterfeit tax stamps were on the packages that had spilled out of the broken cartons, not on the cartons themselves. Choice (B) makes an unwarranted assumption. Maybe Cook really did not know. It is reasonable to assume that the truck with rear end damage was hit by the overturned truck.

Exercise 3

1. **(D)**   The passage begins by saying that the artist must simplify and find the common denominator. It then says that the artist must draw upon the common denominator to produce something that separates us. This act of separation presumably involves adding to the common denominator, and thus may be considered as a complicating act. Answer choices (A), (B), and (E) have no relation to the passage. (C) is presumably derived from the statement that "each of us must be able to *see* something different in the work." This statement uses *see* in a broader sense than mere visual perception.

2. **(C)**   The correct answer, (C), is supported by the paragraph's statement that although advertising gives manufacturers considerable control over the consumers' demand for their products, there are still big risks involved in producing and distributing their goods in advance of the consumers' final selection, which implies that manufacturers' ultimate success depends on the consumers. The statement that there are such risks, in spite of advertising, contradicts (A) and (D). There is no support for statement (B), that manufacturers distribute goods *directly* to consumers, or (E), that they are *more* concerned with advertising than production.

3. **(E)**   Answer (E) suggests what the author is most in favor of—finding out how to make people cooperate. Clearly, finding out why people are cooperative or antisocial is a crucial part of this research undertaking. The other choices do not come as close to achieving this goal.

4. **(B)**   The paragraph states that Russia and China are larger than Canada. No other answer to this question is correct. Choices (C) and (D) make statements in direct contradiction to the paragraph. Choice (A) is wrong because the paragraph compares the size of *Canada* with that of Russia and China, not the size of the *British Commonwealth* with Russia and China. It is entirely possible that Americans do know less about Canada than about China or Russia, but choice (E) is not directly supported by the paragraph.

5. **(B)**   According to the paragraph, the government can spend only what it obtains from the people. The government obtains money from the people by taxation. If the people are unwilling to pay taxes, the government has no source of funds.

6. **(B)**   This paragraph takes careful reading, but it clearly states that the planets were thought to be in heaven like the gods, not that they were thought to be gods or that they were worshipped like gods.

7. **(E)**   The final sentence expresses the idea that Monopoly was especially likely to be invented and to be a success in a country suffering from economic woes; choice (E) also expresses this idea. Choice (B) is somewhat similar, but refers to the popularity of Monopoly after it became a success, a subject not addressed in the passage. Answer choices (A), (C), and (D) are far from the author's topic.

8. **(A)**   The statement warns of the dangers that might result from changes in weather and climate. It does not say that we should *never* meddle with the environment.

9. **(A)**   The author stresses the importance of tradition, and thus would probably oppose destroying society. The author's opinions on revolution and the relative values of imagination and tradition are not stated or implied. His opinions on veneration (worship) of ancestors are likewise not mentioned; he need not oppose a lack of ancestor-worship simply because he stresses the importance of tradition.

10. **(E)**   The author's conclusion follows from his or her premises only if the mechanization of modern society precludes "first-rate things." Choices (A), (C), and (D) are incorrect because the passage discusses the social climate for appreciating beauty, not the characteristics of artists. (B) is incorrect because the passage describes the prerequisites for the creation of beauty, not a definition of it.

11. **(B)**   If an iceberg towers 300 feet above the water line and only one tenth of its height is visible, its total height might well be 3,000 feet. Choices (A) and (C) are clearly incorrect. Choice (D) might well be a correct statement, but it is not supported by the paragraph. Choice (E) is too limiting. Icebergs range throughout the Antarctic Ocean, not just near the South Pole.

12. **(B)** The argument is a reduction to absurdity. An obviously false conclusion is deduced from the assumption the author wants to disprove, thus implying that it is false. Chioce (A) oversimplifies the argument. Choice (C) states a different argument with a somewhat preposterous conclusion. Choice (D) is wrong, since the argument above makes no appeal to observation. Answer choice (E) is at best a parody of the argument.

13. **(D)** The war-peace topic of the sentence is compared to a football game. Choice (A) is clearly incorrect. Choice (B) is incorrect because the author does not clearly approve of nuclear weapons *per se;* he or she approves of their introduction into the area, a view based on the assumption that the weapons exist. Choice (C) is incorrect because the author does not deny that nuclear weapons would destabilize the area. Similarly, (E) is wrong because the question of safety is not addressed. It may be assumed that the author believes that at least *some* inhabitants of the area would be made safer if nuclear weapons were introduced, but it is possible that the author believes that the inhabitants of countries lacking such weapons would be less safe.

14. **(C)** The author points out an example of unsupported inference from the field of psychology. It would be inconsistent for him or her not to deplore such behavior in other branches of science. Since the author objects to jumping to conclusions, he or she would not support choices (A), (D), or (E). Choice (B) is in contradiction to the author's attitude.

15. **(D)** The third sentence of the passage states that bad guys are aggressive and ambitious and implies that nice guys lack these qualities. The passage does not suggest that many people are neither good nor bad, as in (A). No value judgment is offered about the goodness of being a bad guy, as suggested in (B). Choice (C) is probably true only in that sports success might correlate, in the author's view, with success in other aspects of life in the author's distinction between nice and bad guys. The author does not suggest that nice guys never marry, as does (E).

16. **(C)** It is likely that if the human rights campaign winds up with a lot of sympathizers, as the passage states, that it is approved of by many people. Choice (A) is probably correct only if it is further assumed that the speaker has the best interests of the United States at heart. Choice (B) goes too far— the author may believe that some political leaders are now sympathetic to the human rights campaign, but never states that they will fall from power if their sympathy persists. Choice (D) is wrong because it does not contain the provision that the human rights campaign is continued, an essential part of the author's argument. Choice (E) is not supported by the statement.

ARITHMETIC REASONING

The two words, "arithmetic reasoning," strike terror into the hearts of people who have been out of school for a while or who have concentrated their studies in the humanities. With respect to the TEA, this fear is unfounded. The arithmetic reasoning on the TEA does not require you to understand intricate mathematical procedures nor to have memorized complicated formulas. You can solve the problems arithmetically or by using some simple algebra.

Each problem is presented as a short verbal description of a situation that includes some numerical facts. You must read the problem over—several times, if necessary—to be certain exactly what the question is. If a series of calculations will be required, you do not want to stop short of the answer because you misinterpreted the question. Likewise, you do not want to waste time going beyond what is asked.

Once you have determined what the question asks, you must settle on the best route for arriving at the answer and set the problem up accordingly. Finally, you must perform the calculations. The TEA arithmetic reasoning questions all offer "none of these" as the (E) choice. That means you must perform all calculations carefully. You cannot afford to estimate or approximate.

The remainder of this chapter gives simple, to-the-point instruction in the areas tested in TEA arithmetic reasoning, followed by practice problems and solutions. When you have completed this chapter, you should be thoroughly prepared for the 20 arithmetic reasoning questions you must face.

Reminder: Do all the practice exercise questions with pencil on scratch paper. You will not be permitted to use a calculator at the exam, so get used to doing arithmetic without it. Answer questions in the practice exercises by circling the letter of your choice.

Ratio and Proportion

RATIO

1. A **ratio** expresses the relationship between two (or more) quantities in terms of numbers. The mark used to indicate ratio is the colon (:) and is read "to."
   Example: The ratio 2:3 is read "2 to 3."
2. A ratio also represents division. Therefore, any ratio of two terms may be written as a fraction, and any fraction may be written as a ratio.

   Example: $3:4 = \frac{3}{4}$

   $\frac{5}{6} = 5:6$

3. To simplify any complicated ratio of two terms containing fractions, decimals, or percents:
   a. Divide the first term by the second.
   b. Write as a fraction in lowest terms.
   c. Write the fraction as a ratio.

   Illustration: Simplify the ratio $\frac{5}{6} : \frac{7}{8}$

   Solution: $\frac{5}{6} \div \frac{7}{8} = \frac{5}{6} \times \frac{8}{7} = \frac{20}{21}$

   $\frac{20}{21} = 20:21$

   Answer: 20:21

4. To solve problems in which the ratio is given:
   a. Add the terms in the ratio.
   b. Divide the total amount that is to be put into a ratio by this sum.
   c. Multiply each term in the ratio by this quotient.
   Illustration: The sum of $360 is to be divided among three people according to the ratio 3:4:5. How much does each one receive?

   > *Solution:* 3 + 4 + 5 = 12
   > $360 ÷ 12 = $30
   > $30 × 3 = $90
   > $30 × 4 = $120
   > $30 × 5 = $150

   Answer: The money is divided thus: $90, $120, $150.

PROPORTION

5. a. A **proportion** indicates the equality of two ratios.
   Example: 2:4 = 5:10 is a proportion. This is read "2 is to 4 as 5 is to 10."
   b. In a proportion, the two outside terms are called the **extremes,** and the two inside terms are called the **means.**
   Example: In the proportion 2:4 = 5:10, 2 and 10 are the extremes, and 4 and 5 are the means.
   c. Proportions are often written in fractional form.
   Example: The proportion 2:4 = 5:10 may be written $\frac{2}{4} = \frac{5}{10}$.
   d. In any proportion, the product of the means equals the product of the extremes. If the proportion is in fractional form, the products may be found by cross-multiplication.
   Example: In $\frac{2}{4} = \frac{5}{10}$, $4 \times 5 = 2 \times 10$.
   e. The product of the extremes divided by one mean equals the other mean; the product of the means divided by one extreme equals the other extreme.

6. Many problems in which three terms are given and one term is unknown can be solved by using proportions. To solve such problems:
   a. Formulate the proportion very carefully according to the facts given. (If any term is misplaced, the solution will be incorrect.) Any symbol may be written in place of the missing term.
   b. Determine by inspection whether the means or the extremes are known. Multiply the pair that has both terms given.
   c. Divide this product by the third term given to find the unknown term.
   Illustration: The scale on a map shows that 2 cm represents 30 miles of actual length. What is the actual length of a road that is represented by 7 cm on the map?
   Solution: The map lengths and the actual lengths are in proportion; that is, they have equal ratios. If *m* stands for the unknown length, the proportion is:

   $\frac{2}{7} = \frac{30}{m}$

   As the proportion is written, *m* is an extreme and is equal to the product of the means, divided by the other extreme:

   $m = \frac{7 \times 30}{2}$

   $m = \frac{210}{2}$

   $m = 105$

Answer: 7 cm on the map represents 105 miles.

Illustration: If a money bag containing 500 nickels weighs 6 pounds, how much will a money bag containing 1600 nickels weigh?

Solution: The weights of the bags and the number of coins in them are proportional. Suppose *w* represents the unknown weight. Then

$$\frac{6}{w} = \frac{500}{1600}$$

The unknown is a mean and is equal to the product of the extremes, divided by the other mean:

$$w = \frac{6 \times 1600}{500}$$

$$w = 19.2$$

Answer: A bag containing 1600 nickels weighs 19.2 pounds.

EXERCISE

1. The ratio of 24 to 64 is
    (A) 8:3
    (B) 24:100
    (C) 3:8
    (D) 64:100

2. The Baltimore Colts won 8 games and lost 3. The ratio of games won to games played is
    (A) 8:11
    (B) 3:11
    (C) 8:3
    (D) 3:8

3. The ratio of $\frac{1}{4}$ to $\frac{3}{5}$ is
    (A) 1 to 3
    (B) 3 to 20
    (C) 5 to 12
    (D) 3 to 4

4. If there are 16 boys and 12 girls in a class, the ratio of the number of girls to the number of children in the class is
    (A) 3 to 4
    (B) 3 to 7
    (C) 4 to 7
    (D) 4 to 3

5. 259 is to 37 as
    (A) 5 is to 1
    (B) 63 is to 441
    (C) 84 is to 12
    (D) 130 is to 19

6. 2 dozen cans of dog food at the rate of 3 cans for $1.45 would cost
   (A) $10.05
   (B) $11.20
   (C) $11.60
   (D) $11.75

7. A snapshot measures $2\frac{1}{2}$ inches by $1\frac{7}{8}$ inches. It is to be enlarged so that the longer dimension will be 4 inches. The length of the enlarged shorter dimension will be

   (A) $2\frac{1}{2}$ inches

   (B) 3 inches

   (C) $3\frac{3}{8}$ inches

   (D) none of these

8. Men's white handkerchiefs cost $2.29 for 3. The cost per dozen handkerchiefs is
   (A) $27.48
   (B) $13.74
   (C) $9.16
   (D) $6.87

9. A certain pole casts a shadow 24 feet long. At the same time another pole 3 feet high casts a shadow 4 feet long. How high is the first pole if the heights and shadows are in proportion?
   (A) 18 feet
   (B) 19 feet
   (C) 20 feet
   (D) 21 feet

10. The actual length represented by $3\frac{1}{2}$ inches on a drawing having a scale of $\frac{1}{8}$ inch to the foot is
    (A) 3.75 feet
    (B) 28 feet
    (C) 360 feet
    (D) 120 feet

11. Aluminum bronze consists of copper and aluminum, usually in the ratio 10:1 by weight. If an object made of this alloy weighs 77 pounds, how many pounds of aluminum does it contain?
    (A) 7.7
    (B) 7.0
    (C) 70.0
    (D) 62.3

12. It costs 31 cents a square foot to lay vinyl flooring. To lay 180 square feet of flooring, it will cost
    (A) $16.20
    (B) $18.60
    (C) $55.80
    (D) $62.00

13. If a per diem worker earns $352 in 16 days, the amount that he will earn in 117 days is most nearly
    (A) $3,050
    (B) $2,574
    (C) $2,285
    (D) $2,080

14. Assuming that on a blueprint $\frac{1}{8}$ inch equals 12 inches of actual length, the actual length in inches of a steel bar represented on the blueprint by a line $3\frac{3}{4}$ inches long is
    (A) $3\frac{3}{4}$
    (B) 30
    (C) 450
    (D) 360

15. A, B, and C invested $9,000, $7,000, and $6,000, respectively. Their profits were to be divided according to the ratio of their investment. If B uses his share of the firm's profit of $825 to pay a personal debt of $230, how much will he have left?
    (A) $30.50
    (B) $32.50
    (C) $34.50
    (D) $36.50

ANSWER KEY

1. C	3. C	5. C	7. B	9. A	11. B	13. B	15. B
2. A	4. B	6. C	8. C	10. B	12. C	14. D	

EXPLANATIONS

1. **(C)** The ratio 24 to 64 may be written 24:64 or $\frac{24}{64}$. In fraction form, the ratio can be reduced:

    $$\frac{24}{64} = \frac{3}{8} \text{ or } 3:8$$

2. **(A)** The number of games played was $3 + 8 = 11$. The ratio of games won to games played is 8:11

3. **(C)** $\frac{1}{4} : \frac{3}{5} = \frac{1}{4} \div \frac{3}{5}$

    $$= \frac{1}{4} \times \frac{5}{3}$$

    $$= \frac{5}{12}$$

    $$= 5:12 \text{ or } 5 \text{ to } 12$$

4. **(B)** There are $16 + 12 = 28$ children in the class. The ratio of number of girls to number of children is 12:28

    $$\frac{12}{28} = \frac{3}{7} \text{ or } 3 \text{ to } 7$$

5. **(C)** The ratio $\frac{259}{37}$ reduces by 37 to $\frac{7}{1}$. The ratio $\frac{84}{12}$ also reduces to $\frac{7}{1}$. Therefore, $\frac{259}{37} = \frac{84}{12}$ is a proportion, reading 84 is to 12.

6. **(C)** The number of cans is proportional to the price. Let p represent the unknown price:

    Then $\frac{3}{24} = \frac{1.45}{p}$

    $$p = \frac{1.45 \times 24}{3}$$

    $$p = \frac{34.80}{3}$$

    $$= \$11.60$$

7. **(B)** Let s represent the unknown shorter dimension:

$$\frac{2\frac{1}{2}}{4} = \frac{1\frac{7}{8}}{s}$$

$$s = \frac{4 \times 1\frac{1}{7}}{2\frac{1}{2}}$$

$$= \frac{4 \cdot \frac{15}{8}^{1}_{2}}{2\frac{1}{2}}$$

$$= \frac{15}{2} \div 2\frac{1}{2}$$

$$= \frac{15}{2} \div \frac{5}{2}$$

$$= \frac{15}{2} \times \frac{2}{5}$$

$$= 3 \text{ inches}$$

8. **(C)** If p is the cost per dozen (12):

$$\frac{3}{12} = \frac{2.29}{p}$$

$$p = \frac{\overset{4}{12} \times 2.29}{\underset{1}{3}}$$

$$= 9.16$$

9. **(A)** If f is the height of the first pole, the proportion is:

$$\frac{f}{24} = \frac{3}{4}$$

$$f = \frac{\overset{6}{24} \times 3}{\underset{1}{4}}$$

$$= 18 \text{ feet}$$

10. **(B)** y is the unknown length:

$$\frac{3\frac{1}{2}}{\frac{1}{8}} = \frac{y}{1}$$

$$y = \frac{3\frac{1}{2} \times 1}{\frac{1}{8}}$$

$$= 3\frac{1}{2} \div \frac{1}{8}$$

$$= \frac{7}{2} \times \frac{8}{1}$$

$$= 28 \text{ feet}$$

11. **(B)** Since only two parts of a proportion are known (77 is total weight), the problem must be solved by the ratio method. The ratio 10:1 means that if the alloy were separated into equal parts, 10 of those parts would be copper and 1 would be aluminum, for a total of 10 + 1 = 11 parts.

$77 \div 11 = 7$ lb per part

The alloy has 1 part aluminum.

$7 \times 1 = 7$ lb aluminum

12. **(C)** The cost (c) is proportional to the number of square feet.

$$\frac{\$.31}{c} = \frac{1}{80}$$

$$c = \frac{\$.31 \times 180}{1}$$

$$= \$55.80$$

13. **(B)** The amount earned is proportional to the number of days worked. If a is the unknown amount:

$$\frac{\$352}{a} = \frac{16}{117}$$

$$a = \frac{\$352 \times 117}{16}$$

$$a = \$2574$$

14. **(D)** If n is the unknown length:

$$\frac{\frac{1}{8}}{3\frac{3}{4}} = \frac{12}{n}$$

$$n = \frac{12 \times 3\frac{3}{4}}{\frac{1}{8}}$$

$$= \frac{\overset{3}{12} \times \frac{15}{\underset{1}{4}}}{\frac{1}{8}}$$

$$= \frac{45}{\frac{1}{8}}$$

$$= 45 \div \frac{1}{8}$$

$$= 45 \times \frac{8}{1}$$

$$= 360$$

15. **(B)**   The ratio of investment is:

9,000:7,000:6,000 or 9:7:6

9 + 7 + 6 = 22

$825 ÷ 22 = $37.50 each share of profit

7 × $37.50 = $262.50 B's share of profit

$262.50
–230.00
‾‾‾‾‾‾‾
$32.50 amount B has left

WORK PROBLEMS

1. a.   In work problems, there are three items involved: the number of people working, the time, and the amount of work done.
   b.   The number of people working is directly proportional to the amount of work done; that is, the more people on the job, the more the work that will be done, and vice versa.
   c.   The number of people working is inversely proportional to the time; that is, the more people on the job, the less time it will take to finish it, and vice versa.
   d.   The time expended on a job is directly proportional to the amount of work done; that is, the more time expended on a job, the more work that is done, and vice versa.

WORK AT EQUAL RATES

2. a.   When given the time required by a number of people working at equal rates to complete a job, multiply the number of people by their time to find the time required by one person to do the complete job.
   Example: If it takes 4 people working at equal rates 30 days to finish a job, then one person will take 30 × 4 or 120 days.
   b.   When given the time required by one person to complete a job, to find the time required by a number of people working at equal rates to complete the same job, divide the time by the number of people.
   Example: If 1 person can do a job in 20 days, it will take 4 people working at equal rates 20 ÷ 4 or 5 days to finish the job.
   3.   To solve problems involving people who work at equal rates:
   a.   Multiply the number of people by their time to find the time required by 1 person.
   b.   Divide this time by the number of people required.
   Illustration: Four workers can do a job in 48 days. How long will it take 3 workers to finish the same job?
   Solution: One worker can do the job in 48 × 4 or 192 days.
   3 workers can do the job in 192 ÷ 3 = 64 days.
   Answer: It would take 3 workers 64 days.

4. In some work problems, the rates, though unequal, can be equalized by comparison. To solve such problems:
    a.   Determine from the facts given how many equal rates there are.
    b.   Multiply the number of equal rates by the time given.
    c.   Divide this by the number of equal rates.

    Illustration: Three workers can do a job in 12 days. Two of the workers work twice as fast as the third. How long would it take one of the faster workers to do the job himself?

    Solution: There are two fast workers and one slow worker. Therefore, there are actually five slow workers working at equal rates.

    1 slow worker will take 12×5 or 60 days.

    1 fast worker = 2 slow workers; therefore, he will take $60 \div 2$ or 30 days to complete the job.

    Answer: It will take 1 fast worker 30 days to complete the job.

5. Unit time is time expressed in terms of 1 minute, 1 hour, 1 day, etc.

6. The rate at which a person works is the amount of work he can do in unit time.

7. If given the time it will take one person to do a job, then the reciprocal of the time is the part done in unit time.

    Example: If a worker can do a job in 6 days, then he can do $\frac{1}{6}$ of the work in 1 day.

8. The reciprocal of the work done in unit time is the time it will take to do the complete job.

    Example: If a worker can do $\frac{3}{7}$ of the work in 1 day, then he can do the whole job in $\frac{7}{3}$ or $2\frac{1}{3}$ days.

9. If given the various times in which each of a number of people can complete a job, to find the time it will take to do the job if all work together:
    a.   Invert the time of each to find how much each can do in unit time.
    b.   Add these reciprocals to find what part all working together can do in unit time.
    c.   Invert this sum to find the time it will take all of them together to do the whole job.

    Illustration: If it takes A 3 days to dig a certain ditch, whereas B can dig it in 6 days, and C in 12, how long would it take all three to do the job?

    Solution: A can do it in 3 days; therefore, he can do $\frac{1}{3}$ in one day. B can do it in 6 days; therefore, he can do $\frac{1}{6}$ in one day. C can do it in 12 days; therefore, he can do $\frac{1}{12}$ in one day.

    $$\frac{1}{3} + \frac{1}{6} + \frac{1}{12} = \frac{7}{12}$$

    A, B, and C can do $\frac{7}{12}$ of the work in one day; therefore, it will take them $\frac{12}{7}$ or $1\frac{5}{7}$ days to complete the job.

    Answer: A, B, and C, working together, can complete the job in $1\frac{5}{7}$ days.

10. If given the total time it requires a number of people working together to complete a job, and the times of all but one are known, to find the missing time:
    a.   Invert the given times to find how much each can do in unit time.
    b.   Add the reciprocals to find how much is done in unit time by those whose rates are known.
    c.   Subtract this sum from the reciprocal of the total time to find the missing rate.
    d.   Invert this rate to find the unknown time.

    Illustration: A, B, and C can do a job in 2 days. B can do it in 5 days, and C can do it in 4 days. How long would it take A to do it himself?

    Solution: B can do it in 5 days; therefore, he can do $\frac{1}{5}$ in one day. C can do it in 4 days; therefore, he can do $\frac{1}{4}$ in one day. The part that can be done by B and C together in 1 day is:

    $$\frac{1}{5} + \frac{1}{4} = \frac{9}{20}$$

    The total time is 2 days; therefore, all can do $\frac{1}{2}$ in one day.

    $$\frac{1}{2} - \frac{9}{20} = \frac{1}{20}$$

A can do $\frac{1}{20}$ in 1 day; therefore, he can do the whole job in 20 days.

Answer: It would take A 20 days to complete the job himself.

11. In some work problems, certain values are given for the three factors[md]number of workers, the amount of work done, and the time. It is then usually required to find the changes that occur when one or two of the factors are given different values.

One of the best methods of solving such problems is by directly making the necessary cancellations, divisions, and multiplications.

In this problem it is easily seen that more workers will be required since more houses are to be built in a shorter time.

Illustration: If 60 workers can build 4 houses in 12 months, how many workers would be required to build 6 houses in 4 months?

Solution: To build 6 houses instead of 4 in the same amount of time, we would need $\frac{6}{4}$ of the number of workers.

$\frac{6}{4} \times 60 = 90$

Since we now have 4 months where previously we needed 12, we must triple the number of workers.

$90 \times 3 = 270$

Answer: 270 workers will be needed to build 6 houses in 4 months.

EXERCISE

1. If 314 clerks filed 6594 papers in 10 minutes, what is the number filed per minute by the average clerk?
    (A) 2
    (B) 2.4
    (C) 2.1
    (D) 2.5

2. Four men working together can dig a ditch in 42 days. They begin, but one man works only half-days. How long will it take to complete the job?
    (A) 48 days
    (B) 45 days
    (C) 43 days
    (D) 44 days

3. A clerk is requested to file 800 cards. If he can file cards at the rate of 80 cards an hour, the number of cards remaining to be filed after 7 hours of work is
    (A) 140
    (B) 240
    (C) 260
    (D) 560

4. If it takes 4 days for 3 machines to do a certain job, it will take two machines
    (A) 6 days
    (B) $5\frac{1}{2}$ days
    (C) 5 days
    (D) $4\frac{1}{2}$ days

5. A stenographer has been assigned to place entries on 500 forms. She places entries on 25 forms by the end of half an hour, when she is joined by another stenographer. The second stenographer places entries at the rate of 45 an hour. Assuming that both stenographers continue to work at their respective rates of speed, the total number of hours required to carry out the entire assignment is
   (A) 5
   (B) $5\frac{1}{2}$
   (C) $6\frac{1}{2}$
   (D) 7

6. If in 5 days a clerk can copy 125 pages, 36 lines each, 11 words to the line, how many pages of 30 lines each and 12 words to the line can he copy in 6 days?
   (A) 145
   (B) 155
   (C) 160
   (D) 165

7. A and B do a job together in two hours. Working alone, A does the job in 5 hours. How long will it take B to do the job alone?
   (A) $3\frac{1}{3}$ hours
   (B) $2\frac{1}{4}$ hours
   (C) 3 hours
   (D) 2 hours

8. A stenographer transcribes her notes at the rate of one line typed in ten seconds. At this rate, how long (in minutes and seconds) will it take her to transcribe notes, which will require seven pages of typing, 25 lines to the page?
   (A) 29 minutes 10 seconds
   (B) 17 minutes 50 seconds
   (C) 40 minutes 10 seconds
   (D) 20 minutes 30 seconds

9. A group of five clerks has been assigned to insert 24,000 letters into envelopes. The clerks perform this work at the following rates of speed: Clerk A, 1100 letters an hour; Clerk B, 1450 letters an hour; Clerk C, 1200 letters an hour; Clerk D, 1300 letters an hour; Clerk E, 1250 letters an hour. At the end of two hours of work, Clerks C and D are assigned to another task. From the time that Clerks C and D were taken off the assignment, the number of hours required for the remaining clerks to complete this assignment is
   (A) less than 3 hours
   (B) 3 hours
   (C) more than 3 hours, but less than 4 hours
   (D) more than 4 hours

10. If a certain job can be performed by 18 workers in 26 days, the number of workers needed to perform the job in 12 days is
    (A) 24
    (B) 30
    (C) 39
    (D) 52

11. A steam shovel excavates 2 cubic yards every 40 seconds. At this rate, the amount excavated in 45 minutes is
    (A) 90 cubic yards
    (B) 135 cubic yards
    (C) 900 cubic yards
    (D) 3600 cubic yards

12. An oil burner in a housing development burns 76 gallons of fuel oil per hour. At 9 A.M. on a very cold day the superintendent asks the housing manager to put in an emergency order for more fuel oil. At that time, the superintendent reports that he has on hand 266 gallons. At noon, he again comes to the manager, notifying her that no oil has been delivered. The maximum amount of time that the superintendent can continue to furnish heat without receiving more oil is
    (A) $\frac{1}{2}$ hour
    (B) 1 hour
    (C) $1\frac{1}{2}$ hours
    (D) 2 hours

ANSWER KEY

1. C	3. B	5. B	7. A	9. B	10. C	11. B	12. A
2. A	4. A	6. D	8. A				

EXPLANATIONS

1. **(C)**   6594 papers ÷ 314 clerks = 21 papers per clerk in 10 minutes.

    21 papers ÷ 10 minutes = 2.1 papers per minute filed by the average clerk.

2. **(A)**   It would take 1 man $42 \times 4 = 168$ days to complete the job, working alone. If $3\frac{1}{2}$ men are working (one man works half-days, the other 3 work full days), the job would take $168 \div 3\frac{1}{2} = 48$ days.

3. **(B)**   In 7 hours the clerk files $7 \times 80 = 560$ cards. Since 800 cards must be filed, there are $800 - 560 = 240$ remaining.

4. **(A)**   It would take 1 machine $3 \times 4 = 12$ days to do the job. Two machines could do the job in $12 \div 2 = 6$ days.

5. **(B)**   At the end of the first half-hour, there are $500 - 25 = 475$ forms remaining. If the first stenographer completed 25 forms in half an hour, her rate is $25 \times 2 = 50$ forms per hour. The combined rate of the two stenographers is $50 + 45 = 95$ forms per hour. The remaining forms can be completed in $475 \div 95 = 5$ hours. Adding the first half-hour, the entire job requires $5\frac{1}{2}$ hours.

6. **(D)**   36 lines × 11 words = 396 words on each page.

    125 pages × 396 words = 49,500 words in 5 days.

    49,500 ÷ 5 = 9,900 words in 1 day.

    12 words × 30 lines = 360 words on each page

    $9,900 \div 360 = 27\frac{1}{2}$ pages in 1 day.

    $27\frac{1}{2} \times 6 = 165$ pages in 6 days.

7. **(A)**   If A can do the job alone in 5 hours, A can do $\frac{1}{5}$ of the job in 1 hour. Working together, A and B can do the job in 2 hours; therefore, in 1 hour they do $\frac{1}{2}$ the job.

    In 1 hour, B alone does

    $$\frac{1}{2} - \frac{1}{5} = \frac{5}{10} - \frac{2}{10}$$

$= \frac{3}{10}$ of the job.

It would take B $\frac{10}{3}$ hours $= 3\frac{1}{2}$ hours to do the whole job alone.

8. **(A)** She must type $7 \times 25 = 175$ lines. At the rate of 1 line per 10 seconds, it will take $175 \times 10 = 1750$ seconds.

   1750 seconds $\div 60 = 29\frac{1}{6}$ minutes

   $= 29$ min. 10 sec.

9.   **(B)** *Clerk*   *Number of letters per hr*

Clerk	Number of letters per hr
A	1100
B	1450
C	1200
D	1300
E	+ 1250
	Total = 6300

All 5 clerks working together process a total of 6300 letters per hour. After 2 hours, they have processed $6{,}300 \times 2 = 12{,}600$. Of the original 24,000 letters there are

   24,000
   –12,600
   11,400 letters remaining

Clerks A, B, and E working together process a total of 3800 letters per hour. It will take them $11{,}400 \div 3{,}800 = 3$ hours to process the remaining letters.

10. **(C)** The job could be performed by 1 worker in 18×26 days $= 468$ days. To perform the job in 12 days would require $468 \div 12 = 39$ workers.

11. **(B)** The shovel excavates 1 cubic yard in 20 seconds.

There are $45 \times 60 = 2700$ seconds in 45 minutes.

In 2700 seconds the shovel can excavate $2700 \div 20 = 135$ cubic yards.

12. **(A)** If 76 gallons are used per hour, it will take $266 \div 76 = 3\frac{1}{2}$ hours to use 266 gallons.

From 9 A.M. to noon is 3 hours; therefore, there is only fuel for $\frac{1}{2}$ hour more.

DISTANCE

1. In distance problems, there are usually three quantities involved: the distance (in miles), the rate (in miles per hour—mph), and the time (in hours).
   a.   To find the distance, multiply the rate by the time.
   Example: A man traveling 40 miles an hour for 3 hours travels 40×3 or 120 miles.
   b.   The rate is the distance traveled in unit time. To find the rate, divide the distance by the time.
   Example: If a car travels 100 miles in 4 hours, the rate is $100 \div 4$, or 25 miles an hour.
   c.   To find the time, divide the distance by the rate.
   Example: If a car travels 150 miles at the rate of 30 miles an hour, the time is $150 \div 30$ or 5 hours.

COMBINED RATES

2. a.   When two people or objects are traveling towards each other, the rate at which they are approaching each other is the sum of their respective rates.
   b.   When two people or objects are traveling in directly opposite directions, the rate at which they are separating is the sum of their respective rates.
3. To solve problems involving combined rates:
   a.   Determine which of the three factors is to be found.
   b.   Combine the rates and find the unknown factor.
   Illustration: A and B are walking towards each other over a road 120 miles long. A walks at a rate of 6 miles an hour, and B walks at a rate of 4 miles an hour. How soon will they meet?
   Solution: The factor to be found is the time.
   Time = distance ÷ rate
   Distance = 120 miles
   Rate = 6 + 4 = 10 miles an hour
   Time = 120 ÷ 10 = 12 hours
   Answer: They will meet in 12 hours.
   Illustration: Joe and Sam are walking in opposite directions. Joe walks at the rate of 5 miles an hour, and Sam walks at the rate of 7 miles an hour. How far apart will they be at the end of 3 hours
   Solution: The factor to be found is distance.
   Distance = time × rate
   Time = 3 hours
   Rate = 5 + 7 = 12 miles an hour
   Distance = 12 × 3 = 36 miles
   Answer: They will be 36 miles apart at the end of 3 hours.
4. To find the time it takes a faster person or object to catch up with a slower person or object:
   a.   Determine how far ahead the slower person or object is.
   b.   Subtract the slower rate from the faster rate to find the gain in rate per unit time.
   c.   Divide the distance that has been gained by the difference in rates.
   Illustration: Two automobiles are traveling along the same road. The first one, which travels at the rate of 30 miles an hour, starts out 6 hours ahead of the second one, which travels at the rate of 50 miles an hour. How long will it take the second one to catch up with the first one?
   Solution: The first automobile starts out 6 hours ahead of the second. Its rate is 30 miles an hour. Therefore, it has traveled 6×30 or 180 miles by the time the second one starts. The second automobile

travels at the rate of 50 miles an hour. Therefore, its gain is 50 – 30, or 20 miles an hour. The second auto has to cover 180 miles. Therefore, it will take 180 ÷ 20, or 9 hours, to catch up with the first automobile.

Answer: It will take the faster auto 9 hours to catch up with the slower one.

AVERAGE OF TWO RATES

5. In some problems, two or more rates must be averaged. When the times are the same for two or more different rates, add the rates and divide by the number of rates.

   Example: If a man travels for 2 hours at 30 miles an hour, at 40 miles an hour for the next 2 hours, and at 50 miles an hour for the next 2 hours, then his average rate for the 6 hours is (30 + 40 + 50) ÷ 3 = 40 miles an hour.

6. When the terms are not the same, but the distances are the same:
   a.   Assume the distance to be a convenient length.
   b.   Find the time at the first rate.
   c.   Find the time at the second rate.
   d.   Find the time at the third rate, if any.
   e.   Add up all the distances and divide by the total time to find the average rate.

   Illustration: A boy travels a certain distance at the rate of 20 miles an hour and returns at the rate of 30 miles an hour. What is his average rate for both trips?

   Solution: The distance is the same for both trips. Assume that it is 60 miles. The time for the first trip is 60 ÷ 20 = 3 hours. The time for the second trip is 60 ÷ 30 = 2 hours. The total distance is 120 miles. The total time is 5 hours. Average rate is 120 ÷ 5 = 24 miles an hour.

   Answer: The average rate is 24 miles an hour.

7. When the times are not the same and the distances are not the same:
   a.   Find the time for the first distance.
   b.   Find the time for the second distance.
   c.   Find the time for the third distance, if any.
   d.   Add up all the distances and divide by the total time to find the average rate.

   Illustration: A man travels 100 miles at 20 miles an hour, 60 miles at 30 miles an hour, and 80 miles at 10 miles an hour.

   The total time is 15 hours. Average rate is 240 ÷ 15 = 16 hours.

   Answer: The average rate for the three trips is 16 miles an hour.

GASOLINE PROBLEMS

8. Problems involving miles per gallon (mpg) of gasoline are solved in the same way as those involving miles per hour. The word "gallon" simply replaces the word "hour."

9. Miles per gallon = distance in miles ÷ no. of gallons

   Example: If a car can travel 100 miles using 4 gallons of gasoline, then its gasoline consumption is 100 ÷ 4, or 25 mpg.

EXERCISE

1. A ten-car train took 6 minutes to travel between two stations that are 3 miles apart. The average speed of the train was
   (A) 20 mph
   (B) 25 mph
   (C) 30 mph
   (D) 35 mph

2. A police car is ordered to report to the scene of a crime 5 miles away. If the car travels at an average rate of 40 miles per hour, the time it will take to reach its destination is
   (A) 3 minutes
   (B) 7.5 minutes
   (C) 10 minutes
   (D) 13.5 minutes

3. If the average speed of a train between two stations is 30 miles per hour and the two stations are $\frac{1}{2}$ mile apart, the time it takes the train to travel from one station to the other is
   (A) 1 minute
   (B) 2 minutes
   (C) 3 minutes
   (D) 4 minutes

4. A car completes a 10-mile trip in 20 minutes. If it does one-half the distance at a speed of 20 miles an hour, its speed for the remainder of the distance must be
   (A) 30 mph
   (B) 40 mph
   (C) 50 mph
   (D) 60 mph

5. An express train leaves one station at 9:02 and arrives at the next station at 9:08. If the distance traveled is $2\frac{1}{2}$ miles, the average speed of the train (mph) is
   (A) 15 mph
   (B) 20 mph
   (C) 25 mph
   (D) 30 mph

6. A motorist averaged 60 miles per hour in going a distance of 240 miles. He made the return trip over the same distance in 6 hours. What was his average speed for the entire trip?
   (A) 40 mph
   (B) 48 mph
   (C) 50 mph
   (D) 60 mph

7. A city has been testing various types of gasoline for economy and efficiency. It has been found that a police radio patrol car can travel 18 miles on a gallon of Brand A gasoline, costing $1.30 a gallon, and 15 miles on a gallon of Brand B gasoline, costing $1.25 a gallon. For a distance of 900 miles, Brand B will cost

(A) $10 more than Brand A
(B) $10 less than Brand A
(C) $100 more than Brand A
(D) the same as Brand A

8. A suspect arrested in New Jersey is being turned over by New Jersey authorities to two New York City police officers for a crime committed in New York City. The New York officers receive their prisoner at a point $18\frac{1}{2}$ miles from their precinct station house, and travel directly toward their destination at an average speed of 40 miles an hour except for a delay of 10 minutes at one point because of a traffic tie-up. The time it should take the officers to reach their destination is, most nearly,

(A) 18 minutes
(B) 22 minutes
(C) 32 minutes
(D) 38 minutes

9. The *Mayflower* sailed from Plymouth, England, to Plymouth Rock, a distance of approximately 2800 miles, in 63 days. The average speed was closest to which one of the following?

(A) $\frac{1}{2}$ mph
(B) 1 mph
(C) 2 mph
(D) 3 mph

10. If a vehicle is to complete a 20-mile trip at an average rate of 30 miles per hour, it must complete the trip in

(A) 20 minutes
(B) 30 minutes
(C) 40 minutes
(D) 50 minutes

11. A car began a trip with 12 gallons of gasoline in the tank and ended with $7\frac{1}{2}$ gallons. The car traveled 17.3 miles for each gallon of gasoline. During the trip, gasoline was bought for $10.00, at a cost of $1.25 per gallon. The total number of miles traveled during this trip was most nearly

(A) 79
(B) 196
(C) 216
(D) 229

12. A man travels a total of 4.2 miles each day to and from work. The traveling consumes 72 minutes each day. Most nearly, how many hours would he save in 129 working days if he moved to another residence so that he would travel only 1.7 miles each day, assuming he travels at the same rate?
    (A) 92.11
    (B) 93.62
    (C) 95.35
    (D) 98.08

13. A man can travel a certain distance at the rate of 25 miles an hour by automobile. He walks back the same distance on foot at the rate of 10 miles an hour. What is his average rate for both trips?
    (A) $14\frac{2}{7}$ mph
    (B) $15\frac{1}{3}$ mph
    (C) $17\frac{1}{2}$ mph
    (D) 35 mph

14. Two trains running on the same track travel at the rates of 25 and 30 miles an hour. If the first train starts out an hour earlier, how long will it take the second train to catch up with it?
    (A) 2 hours
    (B) 3 hours
    (C) 4 hours
    (D) 5 hours

15. Two ships are 1,550 miles apart sailing towards each other. One sails at the rate of 85 miles per day and the other at the rate of 65 miles per day. How far apart will they be at the end of 9 days?
    (A) 180 miles
    (B) 200 miles
    (C) 220 miles
    (D) 240 miles

ANSWER KEY

1. C	3. A	5. C	7. A	9. C	11. C	13. A	15. B
2. B	4. D	6. B	8. D	10. C	12. A	14. D	

EXPLANATIONS

1. **(C)** $6 \text{ min} = \frac{6}{60} \text{ hr} = .1 \text{ hr}$

   Speed (rate) = distance + time

   Speed = $3 \div .1 = 30$ mph

2. **(B)**   Time = distance ÷ rate

   Time = $5 \div 40 = .125$ hr

   $.125 \text{ hr} = .125 \times 60 \text{ min}$

   $= 7.5 \text{ min}$

3. **(A)**   Time = distance ÷ rate

   Time = $\frac{1}{2}$ mi ÷ 30 mph

   $= \frac{1}{60}$ hr

   $\frac{1}{60}$ hr = 1 min

4. **(D)**   First part of trip = $\frac{1}{2}$ of 10 miles

   $= 5$ miles

   Time for first part = $5 \div 20$

   $= \frac{1}{4}$ hour

   $= 15$ minutes

Second part of trip was 5 miles, completed in 20 - 15 minutes, or 5 minutes.

   15 minutes = $\frac{1}{12}$ hour

   Rate = 5 mi ÷ $\frac{1}{12}$ hr

   $= 60$ mph

5. **(C)** Time is 6 minutes, or .1 hour

   Speed = distance ÷ time

   $$= 2\frac{1}{2} \div .1$$

   $$= 2.5 \div .1$$

   $$= 25 \text{ mph}$$

6. **(B)** Time for first 240 mi = 240 ÷ 60

   $$= 4 \text{ hours}$$

   Time for return trip = 6 hours

   Total time for round trip = 10 hours

   Total distance for round trip = 480 mi

   Average rate = 480 mi ÷ 10 hr

   $$= 48 \text{ mph}$$

7. **(A)** Brand A requires 900 ÷ 18 = 50 gal

   50 gal × $1.30 per gal = $65

   Brand B requires 900 ÷ 15 = 60 gal

   60 gal × $1.25 per gal = $75

   $75 – $65 = $10 more than Brand A

8. **(D)** Time = distance ÷ rate

   Time = 18.5 mi ÷ 40 mph

   $$= .4625 \text{ hours}$$

   $$= .4625 \times 60 \text{ minutes}$$

   $$= 27.75 \text{ minutes}$$

   27.75 + 10 = 37.75 minutes

9. **(C)** 63 days = 63 × 24 hours

   = 1512 hours

   Speed = 2800 mi ÷ 1512 hr

   = 1.85 mph

10. **(C)** Time = 20 mi ÷ 30 mph

   $= \frac{2}{3}$ hr

   $\frac{2}{3}$ hr = $\frac{2}{3}$ × 60 min = 40 min

11. **(C)** The car used

   $12 - 7\frac{1}{2} = 4\frac{1}{2}$ gal, plus

   $10.00 ÷ $1.25 per gal = 8 gal,

   for a total of $12\frac{1}{2}$ gal or 12.5 gal used

   12.5 gal × 17.3 mpg = 216.25 mi

12. **(A)** 72 min = $\frac{72}{60}$ hr = 1.2 hr

   Rate = 4.2 mi ÷ 1.2 hr = 3.5 mph

   At this rate it would take 1.7 mi + 3.5 mph

   = .486 hours (approx.) to travel 1.7 miles.

   The daily savings in time is

   1.2 hr − .486 hr = .714 hr

   .714 hr × 129 days = 92.106 hr

13. **(A)** Assume a convenient distance, Say, 50 mi.

   Time by automobile = 50 mi ÷ 25 mph

   = 2 hr

   Time walking = 50 mi ÷ 10 mph

   = 5 hr

$$\text{Total time} = 7 \text{ hours}$$

$$\text{Total distance} = 100 \text{ mi}$$

$$\text{Average rate} = 100 \text{ mi} \div 7 \text{ hr}$$

$$= 14\tfrac{2}{7} \text{ mph}$$

14. **(D)** 30 mi – 25 mi = 5 mi gain per 1 hr

During first hour, the first train travels 25 miles.

25 mi ÷ 5 mph = 5 hr

15. **(B)** 85 mi × 9 days = 765 mi
65 mi × 9 days = 585 mi
1350 mi

1,550 mi – 1,350 mi = 200 miles apart at end of 9 days.

INTEREST

1. **Interest (I)** is the price paid for the use of money. There are three items considered in interest:
   a. The **principal (p)** is the amount of money bearing interest.
   b. The **interest rate (r)** is expressed in percent on an annual basis.
   c. The **time (t)** during which the principal is used, expressed in terms of a year.
2. The basic formulas used in interest problems are:
   a. $I = prt$
   b. $p = \dfrac{I}{rt}$
   c. $r = \dfrac{I}{pt}$
   d. $t = \dfrac{I}{pr}$
3. a. For most interest problems, the year is considered to have 360 days. Months are considered to have 30 days, unless a particular month is specified.
   b. To use the interest formulas, time must be expressed as part of a year.

   Examples: 5 months = $\dfrac{5}{12}$ year

   36 days = $\dfrac{36}{360}$ year, or $\dfrac{1}{10}$ year

   1 year 3 months = $\dfrac{15}{12}$ year

   c. In reference to time, the prefix "semi" means "every half." The prefix "bi" means "every two."
   Examples: Semiannually means every half-year (every 6 months).
   Biannually means every 2 years.
   Semimonthly means every half-month (every 15 days, unless the month is specified).
   Biweekly means every 2 weeks (every 14 days).

4. There are two types of interest problems:
   a. **Simple interest,** in which the interest is calculated only once over a given period of time.
   b. **Compound interest,** in which interest is recalculated at given time periods based on previously earned interest.

SIMPLE INTEREST

5. To find the interest when the principal, rate, and time are given:
   a. Change the rate of interest to a fraction.
   b. Express the time as a fractional part of a year.
   c. Multiply all three items.
      Illustration: Find the interest on $400 at 11 1/4% for 3 months and 16 days.
      Solution:

      $11 \frac{1}{4}\% = \frac{45}{4}\% = \frac{45}{400}$

      3 months and 16 days = 106 days
      (30 days per month)

      $106 \text{ days} = \frac{106}{360}$ of a year $= \frac{53}{180}$ year
      (360 days per year)

      $^1 400 \times \frac{^1 45}{_1 400} \times \frac{53}{100_4} \quad \frac{53}{4}$

      Answer: Interest = $13.25

6. To find the principal if the interest, interest rate, and time are given:
   a. Change the interest rate to a fraction.
   b. Express the time as a fractional part of a year.
   c. Multiply the rate by the time.
   d. Divide the interest by this product.
      Illustration: What amount of money invested at 6% would receive interest of $18 over 1[1/2] years?
      Solution:

      $$6\% = \frac{6}{100}$$

      $$1\frac{1}{2} \text{ years} = \frac{3}{2} \text{ years}$$

      $$\frac{^3 6}{100} \times \frac{3}{2_1} = \frac{9}{100}$$

      $$\$18 \div \frac{9}{100} = {}^2 \$18 \times \frac{100}{9_1}$$

      $$= \$200$$

      Answer: Principal = $200

7. To find the rate if the principal, time, and interest are given:
   a. Change the time to a fractional part of a year.
   b. Multiply the principal by the time.
   c. Divide the interest by this product.
   d. Convert to a percent.
      Illustration: At what interest rate should $300 be invested for 40 days to accrue $2 in interest?
      Solution:

$$40 \text{ days} = \frac{40}{360} \text{ of a year}$$

$$^5 300 \times \frac{\overset{20}{40}}{\underset{6\ 3}{30}} = \frac{100}{3}$$

$$\$2 \div \frac{100}{3} = {}^{1}2 \times \frac{3}{100 \ 50}$$

$$= \frac{3}{50}$$

$$\frac{3}{50} = 6\%$$

Answer: Interest rate = 6%

8. To find the time (in years) if the principal, interest, and interest rate are given:
   a. Change the interest rate to a fraction (or decimal).
   b. Multiply the principal by the rate.
   c. Divide the interest by this product.
      Illustration: Find the length of time for which $240 must be invested at 5% to accrue $16 in interest.

Solution:
$$5\% = .05$$
$$240 \times .05 = 12$$
$$16 \div 12 = 1 \tfrac{1}{3}$$

Answer: $\qquad\qquad$ Time = $1 \tfrac{1}{3}$ years

COMPOUND INTEREST

9. Interest may be computed on a compound basis; that is, the interest at the end of a certain period (half year, full year, or whatever time stipulated) is added to the principal for the next period. The interest is then computed on the new increased principal, and for the next period the interest is again computed on the new increased principal. Since the principal constantly increases, compound interest yields more than simple interest.

10. $\quad$ To find the compound interest when given the principal, the rate, and time period:
   a. Calculate the interest as for simple interest problems, using the period of compounding for the time.
   b. Add the interest to the principal.
   c. Calculate the interest on the new principal over the period of compounding.
   d. Add this interest to form a new principal.
   e. Continue the same procedure until all periods required have been accounted for.
   f. Subtract the original principal from the final principal to find the compound interest.

   Illustration: Find the amount that $200 will become if compounded semiannually at 8% for $1 \tfrac{1}{2}$ years.

   Solution: Since it is to be compounded semiannually for $1 \tfrac{1}{2}$ years, the interest will have to be computed 3 times:

Interest for the first period:	$.08 \times \tfrac{1}{2} \times \$200 = \$8$
First new principal:	$\$200 + \$8 = \$208$

Interest for the second period:	$.08 \times \frac{1}{2} \times \$208 = \$8.32$
Second new principal:	$\$208 + \$8.32 = \$216.32$
Interest for the third period:	$.08 \times \frac{1}{2} \times \$216.32 = \$8.6528$
Final principal:	$\$216.32 + \$8.6528 = \$224.9728$

Answer: $224.97 to the nearest cent

BANK DISCOUNTS

11. A promissory note is a commitment to pay a certain amount of money on a given date, called the date of maturity.

12. When a promissory note is cashed by a bank in advance of its date of maturity, the bank deducts a discount from the principal and pays the rest to the depositor.

13. To find the bank discount:

  a. Find the time between the date the note is deposited and its date of maturity, and express this time as a fractional part of a year.

  b. Change the rate to a fraction.

  c. Multiply the principal by the time and the rate to find the bank discount.

  d. If required, subtract the bank discount from the original principal to find the amount the bank will pay the depositor.

Illustration: A $400 note drawn up on August 12, 1980, for 90 days is deposited at the bank on September 17, 1980. The bank charges a $6\frac{1}{2}$% discount on notes. How much will the depositor receive?

Solution: From August 12, 1980, to September 17, 1980, is 36 days. This means that the note has 54 days to run.

$$54 \text{ days} = \frac{54}{360} \text{ of a year}$$

$$6\frac{1}{2}\% = \frac{13}{2}\% = \frac{13}{200}$$

$$\$400 \times \frac{13}{200} \times \frac{54}{360} = \frac{39}{10}$$

$$= \$3.90$$

$$\$400 - \$3.90 = \$396.10$$

Answer: The depositor will receive $396.10

EXERCISE

1. What is the simple interest on $460 for 2 years at $8\frac{1}{2}$%?
    - (A) $46.00
    - (B) $52.75
    - (C) $78.20
    - (D) $96.00

2. For borrowing $300 for one month, a man was charged $6. The rate of interest was
    - (A) $\frac{1}{5}$%
    - (B) 12%
    - (C) 24%
    - (D) 2%

3. At a simple interest rate of 5% a year, the principal that will give $12.50 interest in 6 months is
    - (A) $250
    - (B) $500
    - (C) $625
    - (D) $650

4. Find the interest on $480 at $10\frac{1}{2}$% for 2 months and 15 days.
    - (A) $9.50
    - (B) $10.50
    - (C) $13.25
    - (D) $14.25

5. The interest on $300 at 6% for 10 days is
    - (A) $ .50
    - (B) $1.50
    - (C) $2.50
    - (D) $5.50

6. The scholarship board of a certain college lent a student $200 at an annual rate of 6% from September 30 until December 15. To repay the loan and accumulated interest the student must give the college an amount closest to which one of the following?
    - (A) $202.50
    - (B) $203.00
    - (C) $203.50
    - (D) $212.00

7. If $300 is invested at simple interest so as to yield a return of $18 in 9 months, the amount of money that must be invested at the same rate of interest so as to yield a return of $120 in 6 months is
    - (A) $3000
    - (B) $3300
    - (C) $2000
    - (D) $2300

8. When the principal is $600, the difference in one year between simple interest at 12% per annum and interest compounded semiannually at 12% per annum is
    (A) $2.16
    (B) $21.60
    (C) $ 0.22
    (D) $0.00

9. What is the compound interest on $600, compounded quarterly, at 6% for 9 months?
    (A) $27.38
    (B) $27.40
    (C) $27.41
    (D) $27.42

10. A 90-day note for $1200 is signed on May 12. Seventy-five days later the note is deposited at a bank that charges 8% discount on notes. The bank discount is
    (A) $8.40
    (B) $2.60
    (C) $2.00
    (D) $4.00

ANSWER KEY

1. C   3. B   5. A   6. A   7. A   8. A   9. C   10. D
2. C   4. B

EXPLANATIONS

1. **(C)**   Principal = $460

     Rate = $8\frac{1}{2}\% = .085$

     Time = 2 years

     Interest = $460 \times .085 \times 2$

     = $78.20

2. **(C)**   Principal = $300

     Interest = $6

     Time = $\frac{1}{12}$ year

     $300 \times \frac{1}{12} = $25

     $6 \div $25 = .24 = 24\%$

3. **(B)**   Rate = $5\% = .05$

     Interest = $12.50

     Time = $\frac{1}{2}$ year

     $.05 \times \frac{1}{2} = .025$

     $12.50 \div .025 = $500.00

4. **(B)**   Time: 2 months 15 days

     = 75 days or $\frac{75}{360}$ of a year.

     Rate: $10\frac{1}{2}\% = 2\frac{1}{2}\% = \frac{21}{200}$

     Interest: $480 \times \frac{21}{200} \times \frac{75}{360}$

     = $2\frac{1}{2}$ = $10.50

5. **(A)**   Principal = $300

     Rate = $.06 = \frac{6}{100}$

$$\text{Time} = \frac{10}{360} = \frac{1}{36}$$

$$\text{Interest} = {}^{3}\ \$300 \times \frac{{}^{1}\ 6}{{}_{1}\ 100} \times \frac{1}{{}_{6}\ 36}$$

$$= \frac{3}{6} = \$.50$$

6. **(A)** Principal = $200

Rate = .06 = $\frac{6}{100}$

Time from September 30 until December 15 is 76 days. (31 days in October, 30 days in November, 15 days in December)

76 days = $\frac{76}{360}$ year

$$\text{Interest} = {}^{2}\ \$200 \times \frac{{}^{1}\ 6}{{}_{1}\ 100} \times \frac{76}{300\ {}_{60}}$$

$$= \$\frac{152}{60} = \$2.53$$

$200 + $2.53 = $202.53

7. **(A)** Principal = $300

Interest = $18

Time = $\frac{9}{12}$ years = $\frac{3}{4}$ year 12

$300 × $\frac{3}{4}$ = $225

$18 ÷ $225 = .08

Rate is 8%

To yield $120 at 8% in 6 months,

Interest = $120

Rate = .08

Time = $\frac{1}{2}$ year

.08 × $\frac{1}{2}$ = .04

$120 ÷ .04 = $3000 must be invested

8. **(A)** Simple interest:

Principal = $600

Rate = .12

Time = 1

Interest = $600 × .12 × 1

= $72.00

Compound interest:

$$\text{Principal} = \$600$$

$$\text{Period of compounding} = \tfrac{1}{2} \text{ year}$$

$$\text{Rate} = .12$$

For the first period,

$$\text{Interest} = \$600 \times .12 \times \tfrac{1}{2}$$

$$\text{New principal} = \$600 + \$36$$

$$= \$636$$

For the second period,

$$\text{Interest} = \$636 \times .12 \times \tfrac{1}{2}$$

$$= \$38.16$$

$$\text{New principal} = \$636 + \$38.16$$

$$= \$674.16$$

$$\text{Total interest} = \$74.16$$

$$\text{Difference} = \$74.16 - 72.00$$

$$= \$2.16$$

9. **(C)**

$$\text{Principal} = \$600$$

$$\text{Rate} = 6\% = \tfrac{6}{100}$$

$$\text{Time (period of} = \tfrac{3}{12} \text{ year} = \tfrac{1}{4} \text{ year compounding)}$$

In 9 months, the interest will be computed 3 times.

For first quarter,

$$\text{Interest} = \$600 \times \tfrac{6}{100} \times \tfrac{1}{4}$$

New principal at end of first quarter:

$$\$600 + \$9 = \$609$$

For second quarter,

$$\text{Interest} = \$609 \times \tfrac{6}{100} \times \tfrac{1}{4}$$

$$= \$\tfrac{3654}{400} = 9.135, \text{ or } \$9.14$$

New principal at end of second quarter:

$$\$609 + \$9.14 = \$618.14$$

For third quarter,

$$\text{Interest} = \$618.14 \times \tfrac{6}{100} \times \tfrac{1}{4}$$

$$= \$ \tfrac{3708.84}{400}$$

$$= \$9.27$$

Total interest for the 3 quarters:

$$\$9 + \$9.14 + \$9.27 = \$27.41$$

10.　　　　　　　　**(D)**　Principal = \$1200

$$\text{Time} = 90 \text{ days - } 75 \text{ days}$$

$$= 15 \text{ days}$$

$$15 \text{ days} = \tfrac{15}{360} \text{ year}$$

$$\text{Rate} = 8\% = \tfrac{8}{100}$$

$$\text{Bank Discount} = {}^{12}\,\$1200 \times \tfrac{8}{100}{}_{1} \times \tfrac{15}{360}{}_{45}$$

$$= \$ \tfrac{180}{45} = \$4$$

TAXATION

1. The following facts should be considered when computing taxation problems:
   a.　Taxes may be expressed as a percent or in terms of money based on a vermin denomination.
   b.　A *surtax* is an additional tax imposed above the regular tax rate.
2. In taxation there are usually three items involved: the amount taxable, called the base, the tax rate, and the tax itself.
3. To find the tax when given the base and the tax rate in percent:
   a.　Change the tax rate to a decimal.
   b.　Multiply the base by the tax rate.
   　　Illustration: How much would be realized on \$4000 if taxed 15%?
   　　Solution: 15% =. 15
   　　\$4000 × .15 = \$600
   　　Answer: Tax = \$600
4. To find the tax rate in percent form when given the base and the tax:
   a.　Divide the tax by the base.
   b.　Convert to a percent.
   　　Illustration: Find the tax rate at which \$5600 would yield \$784.
   　　Solution: \$784 ÷ \$5600 =.14
   　　.14 = 14%
   Answer: Tax rate = 14%
5. To find the base when given the tax rate and the tax:
   a.　Change the tax rate to a decimal.
   b.　Divide the tax by the tax rate.

Illustration: What amount of money taxed 3% would yield $75?

Solution: 3% = .03

$75 ÷ .03 = $2500

Answer: Base = $2500

6. When the tax rate is fixed and expressed in terms of money, take into consideration the denomination upon which it is based; that is, whether it is based on every $100, or $1000, etc.

7. To find the tax when given the base and the tax rate in terms of money:

    a.   Divide the base by the denomination upon which the tax rate is based.

    b.   Multiply this quotient by the tax rate.

    Illustration: If the tax rate is $3.60 per $1000, find the tax on $470,500.

    Solution: $470,500 ÷ $1000 = 470.5

    470.5 × $3.60 = $1,693.80

    Answer: $1,693.80

8. To find the tax rate based on a certain denomination when given the base and the tax derived:

    a.   Divide the base by the denomination indicated.

    b.   Divide the tax by this quotient.

    Illustration: Find the tax rate per $100 that would be required to raise $350,000 on $2,000,000 of taxable property.

    Solution: $2,000,000 ÷ $100 = 20,000

    $350,000 ÷ 20,000 = $17.50

    Answer: Tax rate = $17.50 per $100

9. Since a surtax is an additional tax besides the regular tax, to find the total tax:

    a.   Change the regular tax rate to a decimal.

    b.   Multiply the base by the regular tax rate.

    c.   Change the surtax rate to a decimal.

    d.   Multiply the base by the surtax rate.

    e.   Add both taxes.

    Illustration: Assuming that the tax rate is $2\frac{1}{3}$% on liquors costing up to $3.00, and 3% on those costing from $3.00 to $6.00, and $3\frac{1}{2}$% on those from $6.00 to $10.00, what would be the tax on a bottle costing $8.00 if there is a surtax of 5% on all liquors above $5.00?

    Solution: An $8.00 bottle falls within the category of $6.00 to $10.00. The tax rate on such a bottle is

    $3\frac{1}{2}$ = .035

    $8.00 × .035 = $.28

    surtax rate = 5% = .05

    $8.00 × .05 = $.40

    $.28 + $.40 = $.68

    Answer: Total tax = $.68

EXERCISE

1. Mr. Jones' income for a year is $15,000. He pays $2250 for income taxes. The percent of his income that he pays for income taxes is

    (A) 9

    (B) 12

    (C) 15

    (D) 22

2. If the tax rate is $3\frac{1}{2}\%$ and the amount to be raised is $64.40, what is the base?
    (A) $1800
    (B) $1840
    (C) $1850
    (D) $1860

3. What is the tax rate per $1000 if a base of $338,500 would yield $616.07?
    (A) $1.80
    (B) $1.90
    (C) $1.95
    (D) $1.82

4. A man buys an electric light bulb for 54¢, which includes a 20% tax. What is the cost of the bulb without tax?
    (A) 43¢
    (B) 44¢
    (C) 45¢
    (D) 46¢

5. What tax rate on a base of $3650 would raise $164.25?
    (A) 4%
    (B) 5%
    (C) $4\frac{1}{2}\%$
    (D) $5\frac{1}{2}\%$

6. A piece of property is assessed at $22,850 and the tax rate is $4.80 per thousand. What is the amount of tax that must be paid on the property?
    (A) $109
    (B) $112
    (C) $109.68
    (D) $112.68

7. $30,000 worth of land is assessed at 120% of its value. If the tax rate is $5.12 per $1000 assessed valuation, the amount of tax to be paid is
    (A) $180.29
    (B) $184.32
    (C) $190.10
    (D) $192.29

8. Of the following real estate tax rates, which is the largest?
    (A) $31.25 per $1000
    (B) $3.45 per $100
    (C) 32¢ per $10
    (D) 3¢ per $1

9. A certain community needs $185,090.62 to cover its expenses. If its tax rate is $1.43 per $100 of assessed valuation, what must be the assessed value of its property?
   (A) $12,900,005
   (B) $12,943,400
   (C) $12,940,000
   (D) $12,840,535

10. A man's taxable income is $14,280. The state tax instructions tell him to pay 2% on the first $3000 of his taxable income, 3% on each of the second and third $3000, and 4% on the remainder. What is the total amount of income tax that he must pay?
    (A) $265.40
    (B) $309.32
    (C) $451.20
    (D) $454.62

ANSWER KEY

1. C   3. D   5. C   6. C   7. B   8. B   9. B   10. C
2. B   4. C

EXPLANATIONS

1. **(C)**   Tax = $2250

      Base = $15,000

    Tax rate = Tax ÷ Base

    Tax rate = $2250 ÷ $15,000 = .15

    Tax rate = .15 = 15%

2. **(B)**   Tax rate = $3 \frac{1}{2}\% = .0352$

      Tax = $64.40

      Base = Tax ÷ Tax rate

      Base = $64.40 ÷ .035

          = $1840

3. **(D)**   Base = $338,500

      Tax = $616.07

   Denomination = $1000

  $338,500 ÷ $1000 = 338.50

  $616.07 ÷ 338.50 = $1.82 per $1000

4. **(C)**   54¢ is 120% of the base (cost without tax)

      Base = 54 ÷ 120%

          = 4 ÷1.20

          = 45¢

5. **(C)**   Base = $3650

      Tax = $164.25

    Tax rate = Tax ÷ Base

          = $164.25 ÷ $3650

          = .045

          = $4 \frac{1}{2}\%$

6. **(C)** Base = $22,850

Denomination = $1000

Tax rate = $4.80 per thousand

$$\frac{\$22,850}{\$1000} = 22.85$$

$22.85 \times \$4.80 = \$109.68$

7. **(B)** Base = Assessed valuation

= 120% of $30,000

= $1.20 \times \$30,000$

= $36,000

Denomination = $1000

Tax rate = $5.12 per thousand

$$\frac{\$36,000}{\$1000} = 36$$

$36 \times \$5.12 = \$184.32$

8. **(B)** Express each tax rate as a decimal:

$31.25 per $1000 = $\frac{31.25}{1000}$ = .03125

$3.45 per $100 = $\frac{3.45}{100}$ = 0345

32¢ per $10 = $\frac{.32}{10}$ = .0320

3¢ per $1 = $\frac{.03}{1}$ = .0300

The largest decimal is .0345.

9. **(B)** Tax rate = $1.43 per $100

= $\frac{1.43}{100}$ = .0143

= 1.43%

Tax = $185,090.62

Base = Tax ÷ Tax rate

= 185,090.62 ÷ .0143

= $12,943,400

10. **(C)**

First $3000:	.02 × $3000 = $60.00
Second $3000:	.03 × $3000 = $90.00
Third $3000:	.03 × $3000 = $90.00
Remainder	
($14,280 − $9000):	.04 × $5280 = $211.20
	Total tax = $451.20

PROFIT AND LOSS

1. The following terms may be encountered in profit and loss problems:
   a. The *cost price* of an article is the price paid by a person who wishes to sell it again.
   b. There may be an *allowance* or *trade discount* on the cost price.
   c. The *list price* or *marked price* is the price at which the article is listed or marked to be sold.
   d. There may be a *discount* or *series of discounts* on the list price.
   e. The *selling price* or *sales price* is the price at which the article is finally sold.
   f. If the selling price is greater than the cost price, there has been a *profit.*
   g. If the selling price is lower than the cost price, there has been a *loss.*
   h. If the article is sold at the same price as the cost, there has been no loss or profit.
   i. Profit or loss may be based either on the cost price or on the selling price.
   j. Profit or loss may be stated in terms of dollars and cents, or in terms of percent.
   k. *Overhead* expenses include such items as rent, salaries, etc. Overhead expenses may be added to cost price to determine total cost when calculating profit or assigning selling price.

2. The basic formulas used in profit and loss problems are:
   Selling price = cost price + profit
   Selling price = cost price – loss
   Example: If the cost of an article is $2.50, and the profit is $1.50, then the selling price is $2.50 + $1.50 = $4.00.
   Example: If the cost of an article is $3.00, and the loss is $1.20, then the selling price is $3.00 – $1.20 = $1.80.

3. a. To find the profit in terms of money, subtract the cost price from the selling price, or selling price – cost price = profit.
   Example: If an article costing $3.00 is sold for $5.00, the profit is $5.00 – $3.00 = $2.00.
   b. To find the loss in terms of money, subtract the selling price from the cost price, or: cost price – selling price = loss.
   Example: If an article costing $2.00 is sold for $1.50, the loss is $2.00 – $1.50 = $.50.

4. To find the selling price if the profit or loss is expressed in percent based on cost price:
   a. Multiply the cost price by the percent of profit or loss to find the profit or loss in terms of money.
   b. Add this product to the cost price if a profit is involved, or subtract for a loss.
   Illustration: Find the selling price of an article costing $3.00 that was sold at a profit of 15% of the cost price.
   Solution: 15% of $3.00 = .15 × $3.00
   = $.45 profit
   $3.00 + $.45 = $3.45
   Answer: Selling price = $3.45
   Illustration: If an article costing $2.00 is sold at a loss of 5% of the cost price, find the selling price.
   Solution: 5% of $2.00 = .05 × $2.00
   = $.10 loss
   $2.00 – $.10 = $1.90
   Answer: Selling price = $1.90

5. To find the cost price when given the selling price and the percent of profit or loss based on the selling price:
   a. Multiply the selling price by the percent of profit or loss to find the profit or loss in terms of money.

b.   Subtract this product from the selling price if profit, or add the product to the selling price if a loss.

Illustration: If an article sells for $12.00 and there has been a profit of 10% of the selling price, what is the cost price?

Solution: 10% of $12.00 = .10 × $12.00

= $1.20 profit

$12.00 − $1.20 = $10.80

Answer: Cost price = $10.80

Illustration: What is the cost price of an article selling for $2.00 on which there has been a loss of 6% of the selling price?

Solution: 6% of $2.00 = .06 × $2.00

= $.12 loss

$2.00 + $.12 = $2.12

Answer: Cost price = $2.12

6. To find the percent of profit or percent of loss based on cost price:

a.   Find the profit or loss in terms of money.

b.   Divide the profit or loss by the cost price.

c.   Convert to a percent.

Illustration: Find the percent of profit based on cost price of an article costing $2.50 and selling for $3.00.

Solution: $3.00 − $2.50 = $.50 profit

$$2.50 \overline{)\,.50\,} = 250 \overline{)\,50.00\,}^{\,.20}$$

.20 = 20%

Answer: Profit = 20%

Illustration: Find the percent of loss based on cost price of an article costing $5.00 and selling for $4.80.

Solution: $5.00 − $4.80 = $.20 loss

$$5.00 \overline{)\,.20\,} = 500 \overline{)\,20.00\,}^{\,.04}$$

.04 = 4%

Answer: Loss = 4%

7. To find the percent of profit or percent of loss on selling price:

a.   Find the profit or loss in terms of money.

b.   Divide the profit or loss by the selling price.

c.   Convert to a percent.

Illustration: Find the percent of profit based on the selling price of an article costing $2.50 and selling for $3.00.

Solution: $3.00 - $2.50 = $.50 profit

$$3.00 \overline{)\,.50\,} = 300 \overline{)\,50.00\,} = .16\tfrac{2}{3}$$

Answer: Profit = $16 \tfrac{2}{3}$%

Illustration: Find the percent of loss based on the selling price of an article costing $5.00 and selling for $4.80.

Solution: $5.00 − $4.80 = $.20 loss

$$4.80\,\overline{)\,.20\,} = 480\,\overline{)\,20.00\,} = .04\tfrac{1}{6}$$

Answer: Loss = $4\tfrac{1}{6}\%$

8. To find the cost price when given the selling price and the percent of profit based on the cost price:
   a.　Establish a relation between the selling price and the cost price.
   b.　Solve to find the cost price.
   Illustration: An article is sold for $2.50, which is a 25% profit of the cost price. What is the cost price?
   Solution: Since the selling price represents the whole cost price plus 25% of the cost price,

$$2.50 = 125\% \text{ of the cost price}$$
$$2.50 = 1.25 \text{ of the cost price}$$
$$\text{Cost price} = 2.50 \div 1.25$$
$$= 2.00$$

   Answer:　Cost price = $2.00

9. To find the selling price when given the profit based on the selling price:
   a.　Establish a relation between the selling price and the cost price.
   b.　Solve to find the selling price.
   Illustration: A merchant buys an article for $27.00 and sells it at a profit of 10% of the selling price. What is the selling price?
   Solution: $27.00 + profit = selling price
   Since the profit is 10% of the selling price, the cost price must be 90% of the selling price.

$$27.00 = 90\% \text{ of the selling price}$$
$$= .90 \text{ of the selling price}$$
$$\text{Selling price} = 27.00 \div .90$$
$$= 30.00$$

   Answer: Selling price = $30.00

TRADE DISCOUNTS

10.　　A *trade discount,* usually expressed in percent, indicates the part that is to be deducted from the list price.
11.　　To find the selling price when given the list price and the trade discount:
   a.　Multiply the list price by the percent of discount to find the discount in terms of money.
   b.　Subtract the discount from the list price.
   Illustration: The list price of an article is $20.00. There is a discount of 5%. What is the selling price?
   Solution: $20.00 × 5% = 20.00 × .05 = $1.00 discount
   　　　$20.00 − $1.00 = $19.00
   Answer:　Selling price = $19.00
   　　　An alternate method of solving the above problem is to consider the list price to be 100%. Then, if the discount is 5%, the selling price is 100% − 5% = 95% of the list price. The selling price is

$$95\% \text{ of } \$20.00 = .95 \times \$20.00$$
$$= \$19.00$$

SERIES OF DISCOUNTS

12.   There may be more than one discount to be deducted from the list price. These are called a *discount series.*

13.   To find the selling price when given the list price and a discount series:

a.   Multiply the list price by the first percent of discount.

b.   Subtract this product from the list price.

c.   Multiply the difference by the second discount.

d.   Subtract this product from the difference. Continue the same procedure if there are more discounts.

Illustration: Find the selling price of an article listed at $10.00 on which there are discounts of 20% and 10%.

Solution: $\$10.00 \times 20\% = 10.00 \times .20 = \$2.00$

$\$10.00 - \$2.00 = \$8.00$

$\$8.00 \times 10\% = 8.00 \times .10 = \$.80$

$\$8.00 - \$.80 = \$7.20$

Answer: Selling price = $7.20

14.   Instead of deducting each discount individually, it is often more practical to find the single equivalent discount first and then deduct. It does not matter in which order the discounts are taken.

15.   The single equivalent discount may be found by assuming a list price of 100%. Leave all discounts in percent form.

a.   Subtract the first discount from 100%, giving the net cost factor (NCF) had there been only one discount.

b.   Multiply the NCF by the second discount. Subtract the product from the NCF, giving a second NCF that reflects both discounts.

c.   If there is a third discount, multiply the second NCF by it and subtract the product from the second NCF, giving a third NCF that reflects all three discounts.

d.   If there are more discounts, repeat the process.

e.   Subtract the final NCF from 100% to find the single equivalent discount.

Illustration: Find the single equivalent discount of 20%, 25%, and 10%.

Solution:

                    100%

                   − 20% first discount

                   80% first NCF

− 25% of 80% =   20%

                   60% second NCF

− 10% of 60% =   6%

                   54% third NCF

100% − 54% = 46% single equivalent discount

Answer: 46%

Illustration: An article lists at $750.00. With discounts of 20%, 25%, and 10%, what is the selling price of this article?

Solution: As shown above, the single equivalent discount of 20%, 25%, and 10% is 46%.

      46% of $750 = $.46 \times \$750$

                 = $345

    $750 − $345 = $405

Answer: Selling price = $405

EXERCISE

1. Dresses are sold at $65.00 each. The dresses cost $50.00 each. The percentage of increase of the selling price over the cost is
    (A) 40
    (B) $33 \frac{1}{3}$
    (C) $33 \frac{1}{2}$
    (D) 30

2. A dealer bought a ladder for $27.00. What must it be sold for if he wishes to make a profit of 40% on the selling price?
    (A) $38.80
    (B) $43.20
    (C) $45.00
    (D) $67.50

3. A typewriter was listed at $120.00 and was bought for $96.00. What was the rate of discount?
    (A) $16 \frac{2}{3} \%$
    (B) 20%
    (C) 24%
    (D) 25%

4. A dealer sells an article at a loss of 50% of the cost. Based on the selling price, the loss is
    (A) 25%
    (B) 50%
    (C) 100%
    (D) none of these

5. What would be the marked price of an article if the cost was $12.60 and the gain was 10% of the cost price?
    (A) $11.34
    (B) $12.72
    (C) $13.86
    (D) $14.28

6. A stationer buys note pads at $.75 per dozen and sells them at 25 cents apiece. The profit based on the cost is
    (A) 50%
    (B) 300%
    (C) 200%
    (D) 100%

7. An article costing $18 is to be sold at a profit of 10% of the selling price. The selling price will be:
   (A) $19.80
   (B) $36.00
   (C) $18.18
   (D) $20.00

8. A calculating machine company offered to sell a city agency 4 calculating machines at a discount of 15% from the list price, and to allow the agency $85 for each of two old machines being traded in. The list price of the new machines is $625 per machine. If the city agency accepts this offer, the amount of money it will have to provide for the purchase of these 4 machines is
   (A) $1785
   (B) $2295
   (C) $1955
   (D) $1836

9. Pencils are purchased at $9 per gross and sold at 6 for 75 cents. The rate of profit based on the selling price is
   (A) 100%
   (B) 67%
   (C) 50%
   (D) 25%

10. The single equivalent discount of 20% and 10% is
    (A) 15%
    (B) 28%
    (C) 18%
    (D) 30%

ANSWER KEY

1. D   3. B   5. C   6. B   7. D   8. C   9. C   10. B
2. C   4. C

EXPLANATIONS

1. **(D)** Selling price – cost = $65 – $50

$$= \$15$$

$$\frac{\$15}{\$50} = .30 = 30\%$$

2. **(C)** Cost price = 60% of selling price, since the profit is 40% of the selling price, and the whole selling price is 100%.

$$\$27 = 60\% \text{ of selling price}$$

$$\text{Selling price} = \$27 \div 60\%$$

$$= \$27 \div .6$$

$$= \$45$$

3. **(B)** The discount was $120 – $96 = $24

$$\text{Rate of discount} = \frac{\$24}{\$120} = .20$$

$$= 20\%$$

4. **(C)** Loss = cost – selling price.

Considering the cost to be 100% of itself, if the loss is 50% of the cost, the selling price is also 50% of the cost. (50% = 100% – 50%)

Since the loss and the selling price are therefore the same, the loss is 100% of the selling price.

5. **(C)** Gain (profit) = 10% of $12.60

$$= .10 \times \$12.60$$

$$= \$1.26$$

$$\text{Selling price} = \text{cost} + \text{profit}$$

$$= \$12.60 + \$1.26$$

$$= \$13.86$$

6. **(B)** Each dozen note pads cost $.75 and are sold for

$$12 \times \$.25 = \$3.00$$

The profit is $3.00 – $.75 = $2.25

$$\text{Profit based on cost} = \frac{\$2.25}{\$.75}$$

$$= 3$$

$$= 300\%$$

7. **(D)** If profit = 10% of selling price,

then cost = 90% of selling price

$18 = 90%$ of selling price

Selling price = $18 \div 90\%$

$$= \$18 \div .90$$

$$= \$20$$

8. **(C)** Discount for each new machine:

15% of $625 = $.15 \times \$625$

$$= \$93.75$$

Each new machine will cost

$625 - $93.75 = \$531.25$

Four new machines will cost

$531.25 \times 4 = \$2125$

But there is an allowance of $85 each for 2 old machines:

$85 \times 2 = 170$

Final cost to city:

$2125 - $170 = \$1955$

9. **(C)**   1 gross = 144 units

Selling price for 6 pencils = $.75

$$\text{Selling price for 1 pencil} = \frac{\$.75}{6}$$

$$\text{Selling price for 1 gross of pencils} = \frac{\$.75}{6_1} \times 144_{24}$$

$$= \$18.00$$

Cost for 1 gross of pencils = $9.00

Profit for 1 gross of pencils = $18.00 - \$9.00$

$$= \$9.00$$

$$\frac{\text{profit}}{\text{selling price}} = \frac{\$9.00}{\$18.00}$$

$$= .5 = 50\%$$

10. **(B)** 100%
                 − 20%
                  80%

− 10% of 80% = − 8%
                 72%

100% − 72% = 28% single equivalent discount

PAYROLL

1. *Salaries* are computed over various time periods: hourly, daily, weekly, biweekly (every 2 weeks), semimonthly (twice each month), monthly, and yearly.

2. *Overtime* is usually computed as "time and a half;" that is, each hour in excess of the number of hours in the standard workday or workweek is paid at $1\frac{1}{2}$ times the regular hourly rate. Some companies pay "double time," twice the regular hourly rate, for work on Sundays and holidays.

   Illustration: An employee is paid weekly, based on a 40-hour workweek, with time and a half for overtime. If the employee's regular hourly rate is $4.50, how much will he earn for working 47 hours in one week?

   Solution: Overtime hours = 47 − 40 = 7 hours

   Overtime pay = $1\frac{1}{2}$ × $4.50 = $6.75 per hour

   Overtime pay for 7 hours: 7 × $6.75 = $47.25
   Regular pay for 40 hours: 40 × $4.50 = $180.00
                  Total pay = $47.25 + $180 = $227.25

   Answer: $227.25

3. a.   In occupations such as retail sales, real estate, and insurance, earnings may be based on *commission,* which is a percent of the sales or a percent of the value of the transactions that are completed.

   b.   Earnings may be from straight commission only, from salary plus commission, or from a commission that is graduated according to transaction volume.

   Illustration: A salesman earns a salary of $200 weekly, plus a commission based on sales volume for the week. The commission is 7% for the first $1500 of sales and 10% for all sales in excess of $1500. How much did he earn in a week in which his sales totaled $3200?

   Solution: $3200 − $1500 = $1700 of excess sales
   .07 × $1500 = $105 commission of first $1500
   .10 × $1700 = $170 commission on excess sales
                + $200 weekly salary
                 $475 total earnings

   Answer: $475

4. *Gross pay* refers to the amount of money earned whether from salary, commission, or both, before any deductions are made.

5. There are several deductions that are usually made from gross pay:

   a.   *Withholding tax* is the amount of money withheld for income tax. It is based on wages, marital status, and number of exemptions (also called allowances) claimed by the employee. The withholding tax is found by referring to tables supplied by the federal, state or city governments.

Example:

MARRIED PERSONS—WEEKLY PAYROLL PERIOD

Wages		Number of withholding allowances claimed				
At least	But less than	0	1	2	3	4
		Amount of income tax to be withheld				
410	420	53	48	42	37	31
420	430	55	49	44	38	32
430	440	56	51	45	40	34
440	450	58	52	47	41	35
450	460	59	54	48	43	37
460	470	61	55	50	44	38
470	480	62	57	51	46	40
480	490	64	58	53	47	41
490	500	65	60	54	49	43
500	510	67	61	56	50	44

Based on the above table, an employee who is married, claims three exemptions, and is paid a weekly wage of $434.50 will have $40.00 withheld for income tax. If the same employee earned $440 weekly, it would be necessary to look on the next line for "at least $440 but less than $450" to find that $41.00 would be withheld.

b.   The FICA (Federal Insurance Contribution Act) tax is also called the Social Security tax. In 1988, the FICA tax was 7.51% of the first $45,000 of annual wages; the wages in excess of $45,000 were not subject to the tax.

The FICA may be found by multiplying the wages up to and including $45,000 by .0751 or by using the table below.

Example:

SOCIAL SECURITY EMPLOYEE TAX TABLE

If wage payment Is—	The employee tax to be deducted is—	If wage payment is—	The employee tax to be deducted is—
$61	$4.58	$81	$6.08
62	4.66	82	6.16
63	4.73	83	6.23
64	4.81	84	6.31
65	4.88	85	6.38
66	4.96	86	6.46
67	5.03	87	6.53
68	5.11	88	6.61
69	5.18	89	6.68
70	5.26	90	6.76
71	5.33	91	6.83
72	5.41	92	6.91
73	5.48	93	6.98

If wage payment Is—	The employee tax to be deducted is—	If wage payment is—	The employee tax to be deducted is—
74	5.56	94	7.06
75	5.63	95	7.13
76	5.71	96	7.21
77	5.78	97	7.28
78	5.86	98	7.36
79	5.93	99	7.43
80	6.01	100	7.51

According to the table above, the Social Security tax, or FICA tax, on wages of $84.00 is $6.31. The FICA tax on $85.00 is $6.38.

Illustration: Based on 1988 tax figures, what is the total FICA tax on an annual salary of $30,000?

Solution: .0751 × $30,000 = $2,253.00

Answer: $2,253.00

c. Other deductions that may be made from gross pay are deductions for pension plans, loan payments, payroll savings plans, and union dues.

6. The *net pay,* or *take-home pay,* is equal to gross pay less the total deductions.

Illustration: Mr. Jay earns $550 salary per week with the following deductions: federal withholding tax, $106.70; FICA tax, $41.31; state tax, $22.83; pension payment, $6.42; union dues, $5.84. How much take-home pay does he receive?

Solution: Deductions $106.70
41.31
22.83
6.42
+ 5.84
$183.10

Gross pay = $550.00
Deductions = −183.10
Net pay = $366.90

Answer: His take-home pay is $366.90

EXERCISE

1. Jane Rose's semimonthly salary is $750. Her yearly salary is
    (A) $9,000
    (B) $12,500
    (C) $18,000
    (D) $19,500

2. John Doe earns $300 for a 40-hour week. If he receives time and a half for overtime, what is his hourly overtime wage?
    (A) $7.50
    (B) $9.25
    (C) $10.50
    (D) $11.25

3. Which salary is greatest?
    (A) $350 weekly
    (B) $1,378 monthly
    (C) $17,000 annually
    (D) $646 biweekly

4. A factory worker is paid on the basis of an 8-hour day, with an hourly rate of $6.00 and time and a half for overtime. Find his gross pay for a week in which he worked the following hours: Monday, 8; Tuesday, 9; Wednesday, $9\frac{1}{2}$; Thursday, $8\frac{1}{2}$; Friday, 9.
    (A) $240
    (B) $266
    (C) $276
    (D) $360

Questions 5 and 6 refer to the following table:

SINGLE PERSONS—WEEKLY PAYROLL PERIOD

Wages		Number of Withholding Allowances Claimed				
At least	But less than	0	1	2	3	4
		Amount of Income to be Withheld				
340	350	49	43	37	32	26
350	360	50	45	39	33	28
360	370	52	46	40	35	29
370	380	55	48	42	36	31
380	390	58	49	43	38	32
390	400	60	51	45	39	34
400	410	63	53	46	41	35
410	420	66	55	48	42	37
420	430	69	58	49	44	38
430	440	72	61	51	45	40

5. If an employee is single and has one exemption, the income tax withheld from his weekly salary of $389.90 is
    (A) $51.00
    (B) $58.00
    (C) $49.00
    (D) $43.00

6. If a single person with two exemptions has $51.00 withheld for income tax, his weekly salary could *not* be
    (A) $430.00
    (B) $435.25
    (C) $437.80
    (D) $440.00

7. Sam Richards earns $1200 monthly. The following deductions are made from his gross pay monthly: federal withholding tax, $188.40; FICA tax, $84.60; state tax, $36.78; city tax, $9.24; savings bond, $37.50; pension plan, $5.32; repayment of pension loan, $42.30. His monthly net pay is
   (A) $795.86
   (B) $797.90
   (C) $798.90
   (D) $799.80

8. A salesman is paid a straight commission that is 23% of his sales. What is his commission on $1260 of sales?
   (A) $232.40
   (B) $246.80
   (C) $259.60
   (D) $289.80

9. Ann Johnson earns a salary of $150 weekly plus a commission of 9% of sales in excess of $500 for the week. For a week in which her sales were $1496, her earnings were
   (A) $223.64
   (B) $239.64
   (C) $253.64
   (D) $284.64

10. A salesperson is paid a 6% commission on the first $2500 of sales for the week, and 7 [1/2]% on that portion of sales in excess of $2500. What is the commission earned in a week in which sales were $3280?
    (A) $196.80
    (B) $208.50
    (C) $224.30
    (D) $246.00

ANSWER KEY

1. C   3. A   5. C   6. D   7. A   8. D   9. B   10. B
2. D   4. C

EXPLANATIONS

1.   **(C)**   A semimonthly salary is paid twice a month. She receives $750 [ts] 2 = $1500 each month, which is $1500 × 12 = $18,000 per year.

2.   **(D)**   The regular hourly rate is $300 ÷ 40 = $7.50

   The overtime rate is

   $$\$7.50 \times 1\tfrac{1}{2} = \$7.50 \times 1.5$$

   $$= \$11.25$$

3.   **(A)**   Write each salary as its yearly equivalent:

$$\$350 \text{ weekly} = \$350 \times 52 \text{ yearly}$$

$$= \$18,200 \text{ yearly}$$

$$\$1378 \text{ monthly} = \$1378 \times 12 \text{ yearly}$$

$$= \$16,536 \text{ yearly}$$

$$\$17,000 \text{ annually} = \$17,000 \text{ yearly}$$

$$\$646 \text{ biweekly} = \$646 \div 2 \text{ weekly}$$

$$= \$323 \text{ weekly}$$

$$= \$323 \times 52 \text{ yearly}$$

$$= \$16,796 \text{ yearly}$$

4.   **(C)**   His overtime hours were:

Monday:	0
Tuesday:	1
Wednesday:	$1\tfrac{1}{2}$
Thursday:	$\tfrac{1}{2}$
Friday:	1
Total:	4 hours overtime

Overtime rate per hour $= 1\tfrac{1}{2} \times \$6.00$

$$= 1.5 \times \$6.00$$

$$= \$9.00$$

$$\text{Overtime pay} = 4 \times \$9.00$$
$$= \$36.00$$

Regular pay for 8 hours per day for 5 days or 40 hours.

$$\text{Regular pay} = 40 \times \$6.00$$
$$= \$240$$

$$\text{Total wages} = \$240 + \$36$$
$$= \$276$$

5. **(C)** The correct amount is found on the line for wages of at least \$380 but less than \$390, and in the column under "1" withholding allowance. The amount withheld is \$49.00

6. **(D)** In the column for 2 exemptions, or withholding allowances, \$51.00 is found on the line for wages of at least \$430, but less than \$440. Choice (D) does not fall within that range.

7. **(A)** Deductions: $188.40
84.60
36.78
9.24
37.50
5.32
+ 42.30
Total $404.14

Gross pay = $1200.00
Total deductions = −404.14
$795.86

8. **(D)** 23% of \$1260 = .23 × \$1260
= \$289.80

9. **(B)** \$1,496 − 500 = \$996 excess sales

9% of \$996 = .09 × \$996
= \$89.64 commission

$150.00 salary
+ 89.64 commission
$239.64 total earnings

10. **(B)** \$3280 - \$2500 = \$780 excess sales

Commission on \$2500:

.06 × \$2500 = \$150.00

Commission on \$780:

.075 × \$780 = + 58.50

Total = \$208.50

FORMULA QUESTIONS
LITERAL EXPRESSIONS

Formula questions appear in two distinct forms. Those described as "literal questions" are expressed mainly in terms of letters. The problem itself is written with no numbers or very few numbers, and the multiple-choice answer must be chosen from a list of formulas which involve manipulation of those letters.

Many individuals, including accountants and other professionals who deal intimately with numbers, have no trouble computing with numbers but panic at the sight of letters. This panic, while understandable, is unnecessary. The letters simply represent the formula used to solve the problem.

1. If you understand the concepts of the problem, you should be able to apply them equally to manipulation of representative letters or to computation with actual figures.
   Illustration: If one book costs c dollars, what is the cost, in dollars, of m books?
   Solution: This is a literal problem at its simplest.
   m books times c dollars $= m \times c = mc$
   If you are truly uncomfortable with this answer, you can easily check it by substituting arbitrary, easy-to-manipulate numbers for the letters. 2 books at $3 each $= 2 \times 3 = \$6$.
2. Understanding the concept is the key. As literal questions become more complex, they require greater concentration and reasoning. And, of course, basic arithmetic knowledge comes into play, as well.
   Illustration: If one book costs c dollars, what is the cost, in cents, of m books?
   Solution: You know that one dollar = 100 cents. Solving the problem, you quite easily expand the earlier solution: $m \times 100c = 100mc$. And you can check, if you wish: 2×300 cents $= 600$ cents $(=\$6)$. Choosing the correct answer from a multiple-choice series, you might pause momentarily to consider $\frac{mc}{100}$, but clear thinking should readily lead you to the correct choice.
3. For test-takers, the multiple-choice format introduces an artificial aura of difficulty to literal questions.
   Illustration: The newly announced toll for the ferry crossing is D dollars for the car and driver and m cents for each additional passenger. Find the charge, in dollars, for a car containing four people.
   (A) $D + .03m$
   (B) $D + 300m$
   (C) $D + 4m$
   (D) $D + \frac{3m}{100}$
   Solution: **(A)** The charge is D dollars for car and driver. The three additional persons pay m cents each, for a total of $3m$ cents. To change this to dollars, divide by 100, for a total of $\frac{3m}{100}$ dollars. In decimal form, this is $.03m$. The total charge in dollars is then $D + .03m$.

The choices offered create visual confusion. The best approach to literal multiple-choice questions is to solve the problem for yourself before looking at the choices offered. If you understand the concept, you are more likely to arrive at the correct answer by not allowing yourself to be misled by seductive suggestions. If your exam offers as the final option "none of these," and your answer is not among those offered, you should try checking your own answer by substituting numbers. If you are right, you can confidently mark "none of these." If not, you can then consider the answers offered.

FORMULA ANSWERS

The other style of formula questions gives the appearance of a routine arithmetical reasoning question. The stem of the question describes a situation and presents a mathematical problem that needs to be solved. The question itself is full of numbers. The answer choices, however, are not final answers. The question does not ask what the answer is, but rather asks how you should find the answer. In other words, the question seeks the process rather than the result. The answer is a mathematical (not an algebraic) formula.

In theory, arithmetic problems that proceed only as far at the formula for their solution should be easier than numerical problems requiring lengthy computations. Indeed, some of these questions you might meet on your exam will involve unwieldy numbers that would be cumbersome to work with under time pressure without a calculator. Obviously, if the answer is to be expressed as a formula, you do not need to do the arithmetic. On the other hand, the concepts underlying formula answer problems tend to be complex and to require a series of steps before the test taker can choose the correct formula. Careful reading and meticulous construction of the problem are key to solution of these questions, as indeed they are to the solution of all arithmetic reasoning problems.

The subject matter of formula questions parallels that of traditional numerical questions: ratio and proportion; work, distance, and gasoline problems; interest and discounts; taxation; profit and loss; etc. Approach the questions in exactly the same way that you approach numerical questions. Setting up the problem requires the same reasoning; the only difference lies in the use of symbolic letters in literal questions and in the stopping point for choosing formula answers.

Illustration: In a group of 22 married couples, 18 people have blond hair, 14 people have gray eyes, and 11 people have both blond hair and gray eyes. How many people have neither blond hair nor gray eyes?

(A) 44 – (7 + 11 + 3)
(B) 22 – (18 + 14 + [11/2])
(C) 18 + 14 + 11
(D) 44 – 2 (18 + 14 – 11)

Solution: First set up the problem so that you can recognize your universe.

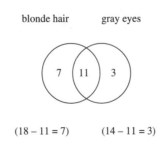

blonde hair   gray eyes

7   11   3

(18 – 11 = 7)   (14 – 11 = 3)

Since there are a total of 44 people (22 couples) the number of people that have neither blond hair nor gray eyes is 44 - (7 + 11 + 3), choice (A).

EXERCISE

1. If a train travels M miles in H hours, how many hours will it take the train to travel the next N miles at the same rate?

   (A) $\dfrac{H}{MN}$

   (B) $\dfrac{HM}{N}$

   (C) $\dfrac{HN}{M}$

   (D) $\dfrac{M}{HN}$

2. If the average of A and B is Q, and the average of C, D, and E is R, what is the average of A, B, C, D, and E in terms of Q and R?

   (A) $\dfrac{Q + R}{2}$

   (B) $\dfrac{2Q + 3R}{5}$

   (C) $\dfrac{2Q + R}{5}$

   (D) $\dfrac{Q + 3R}{5}$

3. A certain truck can travel M miles on G gallons of gasoline. How many gallons of gasoline are needed for 7 of these trucks if each one must travel 300 miles?

   (A) $\dfrac{2100\,G}{M}$

   (B) $\dfrac{2100\,M}{G}$

   (C) $\dfrac{MG}{2100}$

   (D) $\dfrac{GM}{2100}$

4. If a taxi driver charges C cents for the first quarter-mile, and $\dfrac{C}{4}$ cents for each additional quarter-mile, how much does it cost, in cents, for a trip of M miles?

   (A) $C\left(M + \dfrac{1}{4}\right)$

   (B) $\dfrac{C}{4}\left(M + \dfrac{4}{15}\right)$

   (C) $C\left(M + \dfrac{3}{4}\right)$

   (D) $C\left(M - \dfrac{1}{4}\right)$

5. An item which normally sells for X dollars is marked down to Y dollars. What is the percent of markdown?

   (A) $\left(\dfrac{X-Y}{Y}\right)100$

   (B) $\left(\dfrac{Y-X}{Y}\right)100$

   (C) $(X - Y)100$

   (D) $\left(\dfrac{X-Y}{X}\right)100$

6. In a certain company, 5 employees earn $16,000 a year, 3 employees earn $20,000 a year, and 2 employees earn $24,000 a year. What is the average annual salary for these employees?

   (A) ($16,000 + $20,000 + $24,000)(5 + 3 + 2)

   (B) $(5+3+2)(\frac{\$16,000}{5} + \frac{\$20,000}{3} + \frac{\$24,000}{2})$

   (C) $\frac{5(\$16,000) + 3(\$20,000)2(\$24,000)}{5 + 3 + 2}$

   (D) $\frac{(5 + 3 + 2)(\$16,000 + \$20,000 + \$24,000)}{5 + 3 + 2}$

7. A Deputy U.S. Marshal is 24 years older than her son. In eight years, the deputy marshal will be twice as old as her son will be then. How old is her son now?

   (A) $N + 24 = 2N + 8$

   (B) $N + 24 + 8 = 2(N + 8)$

   (C) $N + 24 = 2(N + 8)$

   (D) $\frac{8N + 24}{2} = 2N + (24 - 8)$

8. In a foreign language school, 64% of the students are studying Spanish, 52% are studying French, and 28% are studying a language other than Spanish or French. What percent of the students at the school are studying both Spanish and French?

   (A) $(100 - 28) - [(72 - 64) + (72 - 52)]$

   (B) $100 - (64 + 52)$

   (C) $(100 - 28) + 64 + 72$

   (D) $(64 + 52 + 28) - [(100) - (100 - 72)]$

9. What is the average of a student who received 90 in English, 84 in Algebra, 75 in French, and 76 in Music, if the subjects have the following weights: English 4, Algebra 3, French 3, and Music 1?

   (A) $\frac{4(90+84+75+76)}{4+3+3+1}$

   (B) $\frac{4(90)+6(84+75)+76}{4 \times 3 \times 3}$

   (C) $\frac{\frac{90+84+75+76}{4}}{4+3+3+1}$

   (D) $\frac{(90\times4)+(84\times3)+(75\times3)+(76\times1)}{4+3+3+1}$

10. A dealer mixes a lbs. of nuts worth b cents per pound with c lbs. of nuts worth d cents per pound. At what price should he sell a pound of the mixture if he wishes to make a profit of 10 cents per pound?

    (A) $\frac{ab+cd}{a+c} + 10$

    (B) $\frac{ab+cd}{a+c} + .10$

    (C) $\frac{b+d}{a+c} + 10$

    (D) $\frac{b+d}{a+c} + .10$

ANSWER KEY

1. C   3. A   5. D   6. C   7. B   8. A   9. D   10. A
2. B   4. C

EXPLANATIONS

1. **(C)** Let x = the number of hours it will take train to travel the next N miles.

$$\frac{\text{miles}}{\text{hours}} \quad \frac{M}{H} = \frac{N}{x} \text{ (cross-multiply)}$$

$$Mx = HN$$

$$x = \frac{HN}{M}$$

2. **(B)** $\frac{A+B}{2} = Q$

$$A + B = 2Q$$

$$\frac{C+D+E}{3} = R$$

$$C + D + E = 3R$$

3. **(A)** Since 7 trucks must each travel 300 miles, the total distance travelled will be 2100 miles. Let x = the number of gallons of gasoline needed to travel 2100 miles.

$$\frac{\text{miles}}{\text{gallons}} = \frac{2100}{x} \text{ (cross-multiply)}$$

$$Mx = 2100G$$

$$x = \frac{2100\,G}{M}$$

4. **(C)** After the first quarter-mile, the number of miles remaining in the trip = $M - \frac{1}{4}$. This is equivalent to $4(M - \frac{1}{4}) = 4M - 1$ quarter-miles.

Total Cost = Cost of first quarter-mile + cost of remaining part

$$= C + \frac{C}{4}(4M - 1)$$

$$= C + CM - \frac{C}{4}$$

$$= C(1 + M - \frac{1}{4})$$

$$= C(M + \frac{3}{4})$$

5. **(D)** Let N = the percent of markdown.

$$\frac{\text{Amount of markdown}}{\text{Original value}} = \frac{\text{Percent of markdown}}{100\%}$$

$$\frac{X-Y}{X} = \frac{N}{100}$$

$$\left(\frac{X-Y}{X}\right)100 = N$$

6. **(C)** Combined Average $= \frac{5\,(\$16,000)+3(20,000)+2(\$24,000)}{5+3+2}$

7. **(B)** Let N = the son's age now and $N + 24$ = the deputy marshal's age now. In 8 years, the son's age will be $N + 8$ and the deputy marshal's age will be $N + 24 + 8$, which will be twice the son's age or $2(N + 8)$. So, $N + 24 + 8 = 2(N + 8)$.

8. **(A)** First you must define your universe.

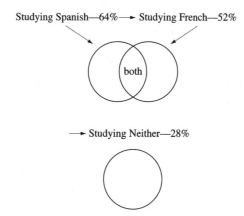

Now, the population with which you are concerned excludes the 28%, so $100\% - 28\% = 72\%$.

With this awareness, you can label the circles and flesh out the formula.

$(100 - 28) - [(72 - 64) + (72 - 52)]$

9. **(D)**

Subject	Grade	Weight
English	90	4
Algebra	84	3
French	75	3
Music	76	1

$$\frac{\text{Sum of weighted grades}}{\text{Sum of weights}} = \frac{(90\times4)+(84\times3)+(75\times3)+(76\times1)}{4+3+3+1}$$

10. **(A)** The a lbs. of nuts are worth a total of ab cents. The c lbs. of nuts are worth a total of cd cents. The value of the mixture is $ab + cd$ cents. Since there are $a + c$ pounds, each pound is worth $\frac{ab+cd}{a+c}$ cents.

Since the dealer wants to add 10 cents to each pound for profit, and the value of each pound is in cents, we add 10 to the value of each pound.

So, $\frac{ab+cd}{a+c+10}$

PROBLEMS FOR INVESTIGATION

How well you do on problems for investigation depends first of all upon how well you read. Reading speed is not crucial; you have 60 minutes in which to read the paragraphs and statements and to ponder the answers to the 30 questions. Accuracy and careful attention to each detail of the reading passage and the statements are essential to scoring high. You can go back and reread and recheck as often as you like while answering these questions.

Clear thinking and total concentration are the keys to doing well on this very significant portion of the exam. You have the time to contemplate the true meaning and the implications of each statement, so ask yourself the following questions:

1. Is this fact? Can the fact be substantiated?
2. Is the statement based on hearsay?
3. Is the statement pure conjecture?
4. How reliable is the source of the evidence?
5. Does the person have a motive for making this statement?

Note time sequences and interrelationships of events. Consider interpersonal relationships, as well, as you try to determine which statements support the questions.

Remain detached from the situation. You might disagree with the actions taken by the agent in regard to handling evidence or questioning witnesses. Don't let such opinions enter into the situation. Concentrate on the description of the events as they are reported, the statements made by witnesses, and the questions that must be supported by statements. In short, be analytical, objective, and very, very careful.

Answer questions in the practice exercises by circling the letter of your choice.

Exercise 1

Directions: *Read the paragraph and statements carefully. Then answer the questions that follow the investigative situation. You may refer to the paragraph and statements as often as needed. Explanations for these questions appear on page 236.*

Isobel Warburton, age 64, wrote a letter to the Social Security Administration requesting a determination of the monthly retirement benefit that she would be eligible to receive at age 65. The letter that she received from Social Security informed Ms. Warburton that her retirement benefits would be minimal because, although she had been a regular contributor to the Social Security system for 26 years, her level of contributions at that time had been very low, and she had made no contributions at all over the last fifteen years. Because Ms. Warburton's contributions had been made before the big inflationary jump in salaries and in most people's contributions and showed increases gained through experience, her benefits were to be calculated on a very low base. Ms. Warburton strongly contested the Social Security determination on the grounds that she had not interrupted her contribution history.

In the course of the investigation, the following statements were made:

(1) Isobel Warburton stated that for the past 15 years she had been employed as supervisor of the cutting room at Torero Dress Manufacturing, Inc.

(2) Herbert Fine, operating manager and chief stockholder of Torero, said that Isobel Warburton had indeed been employed at Torero for the past 15 years.

(3) Isobel Warburton stated that she had had her FICA contribution withheld from every paycheck throughout her working life.

(4) Bob Baroni, bookkeeper, said that Torero was an extremely profitable business.

(5) John Lopez, company treasurer, said that Torero always made timely payments to the IRS to cover employment taxes for all of its employees.

(6) Mama Gatcher, IRS spokesperson, said that Torero filed and paid employment taxes for a very short payroll.

(7) Social Security spokesperson Janet Jankowsky said that in the past 15 years Torero had never filed a W-2 for Isobel Warburton.

(8) Martha Ryan, president of Martha's Lingerie Creations, said that Isobel Warburton had been a fine employee and that she had hated to lose her to Torero 15 years ago, but that she couldn't match Torero's salary offer.

(9) Tom McKinney, auditor, said that Torero's books appeared to be in perfect order.

(10) George Schlitz, a former Torero employee, said that he had left Torero because he felt that there was something illegitimate about the operation.

1. Which two statements together indicate that Isobel Warburton is justified in her protest of the Social Security determination?
    (A) Statements 1 and 3
    (B) Statements 1 and 8
    (C) Statements 2 and 5
    (D) Statements 4 and 10
    (E) Statements 6 and 7

2. Which statement might be classified as a character reference?
    (A) Statement 2
    (B) Statement 5
    (C) Statement 6
    (D) Statement 8
    (E) Statement 10

3. Which statement seems to lend some legitimacy to statement (10)?

(A) Statement 2

(B) Statement 4

(C) Statement 5

(D) Statement 7

(E) Statement 9

4. Which statement casts suspicion on John Lopez?

(A) Statement 4

(B) Statement 6

(C) Statement 7

(D) Statement 9

(E) Statement 10

5. Which statement, along with statement (7), would likely trigger an investigation on suspicion of fraud?

(A) Statement 2

(B) Statement 4

(C) Statement 6

(D) Statement 9

(E) Statement 10

6. Which two statements seem directly contradictory?

(A) Statements 1 and 2

(B) Statements 3 and 7

(C) Statements 4 and 6

(D) Statements 4 and 8

(E) Statements 4 and 9

7. Which statement could indicate either a clever cover-up or collusion?

(A) Statement 3

(B) Statement 4

(C) Statement 6

(D) Statement 8

(E) Statement 9

Exercise 2

Directions: Read the paragraph and statements carefully. Then answer the questions that follow the investigative situation. You may refer to the paragraph and statements as often as needed. Explanations for these questions appear on page 237.

The area had recently been plagued by a rash of cargo pilfering and even large-scale hijackings, so when the giant container ship docked, security was especially tight. At night, city police officers accompanied by dogs patrolled the piers and adjacent warehouses. One night, a stray dog in the area began to act very strangely and erratically. A guard dog sniffed the stray, then led its handler to a crate with a liquid seeping from one corner. Analysis proved that the liquid was whiskey.

In the course of the investigation, the following statements were made:

(1) Police Officer Caleb Hill stated that he had seen the puddle earlier in the evening, but had assumed it was water. He further stated that his guard dog has been well trained and that it eats and drinks only what is served by its handler.

(2) Customs Inspector Hank Holborn stated that the cargo on the dock consisted of automobile parts sent from a manufacturing plant in Europe to an assembly plant in the United States.

(3) Crane operator Marge Marino stated that she did not notice anything unusual in offloading this particular cargo.

(4) Longshoreman Nathan O'Neill stated that every container ship carries some sort of smuggled goods.

(5) DEA Officer Tim Greenes stated that his dogs had sniffed the cargo for narcotics and had found nothing.

(6) Gunnar Gustafson, the shipping company representative, stated that there was one more container on the dock right now than had been officially loaded.

(7) Seaman Tom Tripp stated that Seaman Bill Crooke had told him that he (Crooke) had seen a truck back up to the ship in the night in its European berth and had seen someone handing money to Gunnar Gustafson.

(8) Police Officer Helen Han stated that ship's officer Martin Bligh seemed to spend more time wandering among the containers than was usual practice for ships' officers.

(9) Longshoreman Jim Dunn stated that Gunnar Gustafson's assistant, Thorpe Nichols, seemed excessively agitated when a forklift operator dropped the box now identified as contraband.

(10) First Mate Nelson Sparrow stated that this ship appeared to have an exceptionally hard-drinking crew.

1. Which statement is hearsay?
   (A) Statement 2
   (B) Statement 4
   (C) Statement 7
   (D) Statement 9
   (E) Statement 10

2. Which two statements explain why the dogs did not independently lead police officers to the whiskey?
   (A) Statements 1 and 3
   (B) Statements 1 and 5
   (C) Statements 4 and 5
   (D) Statements 4 and 10
   (E) Statements 5 and 10

3. Which statement, along with statement (8), seems to implicate "management" in the smuggling of whiskey?
   (A) Statement 2
   (B) Statement 4
   (C) Statement 6
   (D) Statement 9
   (E) Statement 10

4. Which statement might be an attempt to divert the investigation?
   (A) Statement 1
   (B) Statement 4
   (C) Statement 5
   (D) Statement 6
   (E) Statement 10

5. Which two statements indicate that law enforcement officers might not have been as thorough as they ought to have been?
   (A) Statements 1 and 2
   (B) Statements 1 and 5
   (C) Statements 2 and 5
   (D) Statements 3 and 5
   (E) Statements 5 and 8

6. Which statement might represent an attempt by the speaker to eliminate himself from suspicion?
   (A) Statement 1
   (B) Statement 3
   (C) Statement 5
   (D) Statement 6
   (E) Statement 10

7. Which two statements, along with statement 4, have no real bearing on this investigation?
   (A) Statements 1 and 2
   (B) Statements 2 and 3
   (C) Statements 5 and 7
   (D) Statements 5 and 10
   (E) Statements 7 and 10

8. Which statement suggests that a ship's officer was doing more than minding official business?
   (A) Statement 3
   (B) Statement 6
   (C) Statement 7
   (D) Statement 8
   (E) Statement 9

Exercise 3

Directions: Read the paragraph and statements carefully. Then answer the questions that follow the investigative situation. You may refer to the paragraph and statements as often as needed. Explanations for these questions appear on pages 238.

The aspiring candidate, we'll call him A, had strong well-defined positions and a personality that magnetized many and quite as forcefully antagonized others. His supporters were visible and audible throughout the land; his detractors were equally apparent. As the convention neared, A and his remaining viable competitors, B and C, campaigned vigorously about the country. In one major city, a few days before a scheduled debate among the three, the daily newspaper published a paid advertisement warning of dire consequences to the party and to the nation if A were to be the party's candidate but making no specific threats against any one person. On the same day, a message arrived at A's local headquarters and another at a radio station. These messages made direct threats against A's person and his family. A's advisors suggested that he bow out of this debate, but A refused to succumb to pressure and threats.

In the course of an investigation to locate the source of the threats and to forestall violence, the following statements were made:

(1) Jean Ramirez, an employee in the newspaper's advertising department, stated that three days before the ad appeared, a man with a bass voice had called and had asked many questions about sizes of ads and relative costs but had not placed an order.

(2) George Tagawa of the newspaper's mailroom stated that the ad had not arrived in the mail but had been slipped through a door slot during the night.

(3) Warren Wiltz, advertising manager of the newspaper, stated that the correct payment, in cash, accompanied copy for the advertisement.

(4) Dan Jenkins, a volunteer in A's headquarters, stated that upon opening the office he had found the threats in an envelope which had been pushed under the door.

(5) Padma Loomba, a forensic expert, stated that the advertisement and the threat appeared to have come from the same typewriter.

(6) Ryan Seltzer of the radio station stated that the threat received at the station was made by telephone and that the caller was a woman.

(7) Joe Dawes, a well-known opponent of A, stated that he had been in another city on business when the threats were delivered.

(8) Betty Maloney, a supporter of C, stated that the ad and threats were planted by A's own committee to elicit extra sympathy for A and to cast vague suspicions about his opponents.

(9) Bob Howard, a homeless person who had previously been a patient in a mental hospital, stated in his bass-pitched voice that he was responsible for the ad and threats.

(10) Molly Yin, a police informer, stated that she could not name her sources, but that a sniper would be stationed in a basement apartment along the route usually taken from the airport to the hotel at which A would be staying.

1. Which statement clearly demands action by local police and by Secret Service?
    (A) Statement 1
    (B) Statement 6
    (C) Statement 8
    (D) Statement 9
    (E) Statement 10

2. Which two statements indicate that more than one person was involved in the intimidation attempt?
    (A) Statements 1 and 3
    (B) Statements 1 and 5
    (C) Statements 1 and 6
    (D) Statements 5 and 9
    (E) Statements 6 and 9

3. Which statement constitutes an alibi?
    (A) Statement 3
    (B) Statement 7
    (C) Statement 8
    (D) Statement 9
    (E) Statement 10

4. Which statement is likely to be of LEAST use in this investigation?
    (A) Statement 1
    (B) Statement 3
    (C) Statement 5
    (D) Statement 8
    (E) Statement 9

5. Which two statements indicate that the threat maker is aware of the law?
    (A) Statements 1 and 3
    (B) Statements 2 and 4
    (C) Statements 3 and 6
    (D) Statements 4 and 7
    (E) Statements 5 and 6

6. Which statement, along with statement (3), indicates that at least part of the intimidation scheme was planned rather than spontaneous?
    (A) Statement 1
    (B) Statement 2
    (C) Statement 4
    (D) Statement 5
    (E) Statement 7

7. Which statement links statement (4) to a man with a high-pitched voice?
   (A) Statement 1
   (B) Statement 3
   (C) Statement 5
   (D) Statement 6
   (E) Statement 7

8. Which statement offers a clue which is probably just coincidental rather than crucial?
   (A) Statement 3
   (B) Statement 5
   (C) Statement 6
   (D) Statement 7
   (E) Statement 9

Exercise 4

Directions: Read the paragraph and statements carefully. Then answer the questions that follow the investigative situation. You may refer to the paragraph and statements as often as needed. Explanations for these questions appear on pages 238 to 239.

Charlie Horton was very upset. His monthly VISA bill had just arrived in the mail with a total far in excess of any charges he could even imagine. Sorting through the enclosed copies of charge slips, he found six unaccountable charge slips with a single distinctive signature of his name that bore no resemblance to his own signature. Further, there were four charges, payable to four different gun shops in Texas, for which no charge slips were enclosed. Evidently the orders had been placed by mail or phone. Horton looked into his wallet. His VISA card was right there in its usual slot. His wife produced her VISA card as well. Mr. Horton immediately called the bankcard company to cancel his cards. Next, he wrote a letter to the card billing address denying knowledge of the charges. Finally, he called the police. The local police told Charlie Horton that the matter was out of their jurisdiction because the card had not been stolen. Horton called the FBI, which referred him to the Secret Service, which deals with credit card fraud; the Bureau of Alcohol, Tobacco, and Firearms, because firearms apparently had been ordered under a false name; and to the Postal Inspector's Office because the mail had probably been used in the fraudulent procurement of firearms.

In the course of the investigation by this team, the following statements were made:

(1) Charlie Horton stated that he usually bought gas at Bill's Service Center where the attendant took his card into the office to run it through the machine.

(2) Mrs. Horton stated that she often had lunch with her friend Lily Bell at the Pickwick Tea Room and occasionally forgot to tear up the carbons.

(3) Jimmy Horton, age 15, stated that he had placed a telephone order for tickets to a hockey game and had given his father's VISA number over the telephone.

(4) Anwar Amin who pumped gas at Bill's Service Center stated that Harvey Brilliant who also worked at Bill's frequently complained that the machine had jammed and made a second impression of a credit card. Amin claimed to never have noticed Brilliant destroying the first impression slip.

(5) Martha Brilliant, Harvey's mother, stated that Harvey had always been a good, hard-working boy but that she did not much care for a new group of friends with whom he had been spending his free time.

(6) Maria Gerardi, waitress at the Pickwick Tea Room, stated that Mrs. Horton was a nice lady but a stingy tipper.

(7) Joyce Shigekawa, supervisor at the ticket agency that handled sports tickets for the community, stated that all the telephone operators in her employ had been fully investigated and were bonded.

(8) Ginny Chen, an operator at the ticket agency, stated that her co-worker Peggy Kowalski seemed to wear an expensive new outfit nearly every day.

(9) Tony Pisano, owner of Hunters' Supply Depot of Laramie, Texas, stated that he adhered strictly to the law in filling orders for guns and ammunition.

(10) Peter VanRijn, manager of Buy Rite Liquors, stated that he was applying for a gun permit because many young toughs in the neighborhood suddenly seemed to have acquired guns, and he was feeling very vulnerable.

1. Which statement, along with statement (3), might link Jimmy Horton's activities to the misuse of his father's card?
   (A) Statement 4
   (B) Statement 5
   (C) Statement 7
   (D) Statement 8
   (E) Statement 10

2. Which statement should prove LEAST helpful to the investigators?
   (A) Statement 2
   (B) Statement 5
   (C) Statement 6
   (D) Statement 7
   (E) Statement 9

3. Which statement is most likely to cause the investigators to concentrate their search for the perpetrator of the credit card fraud right in Horton's hometown?
   (A) Statement 1
   (B) Statement 3
   (C) Statement 5
   (D) Statement 8
   (E) Statement 10

4. Which statement is most likely to remove suspicion from Peggy Kowalski?
   (A) Statement 3
   (B) Statement 4
   (C) Statement 7
   (D) Statement 8
   (E) Statement 9

5. Which two statements, along with statement (3), describe potentially risky practices?
   (A) Statements 1 and 2
   (B) Statements 1 and 4
   (C) Statements 2 and 6
   (D) Statements 4 and 9
   (E) Statements 9 and 10

6. Which single statement casts the greatest suspicion on Harvey Brilliant?
   (A) Statement 1
   (B) Statement 4
   (C) Statement 5
   (D) Statement 9
   (E) Statement 10

7. Which statement might draw state investigators into this case?
   (A) Statement 3
   (B) Statement 5
   (C) Statement 7
   (D) Statement 9
   (E) Statement 10

ANSWER KEY

Exercise 1

| 1. A | 2. D | 3. D | 4. C | 5. A | 6. B | 7. E |

Exercise 2

| 1. C | 2. B | 3. D | 4. E | 5. A | 6. D | 7. D | 8. D |

Exercise 3

| 1. E | 2. C | 3. B | 4. D | 5. B | 6. A | 7. C | 8. E |

Exercise 4

| 1. D | 2. C | 3. E | 4. C | 5. A | 6. B | 7. D |

EXPLANATIONS

Exercise 1

1. **(A)** The fact that she had been working in a supervisory position, presumably at a fairly high salary, for 15 years and the fact that her FICA contribution had regularly been withheld most certainly justified Isobel Warburton's challenge to the Social Security Administration's determination of benefits.

2. **(D)** Basically, Martha Ryan's statement is nothing more than a character reference for Ms. Warburton; however, it does serve to corroborate the fact that Ms. Warburton began work for Torero 15 years ago and that she received a good salary in her position there.

3. **(D)** George Schlitz presents no evidence; his statement is strictly one of opinion. However, the fact that Torero never filed W-2 forms and presumably never paid taxes related to Isobel Warburton's employment and salary, lends credence to Schlitz's hunch that not all aspects of the business were strictly in accordance with law.

4. **(C)** John Lopez, the company treasurer who certainly should have been well-informed as to the financial operations of the company, claimed that employment taxes were paid covering all employees of the company, yet the IRS spokesman stated that Isobel Warburton never appeared on the rolls.

5. **(A)** The fact that a person had worked in one place for 15 years in itself would raise no eyebrows, nor would the fact that no W-2s were filed for any one individual. However, in combination the assertion by the manager of the company that Isobel Warburton was employed by his company and the statement by the Social Security Administration that the company had made no filings on behalf of that individual, should raise suspicions about the company's practices and should immediately trigger an investigation and audit.

6. **(B)** This is quite obvious. Isobel Warburton saw the regular deductions being taken from her paycheck and, presumably, saw the total each year on the W-2 copies that she received, yet the Social Security Administration claimed that the original W-2s had never been filed and that it was unaware of her employment of the last 15 years.

7. **(E)** The auditor, Tom McKinney, stated that the company's books appeared to be in perfect order. Either the fraud was so cleverly executed as to escape detection by the auditor or the auditor was in some way party to the scheme.

Exercise 2

1. **(C)** Tom Tripp is simply repeating a statement made to him. Since Tripp himself did not observe the truck nor the transfer of money, if indeed these occurred at all, his statement is simply hearsay.

2. **(B)** Guard dogs are trained to accept food and drink only from their handlers. The purpose of this training is to protect the dogs from poisoned bait. Statement (1) implies that Officer Hill's dog did not investigate the puddle on its own because it knew not to drink a standing liquid. Once sensitized to the odor, the dog led the officer to the liquor. The dog in statement (5) was trained only to sniff out narcotics, not alcohol.

3. **(D)** As Gustafson's assistant, Thorpe Nichols was part of a management group. Nichols' agitation as the crate that contained the whiskey was dropped implies that he knew of the contents of that particular box and was party to the smuggling scheme.

4. **(E)** The First Mate's mentioning that the crew of the ship did a lot of drinking might be a diversionary tactic, an attempt to suggest that the crew was transporting liquor for its own use or for sale to a stateside contact.

5. **(A)** The puddle abutting the corner of a crate deserved Officer Hill's attention. He should have checked out its nature and not simply assumed that it was water. Customs Inspector Hank Holborn should not have flatly stated what the cargo consisted of without fully checking it out and without a careful count of crates against manifest.

6. **(D)** Gustafson's indication of surprise that there was an extra box on the dock, one more box than he had had loaded, is his means of clearing himself, of telling investigators that he had nothing to do with the illicit whiskey.

7. **(D)** The gratuitous statement that every container ship carries some smuggled goods is completely useless to this investigation. Equally irrelevant is the statement that the DEA dogs did not sniff out any narcotics. The oblique suggestion that a hard-drinking crew had a hand in smuggling a large crate of whiskey is so outlandish as to have no real bearing on this investigation.

8. **(D)** Once the ship has docked and the cargo has been offloaded, the ship's officers have no further responsibility for the cargo. A ship's officer's spending a great deal of time wandering among the crates must raise suspicion that the officer has some personal interest beyond his assigned duties.

Exercise 3

1. **(E)** A police informer must always be taken seriously. The sniper threat may or may not be related to the threats received by the candidate's headquarters and by the radio station, but it must be thoroughly checked by a door-to-door search of basement apartments along the route and possibly averted by change of the route.

2. **(C)** Statement (1) ties the newspaper ad to a man with a bass voice. The phone call to the radio station in statement (6) was made by a woman.

3. **(B)** Joe Dawes' assertion that he was out of town on business at the time that the threats were delivered represents an alibi, albeit not a very good one. From this paragraph and these statements there is no evidence to connect Dawes with the threats, but his being out of town when they were delivered does not preclude his involvement in their preparation.

4. **(D)** Betty Maloney's statement is an expression of her own opinion and nothing more.

5. **(B)** Actually, because the newspaper advertisement did not contain any specific threats, thus making it suitable to print, it could have been sent through the mail. Use of the mail to transmit a real threat subjects the threat-maker to conviction and penalties for mail fraud in addition to violation of the civil rights of the victim. Obviously the threat-maker is aware and wants to expose himself as little as possible to legal action.

6. **(A)** The ad placer called the newspaper to determine exact costs for the ad he wished to place so as to avoid the detection that would come through billing. Then he paid cash so as to eliminate the possibility of being traced through a check.

7. **(C)** Statement (5) identifies both written communications as having been produced on the same typewriter. The man with the bass voice might not have been the actual typist, but he clearly was connected with production of the ad since he was the one who called the newspaper to find out about costs.

8. **(E)** Bob Howard's claim of responsibility must be checked out even if his involvement seems highly unlikely. His bass-pitched voice adds to the possibility that he was the caller, but it is probably mere coincidence. Mentally ill people generally are not taken into the confidence of careful political plotters and schemers. We suspect (see question 2) that the threat-maker did not act alone.

Exercise 4

1. **(D)** Peggy Kowalski's impressive wardrobe implies unlimited funds. It is possible that Peggy, in taking Jimmy's ticket order and credit card number, made note of the number and used it to place telephone orders for clothing. Peggy's occupation exposes her to many credit card numbers and instant suspicion, so her using the card number is highly unlikely, though possible.

2. **(C)** The fact that a waitress considered Mrs. Horton to be pleasant even though a poor tipper really has no bearing on the case.

3. **(E)** The liquor store operator's comment that guns had suddenly appeared in the neighborhood points to the perpetrator of credit card fraud as remaining in the area and as distributing firearms to his or her friends.

4. **(C)** The fact that telephone operators who were privy to patrons' credit card numbers were investigated and bonded, adds to the unlikelihood that Peggy Kowalski is the guilty party.

5. **(A)** All three: Allowing one's credit card to leave one's sight for an impression, leaving legible carbons for another to pick up, and giving a credit card number to a stranger over the telephone are risky practices; however, only the leaving of carbon slips is avoidable.

6. **(B)** Amin's statement that Harvey Brilliant often ran duplicate card impressions through the machine and did not destroy them is, if true, a damaging statement and must be thoroughly investigated.

7. **(D)** One gun dealer stated that he acted within the law in selling guns, but, because guns were obtained from four gun shops by one person, Texas authorities must look into the case to be certain that all four transactions were made in accordance with Texas law.

TEST-TAKING TECHNIQUES

Your last-minute preparations for any exam are based strictly on common sense. They include getting a good night's sleep and leaving home early enough so that you do not need to rush or worry. It is a good idea to wear a watch to your exam so that you can keep track of time on your own and pace yourself. Bring with you to the exam your admission ticket (if you were sent one), identification, and two sharpened pencils with erasers.

Common sense would seem to dictate that you eat a good breakfast before taking an important exam. But, go light on the coffee. After you have been seated in the TEA examination room, you may not leave for any reason. There is no reentry to the examination. You must consider the trade-off, but by the end of the three-plus hours, you will probably be happier having chosen sleepy over squirmy. The adrenaline that naturally flows as you tackle a difficult exam should keep you awake and alert. Of course, you should ask to use the restroom before you are seated in the examination room.

After all examinees are seated in the examination room, the test administrator will hand out the forms and give instructions for filling them out. Listen carefully and follow all instructions. Ask questions if necessary. The administrator will tell you about the procedure that will be followed when the exam begins. He or she will tell you how to recognize the start and stop signals and what warnings will be given. You will learn what to do if all your pencils break or if a page seems to be missing from your test booklet. The instructions should be very clear, but if you are uncertain about anything, do not hesitate to ask.

After you begin the exam, READ every word of every question. Be alert for exclusionary words that might affect your answer—words like "not," "most," "all," "every," and "except."

READ all the choices before you mark your answer. It is statistically true that most errors are made when the last choice is the correct answer. Too many people mark the first answer that seems correct without reading through all the choices to find out which answer is *best*.

The following list consists of important suggestions for taking this exam. Read the suggestions now. Review them before you take the actual exam. You will find them all useful.

Tips for Examination Day

1. Mark your answers by completely blackening the answer space of your choice.
2. Mark only ONE answer for each question, even if you think that more than one answer is correct. You must choose only one. If you mark more than one answer, the scoring machine will mark the question as incorrect, even if one of your answers is correct.
3. If you change your mind, erase completely. Leave no doubt as to which answer you have chosen.
4. If you do any figuring on the scratch paper provided—and you will for the arithmetic reasoning— be sure to mark your answer on the answer sheet. The scratch paper is collected and is thrown away; it is not scored.
5. Check often to be sure that the question number matches the answer space number and that you have not skipped a space by mistake. If you do skip a space, you must erase all the answers after the skip and answer all the questions again in the right places.
6. Within each test section, answer first those questions that seem easiest to you. Then go back and give a little more time to those questions that seem harder. If a question is a real puzzler, do not treat it as a challenge and spend all your time on it. Remember that your task is to answer correctly as many questions as possible. You must apportion your time so as to give yourself a fair chance to answer all the questions. If you skip over an "impossible" question, be sure to skip its answer space, too. Jot

down on your scratch paper the numbers of the question that you skipped so that you can go back and try again if time allows.

7. Guess if you can. If you do not know the answer to a question, eliminate the answers that you know are wrong and guess from among the remaining choices. If you have no idea whatsoever of the answer to a question but choose to guess anyway, choose an answer other than the first. The first choice is generally the correct answer less often than the other choices. If your answer is a guess, an educated guess or a wild one, note the question number on your scratch paper so that you can give it a second try if time for the section permits.

8. Keep track of time. There is no penalty for a wrong guess, so you do not want to leave any question unanswered. Look at your watch as each section begins. Write the time on your scratch paper. For parts A and B, add 50 minutes to the starting time and circle that number. For part C add 60 minutes. Don't be tied to your watch, but do glance at it occasionally. If time for any section is about to run out, mark all the remaining spaces with the same answer. By the law of averages, you should pick up an extra point or two.

9. Stay alert. Be sure you darken the space for the letter of the answer you have chosen. You want to avoid confusion of letters with numbers as might happen in the Problems for Investigation section. If the answer is "(A) Statement (3)," be sure to darken (A). Do not think "3 is the third, therefore (C)."

10. Do not panic. If you cannot finish a section before time is up, do not worry. If you are accurate in the questions that you do answer, and if you guess so as to get whatever credit you can on the remainder, you can do very well without actually reasoning out every question. At any rate, do not let your performance on any one section affect your performance on any other section.

11. Check and recheck. If you finish any section before time is up, check to be sure that each question is answered in the right space and that there is only one answer for each question. Return to the difficult questions that you noted on your scratch paper and try them again. There is no bonus for leaving early, so use all your time to perfect your exam paper.

Good luck!

SELF-DESCRIPTIVE INVENTORIES

Some of the agencies that use the TEA exam as an integral part of the competitive hiring process also make use of a biographical/achievement inventory, a set of self-rating questions. This self-descriptive inventory is designed to look like a multiple-choice test and is timed like a test, but it is not a test at all. There are no right or wrong answers. The examiners are looking for a pattern of achievements, interests, and personality traits that they can compare to the achievement, interest, and personality profiles of persons who are currently active and successful in the position for which you have applied.

You cannot study for a self-descriptive inventory. The only possible preparation is searching out old school records to refresh your own mind as to subjects that you studied—those in which you did well and those that gave you trouble—attendance records, grades, and extracurricular activities and thinking about what you achieved and when. If you cannot find your records, just answer to the best of your ability. Some questions allow for a response of "do not recall"; many require you to choose an answer. Some of the questions offer hard choices, but you do not have time to dwell on the answers. The timing of the inventory is meant to force you to give quick and candid answers.

On a typical self-descriptive inventory, you will find questions about your best and worst grades in school and about your favorite and least favorite subjects; questions about your extracurricular activities in school and college (if you went to college) and about your participation in sports; and questions about attendance, part-time jobs, and leadership positions. Other questions refer to your working life or school relationships. These questions ask what you think your peers think of you; others ask similar questions with respect to your supervisors or teachers. The questions ask how you think your teachers or employers might rate you on specific traits. Similar questions ask you to suggest what your friends might say about you. Still other questions ask how you rate yourself against others. Do not try to "second guess" and give the answers you think the examiners want. Measures of general consistency of answers have been built into the questions. Analysis and calculation are unlikely to do you any good. Just answer quickly and honestly.

The inventories for different positions tend to emphasize different topics, but there is a certain similarity from one to the next. There are no official self-rating sample questions, but the questions that follow offer you a sampling of the types of questions that are often asked.

1. My favorite subject in high school was
   (A) math
   (B) English
   (C) physical education
   (D) social studies
   (E) science

2. My GPA upon graduation from high school (on a 4.0 scale) was
   (A) lower than 2.51
   (B) 2.51 to 2.80
   (C) 2.81 to 3.25
   (D) 3.26 to 3.60
   (E) higher than 3.60

3. In my second year of high school I was absent
    (A) never
    (B) not more than 3 days
    (C) 4 to 10 days
    (D) more often than 10 days
    (E) do not recall

4. My best grades in high school were in
    (A) art
    (B) math
    (C) English
    (D) social studies
    (E) music

5. While in high school I participated in
    (A) one sport
    (B) two sports and one other extracurricular activity
    (C) three nonathletic extracurricular activities
    (D) no extracurricular activities
    (E) other than the above

6. During my senior year in high school I held a paying job
    (A) 0 hours a week
    (B) 1 to 5 hours a week
    (C) 6 to 10 hours a week
    (D) 11 to 16 hours a week
    (E) more than 16 hours a week

7. The number of semesters in which I failed a course in high school was
    (A) none
    (B) one
    (C) two or three
    (D) four or five
    (E) more than five

8. In high school I did volunteer work
    (A) more than 10 hours a week
    (B) 5 to 10 hours a week on a regular basis
    (C) sporadically
    (D) seldom
    (E) not at all

If you did not go to college, skip questions 9–24. Go to question 25.

9. My general area of concentration in college was
    (A) performing arts
    (B) humanities
    (C) social sciences
    (D) business
    (E) none of the above

10. At graduation from college, my age was
    (A) under 20
    (B) 20
    (C) 21 to 24
    (D) 25 to 29
    (E) 30 or over

11. My standing in my graduating class was in the
    (A) bottom third
    (B) middle third
    (C) top third
    (D) top quarter
    (E) top 10 percent

12. In college, I was elected to a major office in a class or in a club or organization
    (A) more than six times
    (B) four or five times
    (C) two or three times
    (D) once
    (E) never

13. In comparison to my peers, I cut classes
    (A) much less often than most
    (B) somewhat less often than most
    (C) just about the same as most
    (D) somewhat more often than most
    (E) much more often than most

14. The campus activities in which I participated most were
    (A) social service
    (B) political
    (C) literary
    (D) did not participate in campus activities
    (E) did not participate in any of these activities

15. My name appeared on the dean's list
    (A) never
    (B) once or twice
    (C) in three or more terms
    (D) in more terms than it did not appear
    (E) do not remember

16. The volunteer work I did while in college was predominantly
    (A) health-care related
    (B) religious
    (C) political
    (D) educational
    (E) did not volunteer

17. While a college student, I spent most of my summers
    (A) in summer school
    (B) earning money
    (C) traveling
    (D) in service activities
    (E) resting

18. My college education was financed
    (A) entirely by my parents
    (B) by my parents and my own earnings
    (C) by scholarships, loans, and my own earnings
    (D) by my parents and loans
    (E) by a combination of sources not listed above

19. In the college classroom I was considered
    (A) a listener
    (B) an occasional contributor
    (C) an average participant
    (D) a frequent contributor
    (E) a leader

20. The person on campus whom I most admired was
    (A) another student
    (B) an athletic coach
    (C) a teacher
    (D) an administrator
    (E) a journalist

21. Of the skills I developed at college, the one I value most is
    (A) foreign language ability
    (B) oral expression
    (C) writing skills
    (D) facility with computers
    (E) analytical skills

22. I made my greatest mark in college through my
    (A) athletic prowess
    (B) success in performing arts
    (C) academic success
    (D) partying reputation
    (E) conciliatory skill with my peers

23. My cumulative GPA (on a 4.0 scale) in courses in my major was
    (A) lower than 3.00
    (B) 3.00 to 3.25
    (C) 3.26 to 3.50
    (D) 3.51 to 3.75
    (E) higher than 3.75

24. While in college I
    (A) worked full-time and was a part-time student
    (B) worked 20 hours a week and was a full-time student
    (C) worked 20 hours a week and was a part-time student
    (D) was a full-time student working more than 10 but less than 20 hours a week
    (E) was a full-time student

25. In the past six months, I have been late to work (or school)
    (A) never
    (B) only one time
    (C) very seldom
    (D) more than five times
    (E) I don't recall

26. My supervisors (or teachers) would be most likely to describe me as
    (A) competent
    (B) gifted
    (C) intelligent
    (D) fast working
    (E) detail oriented

27. My peers would probably describe me as
    (A) analytical
    (B) glib
    (C) organized
    (D) funny
    (E) helpful

28. According to my supervisors (or teachers), my greatest asset is my
    (A) ability to communicate orally
    (B) written expression
    (C) ability to motivate others
    (D) organization of time
    (E) friendly personality

29. In the past two years, I have applied for
    (A) no jobs other than this one
    (B) one other job
    (C) two to four other jobs
    (D) five to eight other jobs
    (E) more than eight jobs

30. In the past year, I read strictly for pleasure
    (A) no books
    (B) one book
    (C) two books
    (D) three to six books
    (E) more than six books

31. When I read for pleasure, I read mostly
    (A) history
    (B) fiction
    (C) poetry
    (D) biography
    (E) current events

32. My peers would say of me that, when they ask me a question, I am
    (A) helpful
    (B) brusque
    (C) condescending
    (D) generous
    (E) patient

33. My supervisors (or teachers) would say that my area of least competence is
    (A) analytical ability
    (B) written communication
    (C) attention to detail
    (D) public speaking
    (E) self-control

34. In the past two years, the number of full-time (35 hours or more) jobs I have held is
    (A) none
    (B) one
    (C) two or three
    (D) four
    (E) five or more

35. Compared to my peers, my supervisors (or teachers) would rank my dependability
    (A) much better than average
    (B) somewhat better than average
    (C) about average
    (D) somewhat less than average
    (E) much less than average

36. In my opinion, the most important of the following attributes in an employee is
    (A) discretion
    (B) loyalty
    (C) open-mindedness
    (D) courtesy
    (E) competence

37. My peers would say that the word that describes me least is
    (A) sociable
    (B) reserved
    (C) impatient
    (D) judgmental
    (E) independent

38. My supervisors (or teachers) would say that I react to criticism with
   (A)   a defensive attitude
   (B)   quick capitulation
   (C)   anger
   (D)   interest
   (E)   shame

39. My attendance record over the past year has been
   (A)   not as good as I would like it to be
   (B)   not as good as my supervisors (or teachers) would like it to be
   (C)   a source of embarrassment
   (D)   satisfactory
   (E)   a source of pride

40. My peers would say that when I feel challenged my reaction is one of
   (A)   determination
   (B)   energy
   (C)   defiance
   (D)   caution
   (E)   compromise

There are no "right" answers to these questions, so there is no answer key.

THE INTERVIEW

The hiring process for Special Agents, Deputy U.S. Marshals, and Criminal Investigators begins with an application and the Treasury Enforcement Agent exam and ends with graduation from the Federal Law Enforcement Training Center at Glynco, Georgia, and swearing in. Earning a superb score on the TEA exam does not automatically mean "you're hired." There are many more steps to take and many more hurdles to cross before you reach appointment to your first duty post. The steps between earning a high score on the TEA exam and entry to a training class at Glynco include medical examination, physical fitness tests, a thorough background investigation, and interviews.

To some extent, all job interviews are similar. The job applicant appears promptly at the appointed hour, well groomed and conservatively dressed. He or she shakes hands firmly, is polite and gracious, speaks distinctly, and answers questions fully and to the best of his or her ability.

But the interview for a federal law enforcement position differs from the conventional job interview in a number of very important aspects. The job interview for a sales, technical, or professional position in the private sector focuses on personal history, education, work experience, and accomplishments. The types of questions asked at the interview for a private sector position, and for many non-federal government positions as well, are fully answered on the federal application forms and by the background investigation.

The interview for a federal law enforcement position is usually conducted by a panel of interviewers rather than by just one person. The questions are not concerned with your past but rather with how you think, speak, and behave right now. Most of the questions pose hypothetical situations and require you to quickly assess the situation, organize your ideas, and articulate a course of action. The main purpose of the interview is to learn how well you can outline your ideas and how you explain the decisions at which you have arrived. Of course, your understanding of the question and grasp of the ramifications of various actions to be taken in response to the situation will make an impression on the interviewers. Likewise, your knowledge of the laws that cover the particular situation and your familiarity with human nature and human behavior cannot escape the notice of the interviewers. The interview is not meant to be a test of knowledge—you will be educated and trained at Glynco—but knowledge implies interest, alertness, and overall suitability for the position under consideration.

The primary goal of the interviewers is to learn how you organize your thoughts and how well you express yourself, but they are also taking close notice of your personality and of your attitude toward the law, as well as your attitude toward lawbreakers and the demands of the job. They want to know how you will bear up under the pressures and dangers you must face and how well you might fit into the law enforcement culture.

A little common sense goes a long way in an interview. You surely do not need to be told to leave politics out of any response. Your party affiliation is irrelevant; your opinion of the current administration—negative or positive—should find no expression here. Stereotyped views of or prejudices toward any ethnic or socioeconomic group must not influence the way you respond in the field; equally, they must not influence your responses to questions posed or to scenarios described.

Some questions that you will face in your interview will be direct questions related to your feelings and attitudes, such as:

- How would you feel about being locked up in a hotel room with two married deputies of the opposite sex and three prisoners?
- Is lawbreaking in the interest of duty ever justified? Explain and give examples.

- What would you do if given an order with which you disagreed on practical grounds? On philosophical grounds?

Give reasoned, logical answers to these questions. Obviously, if you admit that you would be extremely uncomfortable and agitated in the hotel room, you will not impress the interviewers as a likely candidate. But there is quite a bit of latitude in the range of acceptable answers to most questions. The content of your answer, unless it is truly bizarre, is secondary to how well you articulate your reasons and how convincingly you defend your position.

Other questions will take the form of hypothetical situations in which you are asked how to proceed. You might be asked questions like:

- In the course of searching for a fugitive in an airport parking lot, you see the muzzle of a submachine gun poking out from under the seat of an unoccupied locked car. What steps would you take? In what order? With what justification?
- Allegations have reached you that an IRS agent with whom you are personally friendly has been taking bribes and is using tax information to blackmail certain taxpayers. How should you handle this situation?
- An informer on whom your agency has been relying heavily fears that the bootleggers he has been watching have become suspicious. What steps would you take to confirm or allay his fears? What would you do to protect him?

If you know the search and seizure laws that apply, or if you have had experience in similar instances, you can certainly incorporate your knowledge into your responses. On the other hand, hard knowledge is not expected of the untrained applicant. The interviewers are watching for the logic of your reasoning, for the organization of your thoughts, and for the clarity of your explanation.

There is no way to prepare for your interview. You will have no foreknowledge of the questions to be asked or the topics that might be covered. The research about the agency and the position that convinced you that this is the career you want should supply you with the general information and basic foundation for your responses. The following tips should help see you through.

Tips for a Successful Interview

1. Check out the route to the interview location ahead of time. Know exactly where you are going, how to get there, and how long it will take.
2. Get a good night's sleep.
3. Watch your personal hygiene. Nervousness might make you perspire. Use an unscented deodorant and skip the after-shave lotion or perfume. You do not want to offend a sensitive or allergic interviewer.
4. Choose your wardrobe carefully. A well-pressed conservative suit and well-shined shoes are always appropriate. A man should wear a long-sleeved shirt and an interesting, but not flashy, tie. A woman should choose a flattering blouse that is not too low-cut. A man should wear no jewelry other than a wedding band and a watch. A woman should choose jewelry that complements her outfit but that does not make a statement on its own.
5. Leave enough time to get there early. Allow for traffic tie ups or transit delays. Give yourself time to visit the restroom and to give your hair finishing touches.
6. Shake hands firmly and wait to be told to take a seat.
7. Make frequent eye contact. Look directly at the person who is asking the question. When answering, do not avoid making eye contact with any one interviewer.

8. Listen carefully to be certain of exactly what is being asked. Never interrupt.
9. Speak distinctly. Control speed and volume. Avoid slang. Watch your grammar.
10. Sit up straight, but not too stiffly. Try to avoid nervous mannerisms—fidgeting, touching your face, frequently crossing and uncrossing your legs.
11. Smile occasionally.
12. At the end of the interview, thank the interviewers and shake hands again.